NON-
HUMAN

WITNESS-
ING

Thought
in the Act

a series
edited by

Erin
Manning

& Brian
Massumi

DUKE
UNIVERSITY
PRESS

DURHAM
& LONDON

2024

WAR,
DATA, AND

ECOLOGY
AFTER

nonhuman
witnessing

THE
END OF

THE WORLD

MICHAEL
RICHARDSON

© 2024 Duke University Press
All rights reserved

PROJECT EDITOR: MICHAEL TRUDEAU
DESIGNED BY AIMEE C. HARRISON
TYPESET IN MINION PRO AND IBM PLEX MONO
BY WESTCHESTER PUBLISHING SERVICES

Library of Congress Cataloging-in-Publication Data
Names: Richardson, Michael, [date] author.
Title: Nonhuman witnessing : war, data, and ecology after the end of the world / Michael Richardson.
Other titles: Thought in the act.
Description: Durham : Duke University Press, 2024. | Series: Thought in the act | Includes bibliographical references and index.
Identifiers: LCCN 2023015594 (print)
LCCN 2023015595 (ebook)
ISBN 9781478025641 (paperback)
ISBN 9781478020905 (hardcover)
ISBN 9781478027782 (ebook)
Subjects: LCSH: Mass media—Social aspects. | Mass media—Political aspects. | Mass media and technology. | Mass media—Influence. | Information society. | Communication and technology. | Evidence. | Witnesses. | BISAC: SOCIAL SCIENCE / Privacy & Surveillance (see also POLITICAL SCIENCE / Privacy & Surveillance) | SOCIAL SCIENCE / Media Studies.
Classification: LCC P96.S65 R534 2024 (print) | LCC P96.S65 (ebook) | DDC 302.2—DC23/ENG/20231103
LC record available at https://lccn.loc.gov/2023015594
LC ebook record available at https://lccn.loc.gov/2023015595

Cover art: Yhonnie Scarce, *Thunder Raining Poison*, 2015. Blown-glass yams, stainless steel, reinforced wire, dimensions variable. Installation view at Tarnanthi Festival 2015, Art Gallery of South Australia. Photography: Janelle Low. Image courtesy of the artist and THIS IS NO FANTASY, Melbourne.

for adrian
and sacha—

may you witness
many worlds

CONTENTS

Acknowledgments ix

INTRODUCTION 1
nonhuman witnessing

ONE 37
witnessing violence

TWO 80
witnessing algorithms

THREE 112
witnessing ecologies

FOUR 150
witnessing absence

CODA 174
toward a politics
of nonhuman witnessing

Notes 185
Bibliography 207
Index 229

ACKNOWLEDGMENTS

I ACKNOWLEDGE THE UNCEDED SOVEREIGNTY of the Bidjigal and Gadigal people of the Eora Nation on whose lands this book was written. From tens of thousands of years before the settler invasion through today, their knowledge, culture, and customs have protected and nurtured this land, and will continue to do so long into the future. Always was, always will be.

This book responds to a pervading sense of crisis. Its writing began in earnest with the Sydney air thick with bushfire smoke and these words of acknowledgment are typed in the wake of catastrophic flooding and with yet another pandemic wave surging. I was fortunate enough to hold an Australian Research Council Discovery Early Career Research Award from 2019 to 2021 (DE190100486), a research fellowship that spared me the intensity and labor of teaching through the first two years of the COVID-19 pandemic, although not the upheavals, lost jobs, merged faculties, and other stresses of my place of work in those years. That was and remains an immense privilege, one not afforded to the many academics forced to eke out research time under the strain of unsustainable teaching and administration loads.

If this book began anywhere, it was with two questions asked a year apart on separate visits to Freie Universität, Berlin. The first was from Jonas Bens, who asked whether drones might become nonhuman witnesses. The second came after delivering a paper that began to answer that question, when Jan Slaby asked whether the paper would become a book. I am grateful to both Jonas and Jan, but their questions would not have been possible without an invitation from Kerstin Schankweiler to visit Berlin in 2017 for the inspiring Image Testimonies: Witnessing in Times of Social Media symposium and again a year later as a visiting fellow at the Affective Societies Collaborative Research Centre. My deepest appreciation to Kerstin, who has since become my coauthor, coeditor, and friend.

I benefited immensely from the chance to share ideas and words that would become this book at conferences, often on more than one occasion, including 4S, Crossroads in Cultural Studies, Deleuze Studies, Cultural Studies Association of Australasia, the Australasian Society for Continental Philosophy, International Communication Association, the Aesthetics of Drone Warfare, Digital Intimacies, the Australian Sociological Association, World of Drones, Data Futures, Drones in Society, Witnessing and Worlds beyond the Human, and the worlding experience of the Affect WTF and Capacious AIMS conferences organized by the shimmering Greg Seigworth. Thank you also to the many people who invited me to speak on drones, witnessing, and related matters. Kerstin Schankweiler for Image Testimonies at Freie Universität; Elizabeth Stephens for Future Affects at University of Queensland; Kerstin Schankweiler and Tobias Wendl for the art history colloquium at Freie Universität; Lyria Bennett-Moses, Danielle Hynes, and Niamh Stephenson for the Data Injustices Roundtable at UNSW; Vered Maimon at Tel Aviv University; Catherine Rhodes at the Cambridge University's Centre for Existential Risk; Lilie Chouliaraki at the London School of Economics; Carolyn Pedwell and Vince Miller at University of Kent; Shela Sheikh at Goldsmiths; Jonas Wittelman at the Schaufler Lab at TU Dresden; Naoko Abe, Justine Humphry, and Chris Cheshire for Mobile Robotics in Public Space at the University of Sydney; Kerstin Schankweiler (again!) at TU Dresden; Lindsay Kelley for UNFILED at UNSW; Timothy Gregory and Jeremy Moses for the Weapons, Wounds, War seminar series at Auckland University; and Andrew Brooks for the seminar series in my home department at UNSW Sydney. Those prompts to think through theories, themes, and case studies and the generous engagement of the audiences at those talks with the limits and potentials of my thinking made for a much stronger book.

Earlier versions of parts of this book were also published in academic journals but have since been revised extensively. I am immensely grateful to the editors and peer reviewers who guided these texts at a formative stage. Parts of chapter 1 draw from "How to Witness a Drone Strike," *Digital War* (2022), published in a special issue edited by Olga Boichak and Andrew Hoskins. What would eventually become sections of chapter 3 appeared in "Climate Trauma, or the Affects of the Catastrophe to Come," *Environmental Humanities* 10:1 (2018). An earlier version of chapter 4 was published as "Radical Absence: Encountering Traumatic Affect in Digitally Mediated Disappearance," *Cultural Studies* 32:1 (2018), in a special issue on media and affect edited by Sarah Cefai.

I am doubly (if not triply) thankful to Sarah Cefai, who orchestrated my visit to Goldsmiths in 2020, on the cusp of the pandemic, which led to conversations that pushed me to resolve some thorny questions with Joanna Zylinska, Matt Fuller, Chris Woods, Ariel Caine, Eyal Weizman, Susan Schuppli, Shela Sheikh, and Sarah herself.

Conversations large and small, online and off, with a host of interlocutors contributed in large and subtle ways to the ideas in this book or helped cheerlead it into existence. Thank you Adrian Mackenzie, Amy Gaeta, Andrew Yip, Anthony McCosker, Ayesha Jehangir, Baden Pailthorpe, Boram Jeong, Carolyn Pedwell, Casey Boyle, Chad Shomura, Charlotte Farrell, Chris Agius, Chris O'Neill, Chrstine Parker, Crystal Abidin, Declan Kuch, Donovan Schaefer, Edgar Gomez Cruz, Elke Schwarz, Emma Jane, Emma Quilty, Fleur Johns, Gilbert Caluya, Hagit Keysar, Hannah Buck, Heather Horst, Hussein Abbass, Jake Goldenfein, James Parker, Janet Chan, Jathan Sadowski, Jennifer Terry, Jenny Rice, Jodi Brooks, Joel Stern, Joseph DeLappe, Joseph Pugliese, Jussi Parikka, Karin Sellberg, Kat Higgins, Kathrin Maurer, Kathryn Brimblecombe-Fox, Kynan Tan, Larissa Hjorth, Liam Grealy, Lilie Chouliaraki, Lisa Slater, Louise Ravelli, Lyria Bennett-Moses, Mark Andrejevic, Matthew Arthur, Mel Gregg, Michael Balfour, Michal Givoni, Michele Barker, Milissa Dietz, Monique Mann, Nathaniel Rivers, Ned Rossiter, Niamh Stephenson, Nisha Shah, Olga Boichak, Omar Al-Ghazzy, Paul Frosh, Poppy de Souza, Rachel Morley, Rowan Wilken, Sarah Truman, Sonia Qadir, Sukhmani Khorana, Tess Lea, Tim Neale, Tom Sear, Verena Staub, Willy Blomme, Xan Chacko, Yanai Toister, and all those that I have inevitably forgotten. Some of the most rewarding conversations took place with participants in the Drone Cultures symposium that changed incarnation from in-person to online over the course of 2020 and via the Drone Futures seminar series that I ran online through the first year of the pandemic. Special thanks to Ronak Kapadia, Antoine Bousquet, Jairus Grove, J. D. Schnepf,

Kate Chandler, Mahwish Chishty, Thomas Stubblefield, Caren Kaplan, and Alex Edney-Browne. Your presentations and conversations (many of which have continued) all shed new light.

Coauthors and collaborators on other projects also helped me to work through this one. I am immensely grateful to the legends J. D. Schnepf, Beryl Pong, Adam Fish, Heather Ford, Kerstin Schankweiler, Amit Pinchevski, Magdalena Zolkos, Madelene Veber, Anna Jackman, Kyla Allison, and Andrew Brooks.

At UNSW, I'm lucky to work with many wonderful academic and professional colleagues in the School of the Arts and Media, especially my coconspirators in the Media Futures Hub. One of great joys of academic life has been learning from my graduate students Simon Taylor, Meng Xia, Asal Mahmoodi, Theresa Pham, Rachel Rowe, Bron Miller, Kyla Allison, Maddie Hichens, Katariina Rahikainen, and Maryam Alavi Nia.

Remarkable comrades in academic life have enriched my world. Deepest thanks to Anna Gibbs, who set me on the path; Meera Atkinson, my first academic partner in crime; Magdalena Zolkos, for introducing me to affect; Andrew Murphie, for opening the worlds of media; Stephanie Springgay, for wise guidance and late-night bourbon; Rebecca Adelman, for finding joys in email; Elizabeth Stephens, for lifting up others, me included; Ramaswami Harindrinath, for getting me hired (and much more); Helen Groth, for generous mentoring; Tessa Lunney, for laughs and lunches and always remembering; Nick Richardson, for unconditional cheerleading; Collin Chua, for knowing what to read; Caren Kaplan, for solidarity and wisdom; Anna Munster, for the creative energy and collaborative enthusiasm; Tanja Dreher, for believing that change is possible; Thao Phan, for the unerring capacity to ask the right questions; and Greg Seigworth, for endless capaciousness.

Special thanks to the artists who generously gave permission to include their work: Kathryn Brimblecombe-Fox, Baden Pailthorpe, Kynan Tan, Edward Burtynsky, Grayson Cooke, Mahwish Chishty, and Yhonnie Scarce, whose stunning *Thunder Raining Poison* appears on the cover. Particular thanks to Noor Behram for his striking photograph (figure 1.3), used here under fair use guidelines and (I hope) in allegiance with the politics of his work.

A book is nothing without readers, and the writing of this one is indebted to the time, insight, critique, and support of some remarkable ones. The Book Proposal Club of Astrida Neimanis and Lindsay Kelley helped build the framework and find the book a home at Duke. Greg Seigworth, Nathan Snaza, and Tanja Dreher read early, lumpy drafts of the introduction and made it so much stronger through their generous attention to its unformed thoughts and suggestions of further reading. Anna Munster read chapter 3 and homed in on its weakest points with unerring precision, which helped strengthen that chapter greatly.

Research underpinning this book—and especially chapters 1 and 3—was enormously assisted by Madelene Veber, who has worked with me over the last four years and is, among other things, brilliant, indispensable, astute, and creative. I've no doubt that Madelene will soon be writing acknowledgments of her own.

For so many reasons, I am forever in debt to Andrew Brooks and Astrid Lorange, staunchest pals and wisest of readers. Both read the manuscript top to bottom and provided such thoughtful feedback and incisive edits. But more, your fierce politics, love of thought and poetry and language, your convivial joy in snacks, and your friendship have meant everything. Love you. GFFS.

Two anonymous reviewers read both the proposal and eventual manuscript. Their generous, critical, and constructive engagement with the project at proposal stage had a transformative effect on the argument, framework, and analysis. Without them, this book would be much poorer, or not a book at all. All flaws that remain are mine alone. Thank you.

Brian Massumi and Erin Manning believed in this book from the first loose description at a Montreal café in the dead of winter. Brian's work led me to fall for affect theory, for radical empiricism and process philosophy, and for the relationality in all things, and you were both so welcoming to a clueless graduate student at the Into the Diagram workshop in 2011. I am truly honored to be published in your series, alongside so many brilliant others.

At Duke University Press, I am immeasurably thankful to Courtney Berger, whose editorial wisdom and unfailingly warm support for the book made all the difference, editorial assistants Sandra Korn and Laura Jaramillo, and Aimee Harrison for the stunning cover design. As all authors know, a huge amount of unsung work goes into making a book and getting it to readers. Thank you, Michael Trudeau, James Moore, Emily Lawrence, Chad Royal, and the rest of the production and marketing crew for your effort, enthusiasm, attention, and care. Big thanks to Cathy Hannabach and Morgan Genevieve Blue from Ideas on Fire for stellar work producing a rich index.

The Thread—Na'ama, Phil, Astrid, Andrew, Nick, Annie, Zoe—your solidarity, wisdom, humor, advice, and love are beyond measure.

To name all the family and friends who nurtured this book and its author is an impossible task. You know who you are. Mum—you taught me to love learning and to seek justice. Dad—you showed me how to pursue the exact and true. Daniel—I only wish you were nearer so that we could share more joys together.

Finally, my deepest thanks and love go to Zoe, Adrian, and Sacha. There is no one like you, Zoe Horn, so smart, creative, caring, loving, and funny. You keep me on track, you put things in perspective, you teach me again every day what matters most, and you always believe. Adrian and Sacha, this book is for you, for everything you've taught me, and for the desperate need to make new worlds to live and love within.

INTRODUCTION

nonhuman witnessing

AT 6:15 A.M., FEBRUARY 21, 2010, on a deserted stretch of road in the Uruzgan Province of Afghanistan, a convoy of three vehicles slowed to a halt and figures spilled out, clumping and milling as dawn light filtered through the mountains. Captured by the Multi-Spectral Targeting System (MSTS) slung below the nose of the loitering MQ-1 Predator, imagery of the convoy streamed across military networks to screens in the United States and Afghanistan. On the screens, engines and people glowed white against the gray-black landscape as indistinct heat signatures bled into one another in the strange aesthetic of forward-looking infrared (FLIR). Image and control data flowed through the network, moving between different devices, infrastructures, and protocols. Connected by a ku-band satellite link to Ramstein Air Base in Germany, the Predator's data then traveled down optical fiber cable under the Atlantic to the Ground Control Station at Creech Air Force Base outside Las Vegas, Nevada, to image analyst "screeners" in Florida, to command posts and ground stations across the globe, and to an encrypted server farm for archiving, where the video and its accompanying metadata would be logged, recorded, and held for future analysis. Years later, these time-stamped pixel arrays of ones and zeros likely became part of the vast video archive used to train machine learning algorithms to replace the labor of image analysts, a project initiated in partnership with Google and other tech giants in a sign of strengthening ties between the architects of algorithmic enclosure and those of increasingly autonomous warfare.

On that pale morning, one place the video feed failed to reach was the US Special Forces unit conducting an operation against a local Taliban leader in nearby Khod. Afghanistan's weak communications infrastructure and a reliance on satellite bandwidth meant that the imagery never made it to the ground, despite being subject to much debate as it was examined by screeners, operators, and commanders. Conducted by radio and military internet relay chat (mIRC) across discontinuous networks within the operational apparatus, the debate over what the images showed angled ever more inexorably toward violence as the affective surge toward action cohered with the indistinction of the drone's mediations. Alongside the MSTS, the Predator was equipped with GILGAMESH, a sophisticated eavesdropping system capable of blanket signal interception of nearby cellphones. Like the image screeners, analysts combing its data oriented their interpretation toward perceiving the convoy as a node within an enemy network. On the ground, two dozen men, women, and children spread prayer rugs on the dirt, while military personnel on the other side of the planet argued over how to read the varied morphologies produced by the sensor-network-feed. Framed with military discourse, these uncertain bodies were swiftly fixed as "military-aged males" and thus subject to potential elimination.

Prayers complete, the three vehicles continued along the road, veering away from the Special Forces at Khod in what one of the drone crew interpreted as a "flanking" maneuver. The lurking Predator carried only a single missile, so two Kiowa attack helicopters were scrambled into position and a little after 9 a.m., the convoy hit a treeless stretch of road. Guided by the drone's laser targeting system, two AGM-114 Hellfire missiles launched from the Kiowa helicopters and struck the first and third cars, explosive charges in each detonating to fragment the shell casing. Metal and flesh tore apart and fused together. Bodies were everywhere, whole and in pieces. Nasim, a mechanic who survived the blast, later recalled wrecked vehicles, a headless corpse, another body cut in half. On the full-color video feed that the crew switched to after the strike, pixels re-presented themselves as women and, eventually, as children. Later, the Pentagon claimed sixteen dead, including three children; villagers said twenty-three, including two boys named Daoud and Murtaza. A swiftly ordered US Department of Defense investigation traced the tangled lines of communication, the processes of mediation, and the failures of vision and transmission. Its report ran over two thousand pages. When eventually released under a Freedom of Information request filed by the American Civil Liberties Union, the report provided rare insight into the secretive inner workings of drone warfare. Much attention was paid to the transcript of communications between the Predator crew and ground command. Later used to frame both journalistic and scholarly accounts, the transcript distilled the hubris, faith in technology, and tendency toward violence that animates remote war. More than a decade later, the event and its mediations and remediations remain a critical aperture into the drone apparatus.[1]

In all of this, who—or what—bears witness? Human witnesses abound: the victims and survivors, whose flesh and words bear the scars and carry the lived truth of hellfire from above; the pilot and sensor operator, the commanders, military lawyers, image analysts; the military investigators; the documentarians and journalists who will tell the story of what happened, and their audiences across the world; perhaps even the scholars, myself among them, who turn to this moment to help make sense of remote war. Yet what of our nonhuman counterparts? There is the ground soaked in blood, the roadway buckled by the explosive force of two warheads and blackened by fire, and the dirt and stone of the roadside in a land wracked by war, and the carbon-rich atmosphere through which the missile and signals travel, another in the countless processes contributing to the ecological catastrophe that consumes the planet. There is the drone itself, not only the aerial vehicle and its payload of sensors capturing light across the spectrum but its signals relays, and the complex network of technologies, processes, and practices that make up the apparatus. And there are, too, the algorithmic tools for snooping cellphones and scouring video; the data centers sucking power for cooling and expelling heat for stack upon stack of rack-mounted computers; the undersea cables that carry military and civilian data alike. If we extend the assemblage further, we arrive at lithium mines and orbital satellites, image datasets and environmental sensors, cellphone manufacturers and cloud services.

In most accounts of witnessing, much of this would be excluded altogether, relegated to the status of evidence, or assigned the role of intermediary, dependent upon a human expert or interpreter. *Nonhuman Witnessing* refuses that relegation and instead deepens and widens the scope of witnessing to include the nonhuman. Opening witnessing to the nonhuman provides deeper, more finely tuned understandings of events for us humans. But this book goes further, arguing that nonhuman witnessing enables the communicative relations necessary for an alternative and pluriversal politics, founded on the capacity of nonhuman entities of all kinds to witness and through that witnessing compose new ethicopolitical forms. Human witnessing is no longer up to the task of producing the knowledge and forms of relations necessary to overcome the catastrophic crises within which we find ourselves. Only through an embrace of nonhuman witnessing can we humans, if indeed we are still or ever were human, reckon with the world-destroying crises of war, data, and ecology that now envelop us.

NONHUMAN WITNESSING

Witnessing is fundamental to cultures, communities, and polities because it pushes events onto the stage of justice, helps determine significance and truth, contributes to the making of shared knowledge, anchors political subjectivity, and produces responsibility. Necessarily relational, witnessing forges an intensive connection between witness and event, a registering of something happening that forms an address and insists upon a response. Not just any encounter, witnessing exceeds itself and calls others into relation with it. This is why witnessing co-constitutes epistemic and moral communities, and even political subjectivity itself. Witnessing pushes sense-making to grapple with traumas that refuse comprehension. Witnessing responds to violence in all its elusive and terrible forms, but also to wonder, beauty, and even banality. Witnessing precedes what comes to be deemed truth and gifts authority to collective memory, but it also depends on the permeability and fluidity of individual and collective subjectivities.

Witnessing and testimony are found in different guises in court rooms, church halls, human rights tribunals, fiction and poetry, media reports, scientific laboratories, and countless other places. Small wonder, then, that witnessing figures centrally in academic thought, from philosophies of ethics and political theory to media, literary, religious and science and technology studies, to name but a few fields attentive to its normative effects, its constitutive processes, and its historical specificities. Far from a static concept or set of practices, witnessing itself has transformed throughout Western history, taking on new forms and dynamics alongside and in response to changes in technology, politics, sociality, and religion. As both theory and practice, witnessing has proven pervasive and durable, as well as malleable and exploitable. But in an era of interlocking crises of technoscientific war, ecological catastrophe, and algorithmic enclosure, both the theory and practice of witnessing need to reckon far more deeply with the nonhuman.

Nonhuman Witnessing is about what happens when the frame of what counts as witnessing expands, how more-than-human epistemic communities might form, and what this might mean for subjectivity, the nature of justice, and the struggle for more just worlds. I develop nonhuman witnessing as an analytical concept that brings nonhuman entities and phenomena into the space of witnessing and accords them an agency otherwise denied or limited by witnessing theory to date. This strategic gesture makes room for excluded knowledges, subjectivities, and experiences within a wider framework of cosmopolitical justice. It does so through an analysis of technologies, ecologies, events, bodies, materialities, and texts situated in crises of military, algorithmic, and ecological violence. While witnessing can certainly occur separate from violence, this book focuses predominantly on instances of state and corporate violence that occur across a variety of scales, speeds, temporalities, and intensities. This book understands violence as purposive harm inflicted on people, animals, environments, and the ecological relations that make life and nonlife inextricable from one another. Violence thus determines the possibility, capacity, and nature of life for humans and nonhumans alike. This instrumentality means that violence is distinct from mere force and cannot be neatly equated to destruction or death in general. In the way I use it here, *violence* captures environmental, ecological, structural, technological, affective, discursive, and infrastructural forms of instrumental harm, as well as the directly corporeal and material forms that are most obvious and widely accepted. One of my central propositions, then, is that nonhuman witnessing brings more excessive and elusive violence into the frame of witnessing in ways that human witnessing cannot.

What this book proposes is bold: to unknot witnessing, weave it anew as inescapably entangled with the nonhuman, and within the warp and weft of that weaving find a renewed political potential for witnessing after the end of the world. My argument is that understanding witnessing as bound up with nonhuman entities and processes provides new and potentially transformative modes of relating to collective crisis and the role of the human within it. For many on this planet, crisis is neither a new experience nor an exceptional event but rather forms the condition under which life is lived. The book takes as its starting point the presumption that contemporary crises of war, algorithmic enclosure, and ecology are inseparable from the enduring catastrophe of settler colonialism, whether in their connection to extractive industries, colonial militarisms, techniques of control developed in settler states, or the regimes of seeing, knowing, and being that underpin the European modernity that has spread unevenly, violently, and with varying degrees of success across the planet. World-ending crises are all too familiar for First Nations people, who live in what Potawatomi scholar and activist Kyle Whyte calls "ancestral dystopias," or present conditions that would once have been apocalyptic futures.[2] But I also want to emphasize that the subject of History—the figure that enacts and is produced by such structures of violence and control—is neither an accident nor a universal figure. Sylvia Wynter calls this figure Man, the Western bourgeois figure "which overrepresents itself as if it were the human itself."[3] This imposed image of the human as Christian and middle class first emerged in the Renaissance, only to be amended in biological terms by the sciences of the nineteenth century.[4] As I will argue later in this introduction, it is precisely this figure of Man that is the unexamined subject of witnessing. *Nonhuman Witnessing* argues that this dangerous fiction of Man the Witness cannot hold under the dual pressures of existential catastrophe and its own violent contradictions.

The two terms of the main title thus signal the core theoretical interventions and tensions of the book. By putting witnessing and the nonhuman in conversation with each other, I aim to dismantle the humanist frame within which witnessing has been understood until now. This revisioning of witnessing contributes to the larger critical and political project of interrogating fundamental assumptions within the Western tradition and its project of domination. It also speaks to the necessity of building new methods and modes of knowing that can grapple with the injurious impacts of algorithmic enclosure, technowar, and anthropogenic climate change at a time when the illusion of a cohesive world cannot hold. In doing so, *Nonhuman Witnessing* aims to be as generative as it is critical: it is a work of thought in action that seeks new ways of making theory and building concepts.

As an analytic concept, nonhuman witnessing describes the varied material, technical, media-specific and situated relations through which ethicopolitical knowledge, responsibilities and forms are produced in ways that can include but neither require nor privilege human actors. As I define and elaborate the concept, nonhuman witnessing rests on a vitalist conception of existence that understands technics, affects, and materialities as registering and communicating experience in forms that can be deemed witnessing in their own right, prior to and distinct from any semiotic translation or interpretation. In this, I am indebted to philosophies of radical empiricism that stress the movement and relationality through which existence takes shape and meaning. My own intellectual roots are in the processual vitalism of Gilles Deleuze, and particularly its incarnation in the heterogenous field that has come to be known as affect theory. More specifically, my approach to relationality borrows from Brian Massumi's theorizing of affect as intensities of relation between bodies and worlds, whether human or non, corporeal or technical, dominant or fugitive.[5] Parallel to the emphasis throughout on relationality, this book also approaches nonhuman witnessing with a debt to media and cultural studies approaches to media and mediation, as well as witnessing more specifically.

Yet this book is also indebted to encounters with First Nations cosmo-epistemologies that understand animals, plants, rocks, sky, water, and land as forms of life with inherent—rather than granted—rights, agencies, and relations. Academic scholarship all too easily and often adopts an extractivist approach to such knowledges. As an uninvited settler living and working on the unceded land of the Bidjigal and Gadigal peoples of the Eora Nation, in what is now called Sydney, Australia, I engage with these knowledges in a spirit of study without laying claim to traditions that aren't mine. I want to think and inquire with these knowledges, exploring their resonances with the processual empiricism that anchors my own scholarly standpoint. My aim is to show how the exclusion of the nonhuman from witnessing derives from a distinct and narrow approach to both agency and knowledge, a limitation that is endemic to the dominant strain of European philosophy that insists so intently on the discrete and unitary over the relational and emergent.

Nonhuman witnessing elevates the status of the other-than-human in bearing witness, refiguring witnessing as the entanglement of human and nonhuman entities in the making of knowledge claims. In the air strike that killed twenty-three civilians in Uruzgan, Afghanistan, claims to knowledge about what was happening on the ground were animated within the military apparatus by the interdependencies of media technics, environmental conditions, and discursive practices. Violence registers as datalogical and informational before it is kinetic and lethal: witnessing the event of violence cannot be isolated to the drone operators or survivors or the infrared sensors, but rather must be known through the registering of those complex relations within and between human and nonhuman entities. Nonhuman witnessing can be identified in ecological, biological, geological, and even chemical manifestations, but also in technical and aesthetic forms, such as drone sensor assemblages and machine learning algorithms. This means that nonhuman witnessing is inseparable from place, time, media, context, and the other human and nonhuman bodies through and alongside which it takes place. Against the singular world of the scientific or juridical witness inherited from the Enlightenment, nonhuman witnessing coheres with what Mario Blaser and Marisol de la Cadena call a "a world of many worlds."[6] This is, then, one meaning of the temporality of this book's title: a theory of witnessing for a world of many worlds, after the end of the illusion that there is only one.

One consequence is that nonhuman witnessing is rife with practical and conceptual tensions. The very proposition contains within it the irresolvable paradox of identifying a mode of witnessing that must necessarily exceed the capacity to "know" inherited from Western epistemologies. Pursuing witnessing as a relational process, rather than locating it in either the figure of the witness or the act or object of testimony, raises the problem of which encounters constitute witnessing. Where, in other words, is the demarcation between mere registering and the witnessing of an event's occurrence? How is the status of witnessing bestowed and under what criteria? Tempting as it might be to reconcile such tensions or produce checklists of qualification, seeking to do so risks flattening nonhuman witnessing such that it loses purchase on the specificity of media, materials, ecologies, technics, and contexts. Nor is nonhuman witnessing necessarily virtuous. Just as the soldier can witness his own slaughter of innocents, so too the algorithmic witness to drone strikes or environmental violence can be understood as a witness-perpetrator. As with all witnessing, there is no inherent justice to nonhuman witnessing. The task at hand is to ask how nonhuman witnessing pries open conceptual and practical space within how we humans do politics, ethics, and aesthetics.

As a theory of ethical, political, and epistemic formation, nonhuman witnessing responds to a twofold crisis in witnessing itself. Its humanist form cannot reckon with the scale, complexity, intensity, and unknowability of technoscientific war, algorithmic enclosure, and planetary ecological catastrophe. Nor can witnessing hold in the wake of the disruption of "the human" by ecological, technological, and critical-theoretical change, not least under the pressure of critiques by Black and First Nations scholarship. Faced with this crisis of witnessing, we are left with a choice: to reserve witnessing for human contexts and find new concepts to address and respond to new crises, or, as this book argues, reconceive witnessing as entangled with the nonhuman by attending to registrations and relations in the stuff of existence and experience. Precisely because witnessing is so crucial to human—and especially Western—knowledge and politics, there is a strategic imperative to revising its vocabulary to analyze, strengthen, and generate transversal relations with the nonhuman that are ethical, political, and communicative, rather than simply informational or transactional.

This book, then, pursues what nonhuman witnessing *is*, but also what nonhuman witnessing *does* as a concept for crafting knowledge out of which a more just politics might be formed and fought for. Rather than provide a detached and abstract theory, it examines the media-specificity of nonhuman witnessing across a motley archive: the temporal and spatial scales of planetary crisis, the traces of nuclear testing on First Nations land, digital infrastructures that produce traumas in the everyday, deepfakes, scientific imaging that probes beyond the spectrum of the human sensorium, algorithmic investigative tools, the unprecedented surveillance system that is the global climate monitoring regime, and remote warfare enacted through increasingly autonomous drones. It combines close analyses of events, technologies, and ecologies with cultural studies readings of political and creative texts. From poetry to video to sculpture to fiction, creative works play a critical role in this book because they allow me to pursue nonhuman witnessing into speculative domains in which aesthetics and worlds relate to one another in strange, unexpected ways. This approach aims to show both the media dynamics and cultural consequences of nonhuman witnessing. In doing so, nonhuman witnessing emerges as a relational theory for understanding and responding to entangled crises, one that attends to complexity and difference even as it works across divergent domains and dizzying scales.

Rather than stitching together a grand theory, these sites reveal the necessity of capacious, open, situated, and flexible approaches to nonhuman witnessing. What this book pursues are the resonances, overlaps, and unexpected convergences in the kinds of grounded attachments and imaginaries that undo the narrow frame of the human within which witnessing has been understood for too long. This is why I am so insistent throughout on the gerund form of *witnessing* rather than *witness* as either noun or verb. My principal concern is not the figure of the witness as such, although both human and nonhuman witnesses play vital roles in its drama. Nor is this book overtly focused on the forms that testimony can take, although testimonies of many kinds occupy its pages. Nor is it about evidence and its forensic articulation, although such terms are never far away. Rather, I am interested in witnessing as a relational process, as a vital mode of world-making that encompasses both human and non.

In doing so, the book is as attentive as I could make it to differences of capability and process, as well as circumstance. A mountain and a person possess asymmetric capabilities, with one, for instance, able to endure across eons and the other able to marshal linguistic resources that facilitate communication with other people. Pushed to its most speculative ends, nonhuman witnessing might well extend into forms of witnessing that exclude and elude the human entirely. It may well be that witnessing to which we are not party is happening all the time, but of much greater significance are those instances of nonhuman witnessing that seem to be addressed in some way to the human—and through that address insist on both our response and responsibility.

Each chapter is organized around a double meaning: the witnessing of violence, as well as the violence that can be done by witnessing; the witnessing performed by algorithms, as well as the need to witness what algorithms do; witnessing of more-than-human ecologies, as well as ecologies of witnessing; the witnessing of absence, as well as the absence of witnessing. These doublings perform the relational dynamics of nonhuman witnessing itself, reflecting its working as both a critical concept and an emergent phenomenon. But each chapter also elaborates a distinct operative concept for understanding the processual modalities of nonhuman witnessing. Chapter 1, "Witnessing Violence," critiques the violence of increasingly autonomous warfare as it is mediated through technology, bodies, and environments, elaborating the notion of *violent mediation* as constitutive of martial life. Chapter 2, "Witnessing Algorithms," pursues machine learning algorithms that produce techno-affective milieus of witnessing, articulating an account of the *machinic affects* that animate relations within and between technics, bodies, and ecologies. Chapter 3, "Witnessing Ecologies," attends to naturecultures under the strain of climate catastrophe and nuclear war, conceptualizing a distinct form of *ecological trauma* that ruptures vital relations between human and nonhuman. Chapter 4, "Witnessing Absence," conjoins the sites of war, algorithm, and ecology to examine the traumatic absences that circulate in the quotidian of digital media, developing the concept of *radical absence* to show how nonhuman witnessing makes absence intensively present through nonhuman infrastructures.

Each of these analytic concepts—violent mediation, machinic affect, ecological trauma, and radical absence—explicate aspects of the processual dynamics of nonhuman witnessing. But while they intersect with one another in many ways, they don't snap neatly together to provide a unified theory of nonhuman witnessing. These concepts instead name the relational processes that constitute nonhuman witnessing across different contexts. Not all nonhuman witnessing entails violent mediation or radical absence, for example, but the former plays a crucial role in war while the latter is vital to understanding how nonhuman witnessing functions in digital cultures. Throughout the book, I show how these dynamics converge and diverge in productive tension with one another, marshalling varied constellations of them as they obtain to distinct sites of analysis. In the coda, I pull together the conceptual threads of the book to outline in explicit terms how nonhuman witnessing enables a more pluriversal politics that foregrounds communicative justice for more-than-human entities and ecologies.

Upending the long history in theory and philosophy of reserving witnessing for the human subject, I argue that witnessing is and always has been nonhuman. Our contemporary conjuncture makes this much easier to see, precisely because so much of Western ontology and epistemology has been thrown into crisis. If crises of autonomous war, algorithmic enclosure, and environmental catastrophe are indeed converging in the contemporary moment, it is surely in no small part because their roots reach so deep into the historical ground of militarism, capitalism, and settler colonialism. Nonhuman witnessing thus provides purchase on unfolding catastrophic futures, but also on the catastrophes of the past—and on the potential for radical hope, historical acts of resistance, and the making and remaking of more just worlds.

THIS MESS WE'RE IN

Amazon.com is an avatar for the interlocking crises of algorithmic enclosure, ecological catastrophe, and autonomous warfare. Its recommender algorithms and automated warehouses combine with autonomously managed global logistics systems to crowd out small producers and retailers. Its drivers and warehouse workers are tracked with biometric sensors, directed in their movements by algorithmic overseers, expected to meet precisely defined performance metrics, and kept in precarity by zero-hour contracts and just-in-time rostering, their bodies damaged by the dictatorial rule of algorithmic management systems. Its smart-home system, Alexa, provides voice-activated access to Amazon's systems, even as it datafies the fabric of daily life. More profitable even than its e-commerce operations and as vital to the infrastructure of the internet as Google, its Amazon Web Services cloud computing platform powers everything from document storage to facial recognition and is the single biggest service provider to the US military.

All this comes at an astonishing cost to the planet. Amazon's logistics systems alone produce 51.17 million metric tons of carbon, while its AWS data centers produce roughly the same amount of carbon as nine coal-fired plants.[7] Like most smart devices, Alexa relies on lithium and rare earth metals mined at devastating cost to local ecologies and to Indigenous communities, such as the Atacan in Chile.[8] Whether mining users for data or land for lithium, Amazon is ruthlessly extractive, the high-tech successor to the colonial enterprises that coproduced racial capitalism.[9] It has both infiltrated and diverted countless facets of life, and its founder dreams of extending that rapaciousness to the stars. Yet for all this, Amazon still retains much of the veneer of techno-utopian solutionism: a frictionless future of goods, data, and currency flowing through global infrastructures in which human labor is obscured, if not erased from view altogether. The vision of a transcendent future built on material waste and human sweat far more than on computation and abstraction.

To state the obvious: Amazon is neither the architect nor the sole beneficiary of the "modern world system of 'racial capitalism' dependent on slavery, violence, imperialism, and genocide," as Robin D. G. Kelley describes the current global regime.[10] Nor is it the only exemplar of the convergence of crises to which this book is addressed. Since the turn of the millennium and the attacks of 9/11, war and military technologies have undergone dramatic transformations, led by the United States but now sweeping across the globe. Remotely piloted aerial systems, or drones, moved from the margins to become instruments of killing and transform military strategy. Today, autonomous and semiautonomous drones are used by more than one hundred nations for surveillance and by a growing subset for lethal violence, backed by artificial intelligence systems powered by machine learning neural networks that undertake real-time analysis of impossibly large streams of remote sensor and other data. Remote vehicles are used on and above every type of terrain, as well as underwater and underground. Algorithmic selection and targeting systems for drones and other weapons platforms are already here, with fully autonomous weapons systems already emergent, held back less by technical capacity than by military, political, and public unease with the notion of removing human decision making from the act of killing. These changes have, as Jeremy Packer and Joshua Reeves point out, transformed "enemy epistemology and enemy production" in line with specific media logics of "sensation, perception, reason, and comprehension tied to a given medialogical environment."[11] The media-technological production of enemies and knowledge about those enemies is itself inextricable from the determination that certain populations must be controlled or can be killed, whether via the debilitating biopolitics that Jasbir Puar calls "the right to maim" or in the necropolitics of remote warfare with which I opened this book.[12] Consequently, their martial media technics must be read within the context of enduring colonialism.

This martial transformation has been part and parcel of the wider enclosure of life within computational systems and communications technologies, whether at the macroscale of public health databases, citizen registers, and biometric surveillance, or at the personal level with the ubiquitous presence of social media and smartphones across the planet. Logics of surveillance and control that have crept into every dimension of social, political, and economic life are also deeply entwined with histories of anti-Black racism, and the methods of domination applied during and after slavery in the Americas, as Simone Browne persuasively shows.[13] Indebted to wartime initiatives of the 1940s, decades of Cold War arms racing and antagonistic cultural politics that legitimated significant military spending in the United States, and active partnerships between the Defense Advanced Research Projects Agency (DARPA) and what would become Silicon Valley, today's communications technologies also bear the legacy of cybernetics and the effort to craft "infrastructures of sensing and knowing," as Orit Halpern puts it.[14] At the 1970 World Exposition in Osaka, experimental multimedia environments were built to demonstrate the potential for actualizing cybernetic systems in urban architecture and planning. Reflecting on the influence of Expo '70, Yuriko Furuhata argues that "regulatory mechanisms of policing and surveillance, modeled as multimedia systems and aided by networked communications, form a much darker and somber counterpart to the types of artistic multimedia environments that emerged in the 1960s."[15] Japanese architects, theorists, and multimedia artists played a crucial role in this dynamic, inheriting and responding to a different colonial legacy of violence and control.

Algorithmic technologies are now embedded in everything from Amazon's purchase recommendations to the creation of art, from the mining of personal and population data to the provision of welfare services to the structuring of knowledge itself via the search results of Google. But what Paul Edwards calls the "closed world" of Cold War computation also laid the infrastructural foundations for the "vast machine" of atmospheric monitoring that allowed anthropogenic climate change to become more visible and better understood, even as it became both contested and irreversible.[16] Today, ecosystems reel from hotter summers, extreme weather events, failing crops, rising migration, ocean acidification, and atmospheric pollution, to name but a handful of the more striking effects. Whether marked in the geology of the planet or in the biosphere, the sheer scale of ecological crisis (which is really a set of interlocking crises) is its own catastrophe, leading to denials of scientific knowledge, failures of politics, and global paralysis around meaningful response.

Each alone would be more than enough to end countless worlds, but these three crises are also intensifying and accelerating, fueling and fueled by the insatiable expansion of racial capitalism. Advances in machine learning have supercharged both algorithmic enclosure and autonomous warfare. Reliance on mass computing in everything from image recognition to bitcoin mining has combined with an exponential expansion in digital data stored in servers and trafficked across networks to produce a huge carbon footprint for computation. Built into the bedrock of the civilian internet as the host of everything from ebooks to presidential election campaigns to banking, those infrastructures have a massive environmental impact in heat generated and fossil fuel consumed.[17] Those same fossil fuels, of course, power the energy appetite of the US military, the world's largest carbon polluter. Institutionally, economically, and ecologically, Amazon and its ilk are deeply integrated with military apparatuses, especially in the United States where big tech provides everything from enterprise software to cloud storage to strategic guidance through bodies such as the Defense Innovation Board, chaired by ex–Google boss Eric Schmidt. Equivalent dynamics operate at every level, whether in the shared reliance on remote sensors by militarized drones, urban surveillance, and environmental monitoring, or the centrality of extraction to climate change, military industries, and the mining of data.

Despite this tight bind between technology, war, and climate change, ever-more innovation is proposed as the only solution by self-interested luminaries such as Bill Gates. In the most basic material sense, these crises of war, data, and climate and the system of racial capitalism they maintain and depend on are drawing down the finite resources of the planet. Taken together, they are both product and perpetrator of violence, whether structural or infrastructural, environmental or military, algorithmic or interpersonal, kinetic or slow.[18] The very existence of such lists speak to both the ubiquity and variety of violence today and its intimacy with crisis as the condition of life for much of the planet. The explanatory force of nonhuman witnessing resides in part in its capacity to register and communicate those forms of violence that might otherwise be rendered invisible.

Galvanizing the language of crisis, as I have done so far, is not without risk. As Whyte argues, claims of crisis—of food, resources, space, security—have been frequently used to justify colonialism, both in the larger sense of the settler enterprise and in specific instances such as the corporatization of tribal governance in the United States as a response to an "emergency" of poverty.[19] For Whyte, "crisis epistemologies" produce problematic politics that override First Nations concerns, such as in the appropriation of tribal lands for wind farms and other renewable initiatives in response to the exigencies of the climate crisis. Such epistemologies depend on a conception of crisis as aberrant and abnormal, a rupture that must be tamed and contained so that the normal order of things can be restored. Rather than a break from order, crisis is better understood as a condition of existence. "Crisis is not rupture, it is fragmentation," writes Henrik Vigh, "a state of somatic, social or existential incoherence." As such, crisis is "not a short-term explosive situation but a much more durable and persistent circumstance."[20] It is not an event, but the condition and context of life. Lauren Berlant calls this "crisis ordinariness," in which "crisis is not exceptional to history or consciousness but a process embedded in the ordinary that unfolds in stories about navigating what's overwhelming."[21] Thinking about crisis in this way does not require an abandonment of the notion of rupture. But crisis as condition does demand that we see rupture, trauma, violence, dispossession, precarity, and vulnerability as at once pervasive and unevenly distributed. Crisis doesn't punctuate time, so much as shape its passage, lacking any distinct beginning or end, enfolding past and future.

Crisis also enfolds and consumes events, entangles bodies, intensifies the contexts of their occurrence, and cuts through forms of connection to impose new (dis)orders. Andrew Murphie calls this catastrophic multiplicity "a complex storm of feeling, of aspects of world feeling each other in intense, unexpected and constantly mutating ways."[22] Catastrophic multiplicity intensifies, bewilders, and numbs feeling, which makes thinking with and through problems difficult, if not impossible.[23] Knowledge-making as a collective endeavor becomes fraught and frayed. This generalized crisis environment provides fertile conditions for states to harness ontopower, the power to bring into being. Because ontopower targets life as it stirs into activity, it is a form of power that both exceeds and precedes the human. Massumi describes it as the "power to incite and orient emergence that institutes itself into the pores of the world where life is just stirring, on the verge of being what it will become, as yet barely there."[24] Ontopower operates at the processual level of becoming itself. Deploying technoscientific apparatuses of war and governance, states and other actors seek to harness ontopower in attempts to preemptively control the future, as in the drone strike ordered in response to the algorithmic analysis of phone calls and patterns of movement that produce a "signature" deserving of eradication. But in doing so, ontopower also produces crises that themselves escape control, through its continual animation of the forces of state violence, environmental extraction, and algorithmic control. In this sense, ontopower does not replace biopower or necropower but rather operates in concert with them

If I have drawn so many examples from martial contexts, this is because *Nonhuman Witnessing* finds its way into data and climate through war. Like the political theorist Jairus Grove, I take the view that war is a form of life as much as it is a means of death: terrible, ruinous, and endlessly destructive, yet also generative and creative. Applied to geopolitics and indeed to everything from racism to capitalism, "war is not a metaphor; it is the intensive fabric of relations" that form this historical era.[25] What is needed is analysis "characterized by inhuman encounters and deep relational processes across geographical scales rather than a form of political thinking that relies on discreteness, causality, and an exceptional notion of human agency."[26] Also like Grove, I am committed to decentering human actors, but not doing away with human responsibility for the vast assemblages that continue to cause so much damage. As concept, practice, and phenomena, nonhuman witnessing brings such encounters, processes, and scales into conjunction with the relational formation of knowledge and subjectivity. But it does so through committed attention to the processes of mediation that animate and bind together crises of war, data, and climate.

Lively, temporal, and always in flux, mediation is never foreclosed or limited in its potential. Media studies scholarship has much to say on mediation. Sean Cubitt calls it the "effervescent commonality of human, technical, and natural processes."[27] For Sarah Kember and Joanna Zylinska, mediation is crucial to "understanding and articulating our being, becoming with, the technological world, our emergence and ways of intra-acting with it, as well as the acts and processes of temporarily stabilizing the world into media, agents, relations, and networks."[28] In this sense, mediation is always relational, but it is also necessarily nonhuman: even the witness who speaks their testimony entails the mediation of air so that wavelengths of sound can carry from lips to ears. This vitalist understanding of mediation requires an expansive understanding of media forms, one that sees everything from clouds to USB drives to the planet itself as media.[29] In keeping with the crucial work of feminist scholars, this approach to mediation is avowedly material. As Cubitt argues, "Media are finite, in the sense both that, as matter, they are inevitably tied to physics, especially the dimension of time; and that their constituent elements—matter and energy, information and entropy, time and space, but especially the first pair—are finite resources in the closed system of planet Earth."[30] Crises of war, algorithm and ecology are thus also crises of media: of an accelerating consumption that only exacerbates all other crises. In the face of just such a trajectory, Cubitt calls for a renewed and more differentially attuned mode of communication, one that resists the tendency to extract information from nature but not speak back to it. Something like this might be found in the radical empiricist tradition, which Chris Russill argues offers an alternative intellectual history to communication theory via William James, John Dewey, and George Herbert Mead that embraces indeterminacy, incommensurability, and difference.[31] Nonhuman witnessing describes a critical concept and relational practice of a distinct mode of communication, one constituted by an address that demands response but still embraces opacity. It is a transversal opening onto the workings of violence, experiences of precarity, and the shattering of epistemologies; an aperture through which communication might take place in ways that are necessary for care and justice in the aftermath of ended and ending worlds.

AFTER THE END OF THE WORLD

Words that would become this introduction were first written amid bushfires that ravaged Australia in the summer of 2019 and then labored over in the long years of the pandemic. Throughout that summer of smoke and ash, the sun glowed pale red and the density of particulate matter made the air hazardous to breathe. More than a billion animals died, thousands of homes were lost, countless habitats erased. Across traditional and social media, in corridor conversations and at dinner parties, all the talk was about apocalypse, climate change, the failure of normal politics to do much of anything at all. As the pandemic took hold in early 2020 and then wore on through the years, life here began to come undone, but the fabric never tore so deeply, so devastatingly, as it did across much of the globe. With Australia's borders closed for well over year, the sense of an ending world was impossible to escape, even without the massive loss of life experienced in so many places and borne so disproportionately by the already vulnerable and precarious. The very networks of travel and trade that expanded "the world" to fill "the globe" were now a threat to its continuation. What worlds would remain in the aftermath?

Living and working on unceded and sovereign Aboriginal lands, I am enmeshed in ended and ending worlds. Colonial expansion ended the worlds of First Nations peoples in Australia long ago, beginning with the arrival of Captain James Cook in 1770 and eighteen years later with the landing of the First Fleet at Botany Bay, just a few bends of the coast south of my own home. The lines of my own family are bound up with that dispossession, if not at the point of a gun then through the construction of buildings, founding of museums, plying of trade, and service in the military. As my forebears settled this land and built lives and families, the Traditional Owners experienced massacre, epidemic, dispossession, incarceration, starvation, and the stealing of children and the breaking of kinship formations.[32] That ending of worlds continues today, even as Aboriginal people endure and resist in powerful, inspiring, and even beautiful ways. Preoccupations with an apocalypse that is yet to come have a bitter irony in a place where First Nations have spent two-and-a-half centuries surviving the end of the world, struggling for new and old ways of living in this place that always was and always will be Aboriginal land.

After the end of the world: it is a temporality both commonplace and strange. In Western popular culture, apocalypse has been in the air and on the screen and page: zombies running amok, asteroid strikes, AI takeovers, bioengineered crashes, alien invasions. Metaphors of late capitalism, or climate change, or global migration, these end-times imaginaries are no longer the preserve of niche subcultures or millenarian religions but at the heart of the most profitable, most mainstream forms of popular culture. But the estrangement felt from these imaginings, the lure of catharsis in the fictional experience of the end of the world, relies on being situated in relation to a specific telling of history. As Whyte points out, "The hardships many non-Indigenous people dread most of the climate crisis are ones that Indigenous peoples have endured already due to different forms of colonialism: ecosystem collapse, species loss, economic crash, drastic relocation, and cultural disintegration."[33] In this sense, the temporal location in the title of the book—*After the End of the World*—describes a shifting, situated temporality that hinges on *whose world* has ended, to what purpose, and by what hands. As Nick Estes so succinctly makes clear in describing the impact of the Pick-Sloan Dam on the Oceti Sakowin peoples of Dakota in the early twentieth century, "taking away land and water also took away the possibility of a viable future."[34] Now, that ending of worlds has come to the world enders, the colonizers and empire builders who imagined into being a singular, global world and made it so with the rifle, the slave ship, the ledger, and the plantation. Now, de la Cadena and Blaser write, there "is a new condition: now the colonizers are as threatened as the worlds they displaced and destroyed when they took over what they called terra nullius."[35] And yet ending worlds don't always fully end and can be reseeded, as the resilience and endurance of First Nations peoples across the planet makes clear.

Naming this era is no simple matter because to name the problem is also to diagnosis it. Since its popularization by the atmospheric biochemist Paul Crutzen and ecologist Eugene Stoermer in a short article from 2000, the term *Anthropocene* has been widely adopted.[36] While the label is useful because it registers the impact of colonialism and industry on the planet's biological and geological systems, it also risks universalizing and misdiagnosing the problem by naming an undifferentiated Anthropos as the causal agent.[37] In this it serves an ideological function: flattening responsibility onto the human in the broadest sense both hides the histories of extraction, pollution, and violence through which the planet has been transformed and obscures the grossly unequal distribution of the spoils. Critics rightly argue that the term *Anthropocene* risks occluding the originary violence of settler colonialism, without which our era of petrocarbons, plastics, terraforming, species loss, and ocean death might never have been possible at all. Alternatives now abound, many of which attempt to name precisely distinct causal agents: Capitalocene, Plantationocene, Eurocene.[38] For me, deploying the term *Anthropocene* is a necessary strategic decision despite its limitations. Sticking with the Anthropocene allows me to center the Anthropos, understood as the form of Man that has driven colonial and capitalist expansion and, crucially, laid claim to the normative figure of the witness.[39] Conceived in this way, the Anthropocene and Man are co-constitutive. Countering the idea that the Anthropocene begins with the Industrial Revolution or nuclear bomb, Heather Davis and Métis scholar Zoe S. Todd argue that "placing the golden spike at 1610, or from the beginning of the colonial period, names the problem of colonialism as responsible for contemporary environmental crisis."[40] Known as the Columbian Exchange, 1610 marks both the moment when the exchange of biomatter between Europe and the Americas reshaped ecosystems and when carbon dioxide levels dropped in the geologic layer as a consequence of colonial genocide. Dating the Anthropocene in this way ties it both conceptually and historically to Man, and to the ending of worlds that is such an essential dimension of settler colonialism and racial capitalism.

Situating this book after the end of the world is thus a conceptual claim, as well as a historical one: *the world* has long since lost any claim to describe the totality of being. In its place are countless worlds without claim to universality or unity. One of the ways in which the end of the world finds hope is in recognizing that *the world* has always been multiple, a pluriverse produced by the world-making power of countless knowledge systems. Such a multiplicity enables what Kathleen Stewart calls *worldings*, or the "intimate, compositional process of dwelling in spaces that bears, gestures, gestates, worlds."[41] Reflecting on war and its aftermaths, Caren Kaplan writes of the "disturbance of conventions of distance and proximity, the presence of many pasts and places in what we try to think of as the here and now" that make "modernity's everyday aftermaths—the undeclared wars that grieve not only the present absences but the absent presents—not so much a matter of ghosts as multiple worlds that a singular worldview cannot accommodate."[42] The unruly intensities and haunting disruptions of these martial aftermaths are just as evident in the wake of ecological violence, technological enclosure, and colonial dispossession: time, place, space, experience and thought all resist linearity, refuse organization, unsettle the unfolding of life.[43] As a form of worlding after the end of the world, nonhuman witnessing is one means of building a communicative politics that begins with ecological relations and the inherent agencies of nonhuman things, animals, and places.[44]

WITNESSING AND THE NONHUMAN

As crises expand, intensify, and intersect, the capacity of witnessing and testimony to respond has been amplified, multiplied, and diversified by the adoption of new (and sometimes old) technologies, techniques, practices, knowledges, and theories. Open-source investigations led by agencies such as Bellingcat, Airwars, and Forensic Architecture have shown how crowd-sourcing, computational tools, 3D modeling, data analysis, remote sensors, and other technologies and methodologies can be combined with situated testimonies to generate alternative accounts of state and corporate violence. Satellites and drones provide human rights and environmental monitors with rich data that extends and exceeds the perceptual capacity of humans in scale, vantage point, and visibility across a much wider band of the light spectrum. Smartphones and social networks bring a far wider array of voices and images to public attention, shaking the epistemic dominance of traditional media institutions. Cheaper and more accessible sensing technologies have enabled citizen-led projects to monitor local ecologies. Growing recognition within the scientific community about the communicative capacity of plants and ecologies more broadly resonates with the push by First Nations activists to have nonhuman entities recognized by state law, such as the successful attribution of sentience to the Whanganui River in New Zealand following more than a century of struggle by local Māori tribes, led by the Ngāti Hāua. Artists, poets, activists, and creative practitioners of all stripes now engage with technics, ecologies, and politics in a testimonial mode that entangles human and nonhuman actors.

Nonhuman Witnessing conceptualizes and theorizes these developments, both as a means of making sense of these changes in situ and to connect them into a larger project of reckoning with crisis, violence, and trauma. It joins a growing body of critical interventions into the connections between aesthetics, witnessing, and forensics, prominent among them the legal, artistic, and theoretical works of Eyal Weizman and his research agency Forensic Architecture, located at Goldsmiths, University of London. Weizman's *Forensic Architecture* theorizes the application of architectural techniques of siting, sensing, mapping, modeling, and analyzing to the task of uncovering and communicating "violence at the threshold of detectability."[45] Attending to material architectures, media objects, and situated testimonies, forensic architecture is an operative concept that provides a method for investigation. How that method articulates with wider transformations is the subject of Weizman and Matthew Fuller's *Investigative Aesthetics*, which explores how resistant investigations assemble aesthetically to produce what they call an "investigative commons" to challenge state- and court-sanctioned knowledge production and counter the post-truth "anti-epistemologies" of misinformation and disinformation that have undermined trust in shared realities.[46] Aesthetics in their terms comprises both sensing and sense-making, and, as such, is not exclusively human but rather found across all entities in their relational milieus, as I explore in more detail in chapters 1, 2, and 3, including with a close reading of the Forensic Architecture project *Triple Chaser*.

More closely attuned to the questions of witnessing that occupy this book, Susan Schuppli's *Material Witness* combines reflections on her artistic practice and work with Forensic Architecture, which draws on archival and ethnographic research to develop an account of how matter can obtain standing as a witness within public fora such as war crimes tribunals. Her material witnesses are "nonhuman entities and machinic ecologies that archive their complex interactions with the world, producing ontological transformations and informatic dispositions that can be forensically decoded and reassembled back into a history."[47] Material witnesses can express themselves through a technical sensibility rather than speech per se, but "matter becomes a material witness only when the complex histories entangled within objects are unfolded, transformed into legible formats, and offered up for public consideration and debate."[48] Material witnesses appear throughout this book, but particularly in chapter 3 when I turn to the material traces of nuclear testing and their mediation through art.

While Schuppli, Weizman, and Fuller ground their analysis in their own investigative practices in and beyond the academy, Pugliese's *Biopolitics of the More-Than-Human* shares this book's imperative to develop an apparatus for critiquing contemporary warfare and the ruin it does to bodies and ecologies. Discontented with existing practices of evidentiary analysis, Pugliese calls for a "forensic ecology" that can "examine the physical remains, in particular, of more-than-human entities left in the aftermath of the violence and destruction unleashed in militarized zones of occupation."[49] This is resonant with the investigation of drone warfare and its violent mediations in chapter 1, particularly in thinking through the entanglements of technics, bodies, and ecologies.

Witnessing is also an important subfield of inquiry within media studies, producing nuanced empirical and theoretical accounts of distinctive modes and practices of witnessing and testimony. In an influential essay, John Durham Peters defines witnessing as "responsibility to the event" and points out that media must wrestle with the "ground of doubt and distrust" that distance adds to the "veracity gap" inherent to the relay of any testimony.[50] Building on this conception, Paul Frosh and Amit Pinchevski propose the concept of "media witnessing," or "witnessing performed in, by and through media" as essential to contemporary world-making.[51] Media witnessing, Lilie Chouliaraki argues, is a fraught proposition, veering easily into spectatorship as distant audiences are presented with atrocity to which they have few or no avenues of response.[52] New witnessing practices emerged in concert with new media technologies, producing what media studies scholars have variously called mobile witnessing, citizen-camera witnessing, crowd-sourced evidence, digital witnessing, witnessing databases, and data witnessing.[53] These practices have enabled affected individuals and communities to narrate crises in culturally distinctive ways and to self-represent their witnessing, even if they have also produced new expert and intermediary functions for human rights organizations.[54] Throughout *Nonhuman Witnessing*, this research provides valuable insights into distinct witnessing practices related to my lines of inquiry, but also serves as a springboard for thinking past the limits of the human in ways that I hope will in turn be generative for scholarship in media studies.

The works highlighted in the preceding pages share with mine a commitment to interrogating the shibboleths of testimony, evidence, and their relation to politics, technology, and justice. But there are also critical departures. Where Weizman elucidates an existing practice of forensic architecture, this book theorizes a more expansive, ontoepistemological reconception of witnessing as an encounter with and response to violence. Where Fuller and Weizman focus on the theory and process of investigation as a mechanism for assembling aesthetics, this book attends to how the sensing and sense-making of aesthetics produces a witnessing relation that is not dependent upon an investigative team, method, or apparatus. Where Schuppli insists on contestation within public fora as a condition for material witnessing, my approach to nonhuman witnessing insists on witnessing as an experiential relation that can produce contestation but is not dependent on it for its existence or even politics. Where Pugliese centers the law and its enmeshment with military power and colonial structures, my concern is with processes distinct from the juridical domain, and that fail to appear or cohere within legal frames. Where media studies research delves into the complex ensembles of media and human that produce distinct forms of witnessing, it reserves ethical and political standing for human witnesses, intermediaries, and audiences and leaves nonhuman agencies largely out of frame. In short, *Nonhuman Witnessing* contributes to an active project within critical thought in which debates over key concepts remain vibrant. And while the forms of violence and modes of intervention with which all these works are concerned are largely new, they are also embedded in a long history of transformation in the forms and practices of witnessing, who counts as a witness, and how shared knowledge is produced.

In the earliest foundations of the Western legal tradition in Athens and Rome, the wounded body was considered the most reliable witness, which meant torture was central to legal proceedings. Who could be tortured in the name of truth was a matter of importance: the enslaved were often the subject of torture to provoke truthful testimony, not the powerful and propertied.[55] Witnessing was borne on the body up until the Enlightenment, when the law of proof emerged in conjunction with the ocular revolution of the Renaissance and the humanist conception of the dignity of Man.[56] In 1846 the United Kingdom abolished the law of the deodand, a relic of old English jurisprudence that held that an object in motion that has killed a human must be held to account. Consequently, writes Su Ballard, "where once they were able to take responsibility for the harm they have caused, now objects are just another group of silenced witnesses."[57] This sentencing of the memory of objects to evidence accompanied the modern juridical witness taking familiar form: structured by norms, ordered in narrative, and verified by accompanying evidence.[58]

The figure of the witness thus becomes synonymous with Man, which meant certain bodies were again excluded: the enslaved, Indigenous and

Black people, and, often, women and the unpropertied. Unable to become witnesses before the law due to explicit rule or fear of retaliation, their flesh could be made to speak through violent punishment. Hortense Spillers calls the flesh that "zero degree of social conceptualization," left behind in the "theft of the body" that occurred in transatlantic slavery and Indigenous dispossession: "a willful and violent (and unimaginable from this distance) severing of the captive body from its motive will, its active desire."[59] Without will or body, the enslaved and First Nations were rendered illegible to the law as persons, figured as property or inhuman objects. As the philosophical underpinning of imperial and settler colonialism, Man depended on the construction of Black Africans as the ultimate other, the slave, and the assimilation of all dark skinned peoples into the category of "native" as the negative inversion of the imagined normal human.[60] As such, they were also denied witnessing before the law, refused the right to attest to the violence done to them.[61] Thus the humanist figure of the witness fused new notions of the individual, unitary subject of rights and responsibilities with existing regimes of humanity and inhumanity. But it also carried the legacies of monotheistic religion, in which the figure of the witness claims intimacy with the divine.[62] While the testimony of preachers figures prominently in American religious culture, the martyr or blood witness is rooted in the early years of Christianity and carries through—if in radically different ways—to the present in the dead of Auschwitz and the suicide bombers of ISIS.

But the Enlightenment and its rearticulation of Man also produced a new and divergent form of witnessing, one that emerged in the eighteenth and especially into the nineteenth century as markedly free from overt ties to violence and law. With the invention of the scientific method and the establishment of practices of experimentation and observation, science and scientists both invented and claimed mastery over the natural world through the production of knowledge about it. As Lorraine Daston and Peter Galison catalog, the emergence of a new "epistemic virtue" of scientific objectivity was a complex process related to transformations in perspective, understandings of self, and much more.[63] Within this framework, the scientist bears witness, and it is upon their testimony that knowledge builds. Hypothesis, experiment, record, replication, verification, peer review, and scholarly publication built normative guard rails to ensure objectivity, like the swearing of an oath in court.[64] But the scientific witness depended on a host of erasures. Women were excluded, as was embodiment, in the invention of an affectless and cultureless objectivity.[65] Haraway writes that this "gentleman-witness" becomes "the legitimate and authorized ventriloquist for the object world, adding nothing from his mere opinions, from his biasing embodiment."[66] By constructing expert knowledge divorced from opinion and transcendent authority alike, the scientist—by default white and male—became endowed with "the remarkable power to establish facts. He bears witness: he is objective; he guarantees the clarity and purity of objects."[67] This is the figure of the witness capable of the "God-trick" of scientific rationality, which claims an objective, ahistorical, and unbiased viewpoint on the world.[68] This modest witness wins his authority through the performative disavowal of power, and in doing so entrenches science—new though it is—as the authoritative mode of apprehending the world. Against the rich multiplicity of worlds that jostled and warred with one another, this new science and its modest witnesses remade the world as a singular, knowable thing, conquered by colonialism and made profitable by capitalism.

If modern science heightens the power of Man the Witness, then the roughly concurrent emergence of print and then technical media amplifies and extends that authority in time and space, even as it enables new forms and practices of nonhuman witnessing. Media technology had always been bound up with witnessing—consider Moses, who descends from Mount Sinai with the word of God engraved in stone—but the advent of modern communications made bearing witness a form of informational sociality around which shared truths form. No longer a matter for courts, churches, and laboratories alone, witnessing through the printing press, telegraph, and radio imagined nations into being and rendered distant events immediate. No surprise, then, that media studies has had so much to say about witnessing. For John Ellis, television had an even more profound effect on witnessing by placing the viewer in the position of the witness.[69] Mass media made witnessing, as Frosh and Pinchevski put it, a "generalized mode of relating to the world."[70] But this proliferation of media witnessing amplified the "veracity gap" that must be bridged to grant the media narrative its authority as truth, as John Durham Peters explains.[71] Liveness, that new quality of televisual media, stood in as truth's guarantor: How could what is unfolding now before one's very eyes be anything but truth? Yet liveness is no guarantor of the complete picture or the reliability of the witness, nor even—as I will show in chapter 2's examination of deepfake technologies—of the existence of the witness. Liveness, like all media coverage of suffering and violence, can produce spectatorship that dispels action rather than spurs it, presenting mere seeing as sufficient response.[72] Still, media witnessing is often not intended to spark action; its purpose is to bind communities around shared understandings of events, such as the world-shattering nature of the 9/11 attacks for America and much of the West, or the extended intractability of the COVID-19 pandemic. Increasingly, this binding takes place not only through the consumption of images, but also through actively participating in their production and circulation.

In both science and media, witnessing serves as a sociotechnical apparatus that refracts experiment into authority, reportage into truth, science and broadcasting into power.[73] In the twentieth century, a shift took place from transcendental knowledge, continuous media, and analogue technologies to mathematical grids and models, discrete media, and statistical technologies.[74] In *The Practice of Light*, Cubitt argues that the emergence of technical media requires and constitutes a transformation in the processes through which (especially visual) media are produced *and* the underlying epistemic framework.[75] Enumeration, probability, and statistical inference and analysis take hold, backed by mathematical theories of information and markets. With the arrival of the postwar datalogical turn and the claims to potential omniscience that flow from a seeming infinitude of information, the "communicative objectivity" of the cybernetic revolution documented by Halpern began to bind both science and governance ever more tightly to networked systems and screen interfaces. Networked computation applied to a datafied world produced a new kind of observer, one who followed the rules of the new cybernetic order but saw the world through increasingly inhuman modalities of perception.[76] The witness as cyborg, harnessing and harnessed to new technologies of vision began to shape how data was presented and deployed.[77] But it also signaled a deeper infiltration and extension of human perception and action via machine. This technological transformation laid the foundation for smartphones, drones, remote sensors, and even artificial intelligence to become instruments of witnessing, even as they transform the relationship between witnessing and the ground truth against which it is so often measured.[78]

What these changes in media and mediation make clear is that witnessing is a relational process that probes, exposes, and undoes the limits of representational modes of knowing and being.[79] Rather than reinstantiating the authority of the unitary subject or even of language, contemporary witnessing exposes the primacy of relations between bodies, events, environments, worlds, and objects, even if they are obscured, denied, disavowed, or absent. While testimony might take the form of language or a fixed image, the experience of witnessing is always affective, occurring in the encounters through which bodies and worlds emerge within and alongside one another. Witnessing, writes Kelly Oliver, is "the heart of the circulation of energy that connects us, and obligates us, to each other."⁸⁰ But now witnessing must reckon with the unravelling of the ontological and epistemological grounds of knowledge by radical theory on the one hand and the interlocking crises of the contemporary world on the other.

In an evocative, searching essay on the relation between testimony and the witness, Michal Givoni writes that rather than an age of testimony, "ours is an era of becoming a witness, a time in which individuals are called, in greater numbers and intensity and at a growing rate, to fashion themselves as witnesses, while their witness position is never guaranteed and their mode of witnessing is questioned."⁸¹ If becoming-witness is the task set for the human, then what of the agencies that make up more-than-human worlds? If we shift the angle with which we approach witnessing and the human, the scene might be different: Could we not think of witnessing as yet another pressure applied to the human, another dissolving agent working to undo the narrowly inscribed figure of knowing and being that has both enabled remarkable advancement but also done terrible, enduring, and world-ending violence? Or, to put this differently, what if it is not only today's insistent presence of the nonhuman that demands a new understanding of witnessing, but that witnessing carries within itself an unrevealed history, a constitutive nonhumanity?

This choice to bring witnessing into conjunction with the "nonhuman" rather than the more-than-, post-, in- or even de-human was not easily arrived at. For me, nonhuman emphasizes distinction and difference from the human, but retains its necessarily entangled relation to the human and thus asserts the necessity of keeping the human in the frame.⁸² As Richard Grusin observes, "The human has always coevolved, coexisted and collaborated with the nonhuman," and, as such, "the human is characterized precisely by this indistinction from the nonhuman."⁸³ The human is, in this sense, constitutively dependent on complex relations with the nonhuman. This relationality is central to moving to conceptualize nonhuman witnessing, since witnessing itself is a relational practice. But I also find the nonhuman beneficial because it implies no time before, after, or beyond the human.⁸⁴ "Nonhuman" thus avoids the potential to read *post*human as an uncritical desire to move "beyond the human," as Zakkiyah Iman Jackson puts it, which can be an impossible endeavor for those never fully afforded the category of human to begin with, and who might not now wish to receive it, even if only in passing.⁸⁵ As Karen Barad points out, attending to the nonhuman "calls into question the givenness of the differential categories of 'human' and 'nonhuman', examining the practices through which these differential boundaries are stabilized and destabilized."[86] As such, Dana Luciano and Mel Y. Chen argue that "the nonhuman turn marks, for many critics, not a venture 'beyond' the human but a new mode of critical realism, a recognition that the nature of 'reality' itself is changing as power moves away from the individual." Doing so has material consequences.[87] For Shela Sheikh, "where care for both human and nonhuman life is at stake, witness collectivities necessarily entail an expansion beyond the category of the human."[88] This questioning of categories, boundaries, and differences is not only a matter of language, but of the affects, materialities, and mediations of forces, bodies, meanings, experiences, energies, and ecologies.

In this light, *nonhuman* should not be read as a dismissal of the related terms outlined here, nor as a disavowal of the species we call human as a key locus for the struggle for justice. Established practices of witnessing have stratified distinctions between human and the non through an inability to give materiality and relationality their due. Zylinska argues that "embracing nonhuman vision as both a concept and a mode of being in the world will allow humans to see beyond the humanist limitations of their current philosophies and worldview, to unsee themselves in their godlike positioning of both everywhere and nowhere, and to become reanchored and reattached again."[89] As I conceive it, nonhuman witnessing is both a particular form of perception and something else besides, a communicative form shaped by the materiality and affectivity of the world as medium: an ethicopolitical mode of relation for grounding anew how meaning comes to matter in the making and remaking of worlds. Nonhuman witnessing is not an ahistorical or transcendental concept, but rather the naming of a set of interconnected practices and processes of witnessing bound up with evolving epistemic frameworks and forms of mediation.

Nonhuman witnessing is not a free-floating concept but an injunction to the human to become with and alongside the non in far more attentive and attuned ways. Cubitt argues that fundamentally transformed practices of communication offer "the possibility of changing the conduct of relations between human beings and nature, and between both of them and the technologies that so profoundly and multifariously mediate between them."[90] Nonhuman witnessing is thus a historical process, one that has—I would contend—always operated in conjunction with human ethics, politics, and meaning-making but that manifests in new forms, practices, intensities, and dynamics as epistemes and media technics change through time. Nonhuman witnessing in the contemporary conjuncture is thus a response to Man the Witness, but exploits, escapes, and exists beyond the dominance of technical media. Tracing its occurrence in instances as diverse as edge computing weapons targeting and glass-blown art, this book shows how nonhuman witnessing addresses power as process, not solely biopower or necropower, but the ontopower that brings becoming within its ambit. As a modality that operates across multiple levels of sense-, truth- and world-making, opening witnessing to the nonhuman takes up the task of producing new communicative aesthetics, ecologies, and politics in the face of violence and its traumatic aftermaths.

WITNESSING TRAUMA, WITNESSING VIOLENCE

To testify is, in the most basic sense, to insist that something be remembered by someone or something other than the witness. Memory is shared across species, technics, and materials: it is human and animal recall, but also information stored in computation, ammonites fossilized in stone, scars on gumtrees after summer fires. Its politics must be forged; its collectivity brought into being. One means of making memory collective is witnessing. Memorials to wars past bear witness, and statues of slave owners, Confederate generals, and colonial "heroes" remind us of the violence that can be entailed in being called to witness and remember under the normative rule of empire.[91] Memory itself is not normative, but rather attains its ethical or moral weight through its marshalling to cultural or political ends. Witnessing, by contrast, is an ethicopolitical process: it is always and already on the brink of becoming-political, even if its politics remain latent or geared very far from justice. Witnessing orients toward the future, even if it reaches back into the past. This book, then, is not "about" memory, even if memory and its uncertainties feature often. Instead, I am interested in the registering of experience that precedes memory, and of the intimate relation between this witnessing and the violence and trauma to which it so often responds.

For trauma studies in the humanities, the witness to trauma—and to historical trauma and atrocity in particular—lives with the violent event written on and through the body, such that the past is in fact never past at all. Fragments of experience cling to the present and refuse to become memory, continuing as lived remnants of violence. Testimony exposes the failure of language, the stuttering of representation, and the shattering of experience at the heart of trauma.[92] Testimony is thus vital and necessary, even as it cannot ever provide a full accounting of trauma, nor be enough on its own to work through the traumatic event and reconstitute the subject. This is part of why trauma theory has had such influence on literary, film, and cultural theory: art addresses those incidents of history that refuse comprehension, seeking to overcome the collapse of meaning through aesthetic and imaginative force.

In this sense, trauma theory is unabashedly anthropocentric. It might not celebrate a classical humanism, but it is dedicated to the human (in)capacity to speak in the face of that which refuses or resists speech: those traumatic events that most demand voice are also exactly those that refuse representation.[93] If the relation between testimony and traumatic event is necessarily fractured, then how can the witness testify to historical facts? How can history even be written?[94] This fragmenting of the connection between writing or speech and the event throws testimony into crisis: witnessing becomes precisely the urgent task of pursuing the event that will not give itself up to knowing, whose full scope and meaning always eludes the grasp.[95] This necessary failure of witnessing within trauma theory marks the failure of the human: witnessing signals the limit point of what the human can know of itself and what it can become.[96] Trauma can never appear as itself to the knowing subject, it can never be known and rendered speakable. Consequently, the human itself is always bound by this failure to reckon with the traumatic. Witnessing cannot exceed or extend beyond the human because it is constitutive of an incapacity for the human to be fully human in the face of trauma. Positioning both trauma and testimony as operating on the line between human and less-than-human, as trauma theory does, implies that the nonhuman cannot be accorded either trauma or testimony. If witnessing enacts the paradox of the human failure to be fully human, what room is there for the animal, the plant, the stone scorched by exploding fragments of a Hellfire missile? Yet trauma escapes the confines of the subject. It can be climatic, atmospheric, collective, and it can be transmitted between people and across generations. As chapters 3 and 4 argue, trauma can be both affective and ecological. Trauma continually exceeds the human subject, which means that reading the failure of witnessing as a falling short of the human cannot hold. This very proposition is an obscured anthropocentrism that predetermines what witnessing can be.

But all this discussion of testimony and trauma implies an original violence. While trauma and witnessing are often yoked together by theory, relations between violence and witnessing are often assumed, unstated, or unresolved. In part, this is because violence itself is a slippery concept: pervasive, elusive, varied, and resistant to neat formulations. But it is also because witnessing and violence converge and diverge, coming together in some contexts but not at all or only thinly in others. Consider the difference between witnessing police killings and witnessing a volcanic eruption. Both might involve the destruction of life, but only one constitutes violence as such.

Hannah Arendt makes this distinction clear. "Violence," she writes, "is distinguished by its instrumental character," whereas force describes "the energy released by physical or social movements."[97] If violence is instrumental, it is also relational. It might well be that violence is intrinsic to being a body. "The body implies mortality, vulnerability, agency: the skin and the flesh expose us to the gaze of others," observes Judith Butler, "but also to touch, and to violence, and bodies put us at risk of becoming the agency and instrument of all these as well."[98]

But violence can be structural, as well as direct and immediate, "exerted systematically—that is, indirectly—by everyone who belongs to a certain social order," as Paul Farmer observes.[99] Structural violence resists neat ascriptions of blame or responsibility. Its effects are diffuse yet deeply harmful, enabling oppression and working to maintain existing hierarchies of wealth and power.[100] Capitalism and colonialism are forms of structural violence, even if they can also manifest in more kinetic, martial, and immediate forms. This is why Patrick Wolfe describes settler colonialism as a structure, not an event.[101] But other forms of distributed violence feature in this book: symbolic, discursive, infrastructural, environmental, and algorithmic violence, for example. Lacking an obvious originating agent, such violence takes place through institutions, linguistic exclusions, technocratic programs, extractive industries, and other such assemblages, often harnessed to state and corporate power but at times filtered through more ambiguous actors.[102]

Violence is not only distributed, but also differentially experienced. As Saidiya Hartman, Hortense Spillers, and other scholars of slavery and Black life teach us, violence strips away the body and exposes the flesh to injury, often in diffuse and difficult-to-detect ways that permeate the quotidian.[103] Racial violence exemplifies this dynamic because it coalesces the capriciousness of law, the exclusionary force of Man, and the harnessing of relation to produce subjects not governed by the law. Writing on the killing of people of color in Brazil's favelas, Denise Ferreira da Silva argues that "raciality immediately justifies the state's decision to kill" because such "bodies and the territories they inhabit always-already signify violence."[104] Violence exposes the vulnerability of the body, but it distributes that vulnerability in radically unequal ways. To say, then, that the body is defined by its vulnerability to violence makes a necessarily political claim about who gets to possess a body to encase their flesh. This is a question rooted in the Enlightenment conception of the subject, the figure of Man that Wynter ties to European colonial expansion. Binding witnessing to the human means that who witnesses is always contested ground—and witnessing itself can be complicit in the legitimation of violence. After all, can the figure denied humanity bear witness if witnessing belongs to the human? Preceding the body, flesh marked by violence offers a way outside of Man, a fugitive witnessing enabled through the generativity of flesh that refuses to give up its vitality and seeks solidarity, resistance, and joy.

Violence, in other words, is a malleable phenomenon. In war, it can be mechanized and automated, but also intensely intimate. It can unfold slowly, as in the degradation of bodies exposed to radiation or the collapse of environments polluted by toxic. "Violence unfolds on different scales, over different durations, and at different speeds," writes Weizman. "It manifests itself in the instantaneous, eruptive force of the incident, evolves in patterns and repetitions across built-up areas, and then manifests itself in the slower, incremental degradation of large territories along extended timescales."[105] Nor are those forms, modalities, intensities, and speeds separate from one another. Violence flows between states. Buzzing in the sky above, the drone generates fear and abiding anxiety, a kind of diffuse and atmospheric violence, even as its surveillance systems engage in the violence of datafication, transforming the textures of life into metadata. And then, when a target is acquired and a missile launched, violence becomes horrifyingly kinetic. People living under drones in Afghanistan, Yemen, Gaza, or Ukraine witness this violence, as do members of the military apparatus from operators to intelligence analysts to authorizing officers. But when violence is so inseparable from environments and technoscientific systems, there is much that testimonies of the nonhuman can offer. For all the moral force that resides in human rights testimony and the humanitarian witness, the entanglement of the nonhuman in violence suggests the need for nonhuman witnessing as fundamental to healing and repair for human, nonhuman, and the worlds we share.

Oliver's generative attempt at disentangling trauma, violence, and witnessing offers a way through this knot. Writing against the notion that social struggles are struggles for recognition of difference, Oliver develops a theory of the relational formation of subjectivity that turns on the ethicopolitical imperative of witnessing. Drawing on a Levinasian ethic that privileges the other over the self, Oliver argues that "the speaking subject is a subject by virtue of address-ability and response-ability."[106] Both address-ability and response-ability are at the heart of witnessing, and so witnessing is "the basis for all subjectivity; and oppression and subordination work to destroy the possibility of witnessing and thereby undermine subjectivity."[107] The inversion here is crucial: witnessing is not simply a response to violence, but what violence destroys. "While trauma undermines subjectivity and witnessing restores it," she writes, "the process of witnessing is not reduced to the testimony to trauma."[108] Trauma cannot be the foundation of subjectivity because such a move could only engender an impoverished political life. Disaggregated from trauma, witnessing forges bonds that exceed any given situation or singular act of witnessing.

Witnessing is always an open-ended, recursive, and necessarily active process of becoming. But the important move that Oliver makes is to situate witnessing within a relational milieu, arguing that the self develops its capacity as an internal witness through being witnessed by the other and that is how subjectivity emerges from and with social relations. Working within a psychoanalytic framework, Oliver argues that witnessing is essential to working-through hostilities that stem from fear and anxiety over difference. This is a "profoundly ethical operation insofar as it forces us not only to acknowledge our relations and obligations to others" but to transform them.[109] Working-through connects witnessing to sociality and makes transformations—of love, of justice, of respect—possible. Unsurprisingly, Oliver's witnessing is unquestionably human: a process that involves "language and gestures" and an act of "love" in the face of the other and against the dehumanizing power of oppression and violence. Witnessing is intrinsically human such that human subjectivity itself is the "result of a continual process of witnessing."[110] Objects have no capacity to witness precisely because the object cannot speak or gesture.

Despite this avowed humanism, Oliver's account helps elucidate some of the interventions this book makes in thinking witnessing with the nonhuman. First, the rejection of a symbiotic relationship to trauma opens witnessing to world-making in ways that invite richer and more generative potential while not at all foreclosing the necessity of witnessing in response to trauma and violence. Second, the insistence on the relationality of witnessing as enacted through address and response provides a way into what witnessing might be if address and response involve nonhuman animals, machines, entities, and environments, and so on, as long as we understand both address and response outside their familiar anthropocentric frames. Third, the conception of relationality as fundamentally biosocial, affective, and energetic already contains within it a permeability that is almost ecological in its insistence on complexity and process. Fourth, the notion that witnessing forges relations that make working-through hostilities to difference possible offers a way of understanding the dynamism of witnessing and why it makes transformation possible. Taken together, these four implications offer points of departure from the human witness and into the unruly domain of nonhuman witnessing.

In the painting *Theatre of War: Photons Do Not Care,* (figure I.1), Kathryn Brimblecombe-Fox depicts the machinic attempt to make planetary environments subject to martial enclosure. A cluster of drones, networked by fine red lines, looms over a pale dot in a field of rich blues and reds reminiscent of scientific visualizations of cosmic evolution. Viewing the painting, we reside in the cosmic distance, thrown far from any conceivable human perception of the Earth or its technologies of war. And yet the painting calls for us to attend

FIGURE I.1. *Theatre of War: Photons Do Not Care*, oil on linen 92 × 112 cm, Kathryn Brimblecombe-Fox, 2021. Courtesy of the artist.

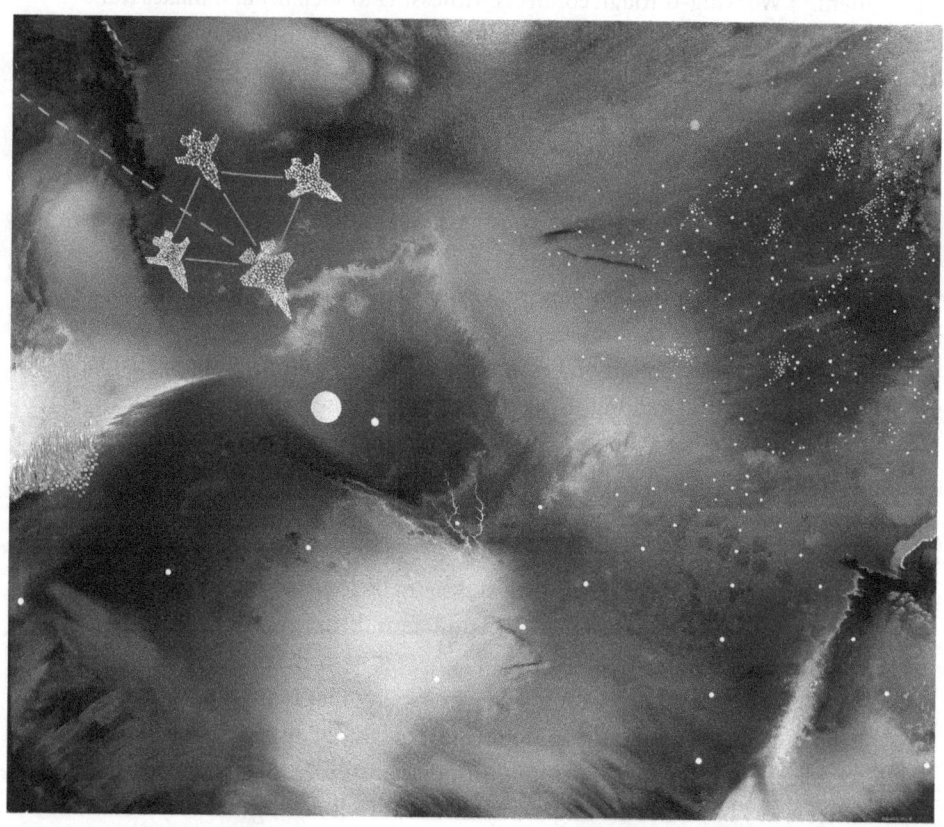

to the planetary nature of military technologies, to their growing tendency to render space-time itself as a site of martial contest. Photons do not care: these massless particles are the raw stuff of the electromagnetic spectrum, transcending national boundaries, the human, and the planet itself. And yet they are also, increasingly, the site of military contestation and intervention, as autonomous and cyber warfare infuses all other forms of martial conflict. Military media, networked systems, and algorithmic assemblages all seek mastery, and in doing so tug us into an age in which the world as target has given way to the planet as an operative medium for targeting any point on or above its surface.[111] The hand of the artist is evident in the occasional unblended brush stroke of oil on linen, and in the uneven stippled dots arranged into the pixelated drones. These pixelated silhouettes of looming drones blur computational mediation with organic representation, human hand, and galactic scale. There is no escaping the human, the painting insists, no release into an existence without responsibility for the crises wrought in the name of economic growth, colonial expansion, state power, and military supremacy. The question is what will happen, down on that pale blue dot, toward survival and a new flourishing of life?

If crisis is the political and ecological condition within which much of the planet lives, the unraveling of the fantasy of a unified, cohesive, and knowable world offers some potential for more just and equitable futures. The enmeshed desire of states and other actors to both produce and control crisis—crisis as a modality of governance that allows for the abrogation of democratic and other responsibilities—is not solely about discourses, institutions, or even technologies that target individuals and populations, whether as biopolitical life-in-the-making or necropolitical death-in-waiting. Ontopower heightens the stakes of contemporary technopolitical power, enabling states and other actors to target the stirring of life within the bare activity of existence. Techniques of ontopower seek to direct being as it becomes, to harness emergence itself to the ends of the already dominant forces of production and control. Such are the promises of the algorithmic technologies of war, governance, culture, and ecology that this book explores, but so too is there the potential in resistant harnessing of technics and aesthetics, algorithmic and otherwise, to produce new modes of surviving with and living beyond the World of Man.

Addressing human responsibility for the existential crises within which we find ourselves—and reckoning with the radically unequal distribution of both responsibility and the effects of crisis—requires us to hold onto the human. But this holding onto the human must also undo the blind privilege, the narrowness of vision, and the closed imagination that undergird an Anthropos that is bound to Man. Oliver writes that "being together is the chaotic adventure of subjectivity."[112] This book calls for witnessing as the foundation of a renewed becoming-together—becoming-environmental, becoming-machinic, becoming-imperceptible—that coheres not on human subjectivity but on the chaotic dance of life and nonlife.

CHAPTER ONE

witnessing violence

TWO MQ-9 REAPERS confront each other nose to nose, simulated aerial vehicles floating above simulated mountainous country. Light bends across the mirrored surface of one; the other is gray and black, a digital replica of its physical counterpart. Interspersed by spinning reflective planes and suspended in inscrutable contemplation, the two machines seem possessed of their own needs and desires. What takes place in this communion of militarized drones? While the drone skinned in military tones and textures is disconcerting if familiar, the mirrored drone is both alluringly beautiful and horrifyingly alien, an other-than-human object across which the gaze slides and fails to stick. Its mirroring offers no clear reflections, but rather refracts its surroundings into distorted fragments—a nonhuman resurfacing, the world rendered into the materiality of the drone as it seeks to become imperceptible. This moment in Australian artist Baden Pailthorpe's *MQ-9 Reaper I–III* (2014–16) captures something of what makes military drones fascinating, disturbing, and urgently in need of critical attention. At once threatening and seductive, the Reaper drone promises an omniscient and yet nonhuman capacity to perceive, know, and kill, one that sanitizes war by making it datalogical, computational, and spatially and affectively remote.

For the militarized drone of the last two decades—exemplified by (but far from limited to) the Predators, Reapers, and Global Hawks operated by the United States, or the Turkish Bayraktar TB2 used by Ukraine—this capacity has depended on its near invisibility, its ability to operate untouched from the atmosphere. As war becomes increasingly autonomous and more centered on great power conflict, the forms and applications of drones are becoming far more varied, ubiquitous, and dependent upon artificial intelligence.

Exhibited at Centre Pompidou, Art Basel Hong Kong, and numerous festivals and galleries, *MQ-9 Reaper I–III* presents drone warfare as violence enacted through the computational simulation of reality (figure 1.1). Built in the modeling program Autodesk 3DS Max, Pailthorpe's project reimagines key locations within the drone apparatus into the air above an environment that references the mountainous terrain of Afghanistan, over which drone warfare took its contemporary form. Shipping containers rotate slowly in the clouds, walls cantilevering open on hydraulics to reveal ground control station cockpits loaded with the screens, controllers, and interfaces needed to crew the Reaper and its siblings. Or they open to expose spare living rooms in which uniformed men perch on beige couches or do jumping jacks, transplanting the suburban life that bookends on-base shifts operating drones from the domestic United States to the atmospheric zone of war. Graphics are realistic but heightened, surreal simulacra of the computational space of war and an aesthetic familiar to both video games and the promotional videos produced by arms manufacturers. Their sterility mimics the rhetoric of precision and hygiene that accumulates around remote warfare and infuses the technocratic and corporate discourses that elide the violence inflicted by lethal strikes.

More than this, the computational materiality of *MQ-9 Reaper* is a stark reminder of the layers of simulation, data, modeling, and algorithms connected by distinct logics and processes that constitute the martial contemporary. Estranging relations between elements within the drone apparatus while insisting on the distortions and reflections produced by its operations, Pailthorpe lays bare the circulatory, diagrammatic flows of the system by shifting the locus of agency away from the human and to networked relations. When soldiers appear on screen to shadowbox and sit at their control stations, they have also entered the space of the drone and become its subject. Yet in taking up the toolkit of modeling, computation, and simulation, Pailthorpe knowingly enters the epistemic regime of contemporary war and so is bound to its informational logics and representational modalities even as they come under scrutiny. How, then, to witness this increasingly autonomous form of

FIGURE 1.1. Still from *MQ-9 Reaper (III)*, Baden Pailthorpe, 2016. Courtesy of the artist.

war? How to grasp the violence its witnessing might do? While Pailthorpe's aesthetic intervention makes for an instructive entry point into the entanglement of aesthetics, war, and computation, this chapter is not about drone art per se.[1] Rather, it pursues these questions of witnessing violence by tracing the violent mediation that is essential to perception, knowledge-making, and communication in contemporary war.

DRONE WAR'S VIOLENT MEDIATION

Violent mediation names those material processes that are constitutively harmful, whether because they cut, target, exclude, define, categorize, or classify in ways that are injurious to human or nonhuman entities and environments. Weapons targeting systems are one such violent mediation in which the flux of light, molecules, and energy captured by computer vision systems are directed through interfaces that enable the selection of entities for lethal assault. But so too are mugshots, colonial land registers, and pesticides. Mediation itself is ambivalent, as Sean Cubitt notes, its flux preceding "all separations, all distinctions, all thingliness, objects, and objectivity."[2] In this sense, "mediation as the very fabric of change, of mutation, is a builder of

Witnessing Violence   39

differences, but as bearer of communication, it also establishes organizational forms with varying degrees of longevity."[3] While mediation can be transformative and generative, enabling deep communication and the flourishing of rich ecologies, it is not bound by moral standards nor intrinsically ethical. Mediation is thus not a normative process. With this concept of violent mediation, I want to distinguish between mediation in general and those instances in which it animates human desires to control, extract, dominate, oppress, and kill. Violent mediation is often most evident through technical systems that subjugate life and nonlife to their ends, but it is also at work in datafication and computation, and in a host of biogeophysical interactions instigated by humans to bring ecologies to heel or direct them to human ends. In this chapter, my focus is on the violent mediations of drone warfare, enacted through its sociotechnical apparatus. Violent mediation is not ancillary to drone warfare, but constitutive of it.

In this, drone warfare is not an outlier within war more generally but rather symptomatic of its media saturation. Martial operations are intensely mediated, bound together through recursive informational flows structured and organized by media technics. "Military knowledge," as Packer and Reeves put it, is primarily "a media problem, as warfare is organized, studied, prepared for, and conducted according to communicative capacities."[4] Military strategy, logistics, and operations are all determined by media technological capacity, but also shape those technologies in turn. The necessity of communication across distance produces semaphore, the telegram, satellites, and the internet, and these then enable naval formations, the coordination of mass armies, the deployment of missile batteries, and the networking of the battlefield via tactical drones, wearables, and mapping systems. This co-constitution of war and media means that human soldiers, pilots, analysts, and even commanders are increasingly ancillary to the workings of the systems themselves. If this was already true in the logistics or command-and-control infrastructures of earlier wars, the intensification and proliferation of automation marks an acceleration of the removal of human agency. No longer the essential component in waging war, the human is increasingly seen as either its most fallible element or its datalogical target. The ballistics revolution reorganized battlefield perception around wider geographies and enabled the infliction of violence at considerable distance, while the nuclear revolution introduced a planetary perception coupled with the potential for violence at a planetary scale. But the emergent AI revolution is reconfiguring perception to be everywhere and nowhere, with the capacity for violence so tightly bound to perception that it too can take place anywhere at any time.

Warfare transforms not only in connection with technological, strategic, or even political change, but also in concert with epistemic shifts in the foundational frameworks, assumptions, and metaphors of scientific knowledge.[5]

From its inception, artillery targeting entailed mediation: the selection of targets, measuring of distances, the translation to maps, the adjustment of machinery, the firing of the gun. But with the emergence of autonomous systems of war—exemplified by the adoption, development, augmentation, and transformation of remotely piloted systems such as drones—mediation takes on a new complexity founded on the imagined and presumed exclusion of the human from its workings. Wide area motion imagery systems track areas as large as small cities at high resolution, identifying and following targets of potential interest that would be difficult if not impossible for human analysts to comprehensively account for. As such systems develop in capacity and autonomy, automated processes of mediation will locate, select, track, and even execute threats that only exist within the framework of the system. Military media are thus "constantly producing new enemies, and new methods of enemy identification stimulate the development of new weapons technologies designed to kill those newly identified enemies."[6] This interconnection between media and what Packer and Reeves call "enemy epistemology" and "enemy production" is not only a question of stabilized media technologies intersecting with military strategic imperatives. It also occurs through material processes of mediation, bounded by instrumental technologies but let loose on the complex terrain of life.

As I theorize it, violent mediation is embedded in a material-ecological understanding of war and the role of technologies of perception within it. In this, it shares much with what Antoine Bousquet terms the "martial gaze," which aligns "perception and destruction" through "sensing, imaging and mapping" that encompasses not just the visual but "the entire range of sensorial capabilities relevant to the conduct of war."[7] As perception and violence are increasingly twinned, mediation functions within those apparatuses to produce violence. Violent mediation is thus intrinsic to the martial gaze. We might think of violent mediation as the connective tissue of such systems, constituting sensing at the material level of technical operation but also stitching sensing into the larger apparatus: the thermal camera of the drone sensing its environment entails violence within its mediating processes, but also in the translation from sensing (thermographic camera) to imaging (decoding for optical display) to targeting (fixing of the reticule on an agglomeration of pixels). Processes of mediation occur within each stage, but also across them and throughout the kill chain. Attending to violent mediation thus means focusing on the movement, use, and structuring of information within the military apparatus, as well as within the elements that compose it. As with the martial gaze, much of this mediation is not visual—or only presented visually for the benefit of human actors within the system. Much of what is violent in such mediation is bound up with the technical processes of datafication, abstraction, analysis, and instrumentalization that increasingly animate military technologies of perception.

This chapter asks how witnessing might take place through the violent mediations of the martial gaze, and how those mediations—and the corporeal, ecological, and affective violence they engender—might be witnessed. It locates remote and increasingly autonomous warfare as both a driver and beneficiary of algorithmic enclosure, while recognizing that it simultaneously responds to and produces ecological crises.[8] Nonhuman witnessing provides an analytic framework for conceiving and excavating the witnessing that takes place in, by, through and, crucially, *of* the drone assemblage. War has always been a form of life, as Grove maintains, but its emergent contemporary forms possess a ubiquity, complexity, variability, autonomy, and technicity unprecedented in human experience. Reckoning with this becoming-war will require a refiguring of the human relation to it, but also a transformative shift in what counts as ethical and political claims to knowledge. This chapter thus lays conceptual foundations for the examinations of algorithms, ecologies, and absences that follow by showing how violent mediation is constitutively imbricated with war.

By attending to the nonhuman of witnessing, I am not dismissing or marginalizing the Afghans, Yemenis, Somalis, Palestinians, Pakistanis, Syrians, Iraqis and others who have given and will continue to give testimonies to reporters and human rights organizations.[9] As Madiha Tahir forcefully points out, "every thing is speaking and talking and witnessing and testifying these days, it seems, except the people whose family members and neighbors have been blown to bits in this war."[10] Hearing those voices louder and in more forums is unquestionably a vital task. Factual in orientation and presented as narrative, many of these testimonies are shaped by the expectations of human rights convent and the norms of tribunals and courts.[11] Their very familiarity, their echoing of testimonies of torture or rape or migration, speaks to the "becoming witness" of international humanitarian politics in the latter half of the twentieth century.[12] Such testimonies intentionally reinforce the humanist, rights-bearing subject because their very efficacy and legitimacy depends on recognition by the institutions and conventions of international humanitarian law, which are themselves interwoven with neoliberal attempts to develop a moral framework for capitalist relations in the wake of World War II.[13] Yet in doing so they seek to make recognizable encounters with nonhuman systems of violence—networked, autonomous, highly technical, and massively distributed in space—that resist the forms of knowing and speaking available to the eyewitness. There is a tension, then, between the necessity and possibility of making drone violence legible within the conventions of human-centered forums, whether international humanitarian law or rights discourses more generally. Within such a framework, drones and their data can only be made evidence, rather than recognized as witnessing in themselves. That is, human witnessing takes precedence and priority, relegating the nonhuman to the status of evidence that must be interpreted. While Pugliese provides a powerful case for a counterforensics that reckons with the more-than-human and Schuppli shows how material witnesses can obtain standing within public and legal fora, this chapter adopts a strategic agnosticism toward the agencies that animate the drone apparatus *and* to the potential for any instance of witnessing taking future shape as testimony. It refuses to deny potential standing as witness to the system (the entire military drone network, for example) nor any given elements of such systems (automated image analysis software, for example), even if they will be hostile witnesses. And it understands nonhuman witnessing as *preceding* the existence of fora for testimony, and so sees witnessing as independent from such fora. This chapter thus attends to the constitutive entanglement of human and nonhuman witnessing as a relational process of mediation through which violence is both registered and enacted on people, places, and ecologies, no matter whether testimony is ever called for.

In the remainder of this chapter, I examine nonhuman witnessing within the widening frame of increasingly autonomous martial systems. First, I consider the multiplying aftermaths of drone violence, attending to the interplay of the survivor testimony, war's material and cultural traces, and the way drone sensors and computational systems perform their own nonhuman witnessing. As a counterpoint to this bleak vision, I then turn to look at drone and remote sensor witnessing of Aleppo, Syria, in the aftermath of war. Moving from the drone war of recent decades to more autonomous futures, I then examine the violent mediations of augmented sensor systems in the case of the Agile Condor targeting system, which I read as an instance of automated media that displaces and disperses witnessing across military architectures and into the preemptive technics of edge-computing targeting systems. Finally, the chapter closes with an extended discussion of witnessing, autonomy, and the martial future of violent mediation.

Drone is the colloquial term for an unmanned or remotely piloted aerial vehicle or—more properly—an unmanned or remotely piloted aerial system. At a minimum, the vehicle requires a controller, network, and signal to operate. Hobby drones typically form a wifi network with a smartphone as controller. Small military drones such as the AeroVironment RQ-11 Raven, a fixed-wing drone designed for tactical battlefield awareness, are launched by hand, and networked to a hardened laptop. The Predator and Reaper commonly associated with drone warfare are more complex, employing a "remote split" system in which the drone is launched from one location before control is handed off via satellite link to an operations crew, typically located in the continental United States. Data feeds from those systems can flow across an array of military institutions and actors, with communications inputs streamed back into the control station via voice and IRC-style text chat. Swarming drones are more complicated still, communicating with one another in the service of a predefined mission and thus even more dependent on software and sensors.

Drone systems are complex media architectures subject to continual transformation, which means they are best understood as hybrid collections of human and nonhuman agents and the relations that bind them.[14] As Anthony McCosker and Rowan Wilken observe, "Drones have emerged as a set of technologies that throw orbital power off its axis through their unfixed, unruly trajectories, their accessibility to ordinary users and their multidirectional motility."[15] Whatever their form, as Lisa Parks and Caren Kaplan write, drones "are loaded with certain assumptions and ideologies."[16] Yet while it is tempting to think of drones as radical departures—as exceptional technologies—undue focus on their newness obscures their debt to histories of airpower, racializing surveillance, and colonial-imperial practices of classification and control.[17]

Figured within the long history of airpower and its relations to visual culture, drones don't so much mark a radical break in the evolution of the martial gaze as coalesce a set of tendencies residing within the technics, imaginaries, and conduct of modern war.[18] This coalescence is particularly evident in their operational combination with the "kill box," the US military term for a temporally limited, geographically specific, and volumetrically defined zone in which deadly force is preauthorized.[19] Defined by a grid reference system and managed computationally through militarized communications systems, the kill box neatly encapsulates the violent mediation constitutive of contemporary war in general and of drone war in particular. The kill box itself is a mediation: an operative transfiguration of world into media. In taking up life and refiguring its relation to death, this mediation is constitutively violent even before it kills, reworking the ontoepistemological status of those within its ambit from life to not-yet-death. Whether in concert with the kill box or operating in a less preauthorized context, the kill chain of the drone is distributed, dispersed, and mobile, producing and responding to emergent threats actualized within and through the network.

In this chapter, I approach the problem of witnessing (drone) violence by understanding it in relation and response to the becoming of war, rather than beginning with an imagined fixity or boundedness to war. Against the idea that the nature of war is given or known in advance, Antoine Bousquet, Jairus Grove, and Nisha Shah propose embracing "war's incessant becoming" such that "its creativity, mutability and polyvalence" are as central to analysis as its destruction.[20] Their "martial empiricism" references philosophies of radical empiricism—particularly Whitehead, James, and Deleuze—that resist any preferential focus on either ontology or epistemology in favor of an open-ended embrace of experience in all its generative mutability. Martial empiricism orients critique toward the processes, relations, affects, sensations, and technicities through which war autopoetically emerges. Such an approach necessarily involves an openness to the incapacity to provide ultimate or definitive answers and demands instead that martial violence be apprehended "as a process of becoming that is suspended between potentiality and actuality," in which the task of critique is "scrutinizing the enfolding of intensities, relations and attributes that give rise to war's givenness."[21] In the context of increasingly autonomous warfare, one starting point for a martial empiricism might be the perceptual relations that cohere around the figure of the drone, itself understood as an unstable and hybrid assemblage through which knowledge is produced and operationalized to violent ends.

My concern here, however, is less the emergent dynamics of autonomous warfare as such but rather how witnessing occurs within this condition of martial violence, and how nonhuman entities and processes engage and enfold human experiencing and witnessing. My pursuit of nonhuman witnessing within this becoming-war takes place through attention to violent mediation as a transversal process that both occurs within and connects distinct formations of martial violence, as well as the bodies, technologies, and situations that compose them. Attending to violent mediations as processes of knowledge-making and communicating opens the terrain on which witnessing can and must take place. As I theorize it here, nonhuman witnessing provides a mode of inquiry into the tensions between actual and virtual in the flux of becoming as it is interrupted, redirected, and mutated by martial violence.

Let us begin, then, with the violent mediations that animate the drone war assemblage by attending first to the shift from optical to datalogical mediations. In their first operational incarnation above the skies of Kosovo in the 1990s and then Afghanistan after 9/11, Predator drones were primarily optical technologies. With full motion video (FMV) and (usually) thermographic sensors, these drones "produce a special kind of intimacy that consistently privileges the view of the hunter-killer," as Derek Gregory puts it in an early and influential critique of drone violence.[22] One operator describes the view from above as "looking through a soda straw" that cuts context and complexity and tends to lock focus on whatever stays within its narrow targeting frame.[23] Limitations of bandwidth and multiple stages of encoding and decoding meant that video imagery was often not received by operators at anywhere close to the high definition in which it was recorded, while the atmospheric location of the sensors meant that people were principally seen from directly above or at a very acute angle, dehumanized pixels rather than recognizable persons. This violent mediation cut, reduced, and blurred complexity in ways that encouraged the infliction of force: rather than generating uncertainty that might discourage lethal action, the mediation of events in the world through the technical apparatus produced degraded information that was read as a threat within the system. While the perceptual capacity of drone sensors has advanced in the last decade, the underlying dynamics of using degraded information to produce threats remains very much in place in contemporary Reapers, Global Hawks, and similar lethal surveillance platforms.

To make sense of the drone as paradigmatic of a particular strand of contemporary war, I want to tease out the *relational processes* that underpin drone violence and in doing so shift the locus of inquiry from image and representation to mediation. Drone vision is digital vision, enabled through sensors that transform light into binary data rather than an analog imprint. Such vision operates through change and transmission of code, mathematical arrangements that can be rendered into pixels for display to human operators. Drone vision is thus operative and actionable, rather than merely representational.[24] That is, we can think of the drone assemblage as not only perceiving but also producing slices of the world upon which operations can be performed. Drones are automated media, oriented toward the future and governed by a logic of preemption that seeks to define and control threat. "Pre-emption operates in the register of the urgency of the imminent threat," writes Mark Andrejevic.[25] Privileging visual representations risks instantiating problematic imaginings of the temporal and spatial dynamics of drone warfare at the expense of properly grasping its networked, mediated, processual, and computational logics as a sociotechnical assemblage. Mediation is the performative transformation of a perceptual encounter, one that occurs in time and exceeds its content. It is a vital process, as well as a technical one: indeed, its technicity is itself a form of life.

Drone mediations are enmeshed with terrestrial surfaces and substrates, aerial atmospheres, built environments, multiple spectrums, and corporeal activities. Parks calls this vertical mediation: "a process that far exceeds the screen and involves the capacity to register the dynamism of occurrences within, upon or in relation to myriad materials, objects, sites, surfaces or bodies on earth."[26] As mediating technologies, "drones do not simply float above—they rewrite and re-form life on earth in a most material way," extending to "where people move and how they communicate, which buildings stand and which are destroyed, who shall live and who shall die."[27] In the context of war, the mediations of the drone apparatus are not solely vertical but also violent, and that violence is bound up with verticality. In perceiving and capturing slices of existence through its perceptual technics, the drone assemblage is at once reductive and productive. Reductive, in that it frames and subordinates life within the narrow aperture, angle, and classificatory mechanisms of militarized knowing. Productive, in that it transforms that life into actionable data crowded with virtual futures of persistent surveillance, active control, and even arbitrary death.

Both the soda straw and bandwidth problems spurred technological developments that marked an important shift in the sensory apparatus of war and an intensification of its violent and vertical mediations. To counter the narrow field of view, DARPA facilitated a series of wide area motion imagery (WAMI) initiatives to equip drones with sensors capable of recording and analyzing hundreds of city blocks within a single frame.[28] In its early forms, WAMI promised to capture everything, but in doing so produced an astonishing amount of data. Automated image analysis tools sought to exploit the totality of the feed, a feat what would require hundreds, if not thousands, of human analysts working in real-time. But bandwidth issues also meant that WAMI was difficult to make operational via the ad-hoc satellite, optical fiber, and wireless relays that compose military network infrastructures. WAMI thus produced spatial and temporal expansions in potential capability and in labor, network, and computational demands. Take the Autonomous Real-Time Ground Ubiquitous Surveillance Imaging System, or ARGUS-IS, which combined 368 overlapping high-definition sensors into the equivalent of a 1.8-billion-pixel camera to provide a high-resolution, full-motion video of up to ten square miles at a ground resolution of six inches per pixel from an altitude of twenty thousand feet (figure 1.2). As it was hyped in the 2013 PBS documentary *Rise of the Drones*, analysts would be able to create video windows, track vehicles, generate 3D models, and access location-specific archives to compare prior activities and track environmental change.

The volume of data produced by the system was astonishing: up to one billion gigabytes of data in twenty-four hours running at full capacity. Such potential perception far outstripped human visual capacities, promising to transform the world and its inhabitants into actionable data that can be called up on demand and rolled back and forward through time. But that technological capacity was never realized in practice due to the massive bandwidth and computational power required to make the system effective. For WAMI to provide its promised ubiquitous surveillance, the problem of getting data to humans in swiftly actionable form needed to be resolved. The obvious answer was to reduce the reliance on humans: new systems are thus built

FIGURE 1.2. Interfacial image from ARGUS-IS presentation, 2013

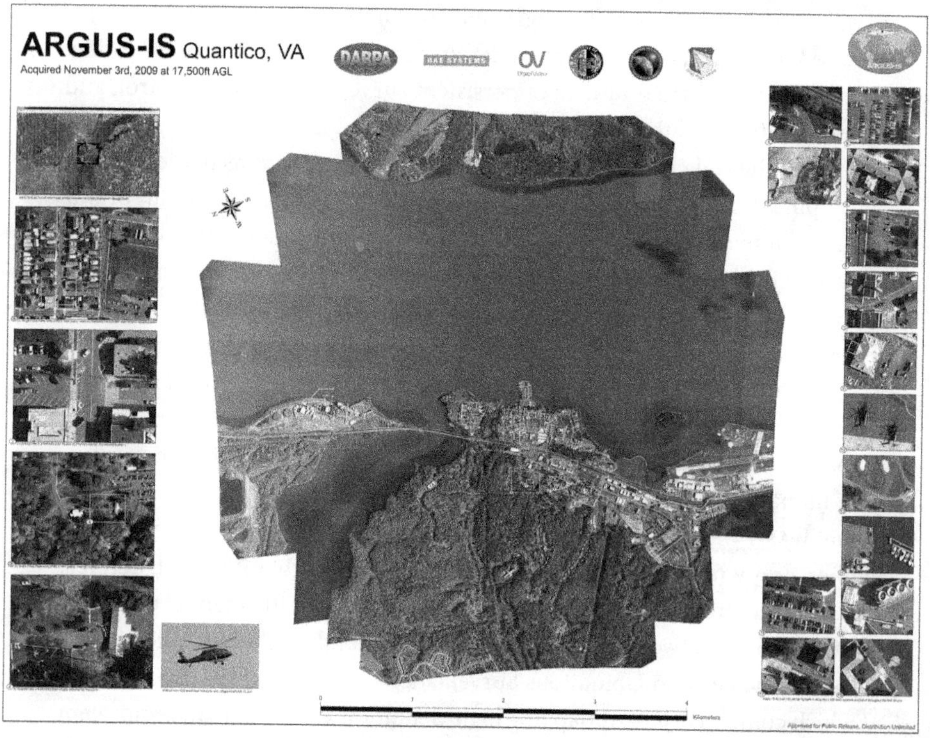

48   Chapter One

around on-board packages that automatically analyze sensor data for items of interest and then push a selected subset of data through to human analysts and operators. These edge computing systems, such as the Agile Condor pod that I discuss later in this chapter, mark an intensified operative role for computation, one in which autonomous software systems not only record and analyze but also present data as actionable, where action can lead to killing. Mediation here takes on an overtly violent tendency, not simply through what it excludes or removes but through the lives that it presents as (potentially) requiring the application of lethal violence. As WAMI, edge computing, machine vision, photogrammetry, and autonomous targeting and navigating systems in general show, violent mediation is increasingly complex, distributed, and thick.[29] The identification, selection, targeting and execution of people depends upon a growing number of systems and technics involving increasingly interoperable components, while at the same time becoming opaquer in its workings. Making remote and increasingly autonomous war sensible—that is, making it graspable and addressable within the terrain of politics rather than its irruption into martial conflict—requires finding ways to witness the workings of these violent mediations. Yet the perceptual operations of violent mediation can themselves produce witnessing: registering and responding to violence, including their own.

TENUOUS AFTERMATHS

Drone warfare seems not to want to produce lasting aftermaths. Drone wars persist, carried on through the open-ended generation of threat, the low cost of involvement for aerial powers, and the ease with which they can be returned to the air above places and populations. This distended temporality is punctuated both by intense periods and sharp instances of violence and textured by the ever-present potential of death from above. Wartime, writes Beryl Pong, "constitutes its own violent, recalcitrant temporality."[30] Living with drone war means living in enduring aftermaths, troughs of grief and ruin that follow from drone strikes and shadow operations yet can never mark an end to wartime. Drone war's aftermaths are rarely spectacular, translated into narrow idioms that commemorate and reinstantiate a lost, yet mythical, past. Instead, the aftermaths of drone war are intimate, contested, and unruly; etched in stones, buildings, gardens, and bodies; seared into the fabric of communities and cultures.

The photojournalism of Noor Behram captures these entangled effects of drone violence throughout Waziristan on the Pakistani border with Afghanistan. Haunted faces of survivors, shattered bodies of victims, broken homes, and fragments of Hellfire missiles—the people and objects documented since 2007 by Behram refuse to go unseen.[31] Among the many arresting images are those of survivors in the ruins of their homes, cracked metal from the shaft of a Hellfire held in their hands like the weight of it might break them all over again. Here is the materiality of remote war, stark matter that belies claims of surgical precision even as, according to Thomas Stubblefield, "these photographs at the same time acknowledge a certain inadequacy of (human) narrative in this system of drone vision." In one potent image, children stare into the lens, pieces of rubble offered to the camera and the remnants of buildings (a home, a school?) all around (figure 1.3). Mark Dorrian argues that the belatedness of the photographs to the act of violence—bodies, homes, and missiles already destroyed—signals the "violent cancellation of the possibility of witnessing" in the face of remote war.[32] But I want instead to suggest that these images confront the limits of human witnessing as the Hellfire fragments, ruined homes, and haunted survivors insist on richly textured, intimate relations shattered by war.[33] They both assert the radical absence of the technical apparatus of the drone on the ground, but also insist on that absence as a site of witnessing: its absence is itself a violent mediation. Against the violent delimitations of the algorithmic systems and militarized modes of analysis that dehumanize people into targets, homes into safe houses, and social relations into signs of threat, the material and affective relations that circulate within and leap from these photographs manifest the more-than-human wounding and trauma that accompanies "precision" warfare—and the inability of military infrastructures to reckon with or even acknowledge its ongoing presence.

Aftermaths such as these almost never disturb Western culture or politics, held at a distance by an apathy toward the unseen. Drone war persistently happens *over there*, despite the ramifications of its racializing technopolitics for publics at home.[34] In her history of war's aerial aftermaths, Caren Kaplan calls for close attention to "unpredictable yet repetitive intensities of time and space, disturbing the singular linear or bounded world that we take for 'reality' in Western culture."[35] Such "rogue intensities" are characteristic of wartime, holding the potential to "disturb the everyday experiences of those who might otherwise believe that they are unscathed or untouched folds places and times onto each other while opening up possible affiliations and historical accountability."[36] Careful attention to the ambivalence, contradiction,

FIGURE 1.3. Photograph from Dande Darpa Khel, August 21, 2009, by Noor Behram

resistance, and uncertainty that marks the visual history of the aerial view is crucial. But this same care can be extended beyond the aerial to its terrestrial reverberations and, in particular, its material, cultural, and affective registrations. Drone war's tenuous aftermaths become more response-able and address-able when their witnessing is not a human project alone, but also heard in the discordant strains of nonhuman witnessing.

In operation, drones flicker on the edge of perception. For people living under drones, encountering them within the visual field is not uncommon, but neither can sight be relied upon to warn of an operation in progress.[37] On American missions, militarized drones usually fly high enough not to be seen at all, or to be caught only in the glint of sunlight in de-icing fluid as it slides across the wings and fuselage of the vehicle. Rain can keep them grounded, while cloudy weather sometimes means lower flights and greater visibility and tends to be avoided by commanders keen not to alert the surveilled to their presence. But the aural presence of drones is far more constant: a whirr that cuts through the hum of daily life and grinds against the mind. One man describes the sound of the drones as "a wave of terror" that sweeps through the community. Another links their buzz both to the permanent affective state of fear and to the strain placed on communal gatherings. "When we're sitting together to have a meeting, we're scared there might be a strike," he tells the researchers. "When you can hear the drone circling in the sky, you think it might strike you. We're always scared. We always have this fear in our head."[38] Alex Edney-Browne notes that one Afghani slang for drones is *bnngina*, after the bnng noise that the drones make.[39] That buzz works its way into bodies. As Mohammad Kausar, father of three, says, "Drones are always on my mind. It makes it difficult to sleep. They are like a mosquito. Even when you don't see them, you can hear them, you know they are there." If the everyday disruptions and anxieties of life under drones is most present in their aural intrusion, then might witnessing not also take place at this level of ears, sound, and material vibration?

For Schuppli, this *earwitnessing* strains the limits of what can count as the material witness of conflict because it leaves no trace, even if when "these low-frequency emissions combine with physical matter, they vibrate the tympanic membrane of the ear, so that hearing becomes a kind of barometer for reading the atmospheric pressure of drone surveillance on the body public."[40] Yet while the lack of trace limits the potential of this aural witnessing to enter the legal domain, we nevertheless need to reckon with its registering in the body as a critical point of contact in witnessing relations. Aural witnessing entails bodily mediation in the now, yet what it mediates is the virtuality of future violence: not simply a *warning* of potential drone strikes, but an impingement of the future on the sensorium in the present. *Bnngina* is the crowding presence of the aftermath to come, the violent mediation of a possible future.

Witnessing drone warfare from below is as much about making sensible the enduring, gradual, and uneven violence done to the fabric of life as it is about registering the spectacular, kinetic violence of the lethal strike. Surviving entails reworking relations of community and the movements of daily life in counter-rhythm to the algorithmic operations of intelligence gathering and analysis. Disruptions to daily life and its communal governance are matters of space and movement, as well as custom, ritual, and routine. No longer socializing after dark, no longer holding community gatherings, no longer undertaking funeral rites: these are restrictions on mobility dictated by the uncertainty of violence from the air.[41] They also reflect intensive, shared learning in response to drone violence, a communal pedagogy of atmospheric war. That pedagogy not only entails reorienting daily life away from those activities that the drone apparatus might mark as threatening—it also involves integrating responsiveness to intelligence gathering into daily life such that the potential presence of the drone reweaves the cultural fabric. This reweaving becomes quite literal in the incorporation of drone iconography into traditional Afghan war rugs, with silhouettes of Predators and Reapers replacing the Soviet tanks and Stinger missiles that found their way into these woven images in the 1980s.

In works by Pakistani American artist Mahwish Chishty, this cultural imbrication of drone violence takes on a more direct critical dimension. Trained in miniature painting at the National College of Arts in Lahore, Chishty turned her attention to drone violence following a visit home in 2011. Combining her training in painting with the ornate folk traditions of Pakistani truck art, Chishty's *Drone Art Paintings* (2011–16) and accompanying installations and video works refigure drone technologies as splendidly visible, captured in the vibrant color and gold leaf of finely wrought bricolage against tea-stained backgrounds. Painted in opaque gouache, the works insist, as Ronak Kapadia points out, on the permanent visibility of the drone: materialized not as technoscientific monstrosity but as contained and owned

FIGURE 1.4. *Reaper*, Mahwish Chishty, gouache and gold flakes on paper, 2015. Courtesy of the artist.

FIGURE 1.5. Image from *Drone Shadows* installation, Mahwish Chishty, 2015. Courtesy of the artist.

by the body of the artist, the thick pigment of the paint, and the textured surface of the paper, exemplified by the painting *Reaper* (figure 1.4).[42] These works are emblematic of what Kapadia calls an "insurgent aesthetics" that seeks to unsettle the racialized, gendered, and colonial dynamics of empire.

Against the smooth, blank dimensionality of the militarized drone, Chishty's paintings segment surfaces into blocks of color, flowers, flag motifs, and eyes and mouths. For her *Drone Shadows* (2015) installation, Chishty painted plastic model kits of Reaper and Predator drones in the bright reds, greens, and yellows of truck art (figure 1.5). Suspending them in Perspex containers and using gallery lights to cast shadows, Chishty puts the (in)visibility of drone warfare in tension with the hypervisibility of the miniatures. In Chishty's work, there is an insistence on returning the nonhuman technics of drone warfare to the embodied scale of craft and paint. In wrestling with how to figure such nonhuman violence, Chishty undertakes a kind of nonhuman witnessing in reverse: testifying aesthetically to the possibility and necessity of making the seemingly invisible technoscientific mechanisms of violence the briefly tamed object of art.[43] This making visible and identifiable is, of course, al-

ways only propositional: an address to imagine otherwise, and to resist the sanitizing discourse that surrounds and obscures drone violence in practice.

Over Afghanistan and in the Federally Administered Tribal Areas (FATA) of Pakistan, drone strikes fit into two broad categories.⁴⁴ While "personality strikes" target specific individuals identified by the US as threats (alleged terrorist or insurgent leaders, for example), "signature strikes" are activated by emergent patterns in accumulated data about movement and communication cross a certain threshold on a predefined decision matrix. Collected by drones carrying the GILGAMESH cell phone snooping equipment, metadata from cellphone tower check-ins, calls, and texts is analyzed by SKYNET software to identify "patterns of life" that could be mapped to potential threats or targets of interest.⁴⁵ But cell phones have strange lives—SIM cards can be swapped, phones shared—and in many places the status of various persons can be multiple and contextual—local elder in one context, warlord in another. Preemption obscures such specificities in favor of what can become operationally subject to tools that identify risk and act to eliminate it.⁴⁶ Even if the technical details aren't known on the ground, the felt force of potential violence permeates daily life. Camouflage is phones changing hands, SIM cards circulating, gatherings avoided. Life's textures transform, binding existence more tightly to war. People on the ground speculated to the Stanford and NYU researchers about paid informants, worried about "chips" and "SIMS" placed in cars and houses, and complained of eroding community trust and an atmosphere of paranoia.[47] The learned protective practices of people under the martial gaze testify to an intensive relation to the potential for death that manifests in the drone apparatus. Movements, changing cultural patterns and practices, a folding into life of the vagaries of the algorithm—these are a kind of collective witnessing to the nonhuman assemblages of signature strikes and their algorithmic architectures of intelligence gathering and objectification.

Surviving drone warfare is, however, as much a matter of chance as anything else.[48] How surveillance analysts and signals intelligence processes capture and classify bodies, movements, and social relations is deeply contingent. Death, too, entails the randomized destruction of living bodies into ruined flesh. Algorithmic killing, or "death by metadata" in Pugliese's formulation, is far from the technocratic ideal. While the language of surgical strikes and precision warfare suggests some sanitized form of violence, the reality on the ground is very different. Lethal strike survivor Idris Farid describes "pieces—body pieces—lying around" and the effort to "identify the pieces and the body parts" to determine "the right parts of the body and the right person."[49] Delving into the horrific violence of an attack on a village in Yemen, Pugliese writes that distinguishing between animal, child, and adult was often impossible, bodies fused into a "composite residue of inextricable flesh. The one melts into the other. The one is buried with the other."[50] While the targeting systems and discursive logic of drone warfare dehumanizes through techniques of gendering and racializing, its violence strips its victims of any corporeal distinction from other animals. Reducing the living to "scattered fragments of undifferentiated flesh," animal and human bodies become what da Silva calls "no-bodies" and Pugliese labels "nothing less than generic, anomic, and wholly killable flesh."[51] Even the land is scarred. As one survivor put it, "The entire place looked as if it was burned completely," so much so that "all the stones in the vicinity had become black."[52]

This ruination to human, animal, plant, and inanimate entities signals the limits of a witnessing that centers the human: How can a narrow humanism account for violence that strikes at the very vitality of more-than-human ecologies? This enfolding of more-than-human environments with human flesh demands what Pugliese calls forensic ecology. His vision of a radical forensics sees testimony as "a relational assemblage of heterogeneous materials that, collectively, is mobilized to speak an evidentiary truth."[53] While mobilization within a framework of laws typically depends upon a speaking subject, the registration of violence enacted on the sites of drone strikes constitute a form of witnessing that both precedes and exceeds the human. It precedes the human because the air's mediation of light in the collection of sensing data and of force in the on-rush of Hellfire missiles is already witnessing ruined flesh, scarred rock, and shattered plant life in the instant of explosion. It exceeds the human because this witnessing occurs below the threshold of detectability—in the faint striations of dirt subject to passing shrapnel, in the misting of viscera, in the ephemerality of heat—and far outside it, too, in the elusive scale of the drone apparatus itself. Translating such witnessing into frameworks of individualized responsibility is impossible, not least when the drone apparatus itself is so dispersed as to make no one singularly responsible for any given strike.[54] Yet while this combination of fused flesh and machinic occlusion of responsibility certainly signals the limitations of rights-based frameworks for dealing with the violence of increasingly autonomous warfare, it also suggests the necessity of a conceptual means of dwelling with the thick and messy confluence of forces that produces these horrors. Such a dwelling-with can only be processual and can only reckon with the violence of drone war as process. As a process of registration—which is to say, of the violent event mediated into the more-than-human flesh of the world—nonhuman witnessing offers critical purchase, insisting on attending to both the thick knots that bind violence, as well as the tenuous strands of relation that shimmer out of reach within ecologies and technical systems alike.

On the other side of the drone sensor array, aftermaths of violence are mediated very differently. In the form that has dominated the last twenty years of remote warfare, drone sensors display sensing data in visual images on the screens of operators located in ground control stations far from the battlefield. Replicated on the terminals of lawyers, commanders, image analysts and, in certain situations, officers commanding troops on the ground, the principal lens for drone operations is either optical or thermal full-motion video overlaid with GIS, timestamp, targeting, and other key information. With the arrival of the war on terror, Parks shows how media coverage "made vertical space intelligible to global publics in new ways and powerfully revealed what is at stake in being able to control the vertical field."[55] Media coverage of the invasions of Afghanistan and then Iraq rendered the aerial view familiar, training publics to recognize and decode new ways of seeing.[56] According to Roger Stahl, drone vision "invited publics to see the drone war through the very apparatus that prosecuted it," and in doing so "framed out those populations who must live and die under this new regime of aerial occupation," rendering them vulnerable, invisible, and ungrievable.[57] When drone war does intrude on the mediascape of the United States, the United Kingdom, Australia, France, Denmark, or elsewhere in the West, it does so through the existing profusion of screens, stories, images, and mediated encounters. Drone warfare presents distinct challenges for witnessing that take place in, by, and through journalistic media.

Visible in YouTube videos of Reaper strikes and part of the visual rhetoric of films such as *Eye in the Sky* (2015), the event of a missile strike overcomes the sensory capacity of the drone: a burst of white, intensities of light that overwhelms the optical camera and of heat that undoes the thermographic sensor.[58] Focalizing infrared radiation through the lens and onto the microbolometers assembled one-per-pixel into the sensor itself, thermographic cameras have to manage wider wavelengths than their optical counterparts. For Nicole Starosielski, "the infrared camera is not just another thermal medium alongside thermostats, sweatboxes, and heat ray guns: it is a technology whose sensing capacities work to transform all matter, whether bodies or buildings, into thermal media itself." The images it produces depend upon the recasting of "the world as a landscape of infrared reflectors and infrared emitters—as a field of thermal communication."[59] Sometimes, that field overwhelms the camera's thermoceptive capacity. When a missile strikes, the combination of limited resolution and intense heat prevents infrared sensors from doing anything but assigning maximal intensities—computer vision cannot resolve what it cannot sense. Whether in optical or infrared, this incapacity to capture the event of the strike means that drone sensors necessarily repeat the erasure of life at the level of sensor process. From within the drone apparatus, the aftermath is always obscured by the destruction itself, the wreckage of buildings and bodies, thick smoke, and the heat of melted matter. Inhuman vision reveals its inhuman sensoria, yet what human sensorium would not be shocked and undone by witnessing such a thing? In the aftermath, sensor operators typically shift to infrared to identify the movements of bodies and the still-warm flesh of the dead. Prescribed by the requirement to count all dead as military-aged males, as threats until proven otherwise, military personnel decipher the aftermath according to a rubric designed to repeat visceral, material violence in informational form. This reading of the scene—a kind of brute forensics—is often yoked to the question of additional strikes. These so-called double taps are often conducted at a delay intended to flush out further threats, but are far more likely to kill or wound anyone who rushes to assist at the scene, a fact that means bystanders often choose to listen to their neighbors die rather than risk being killed themselves.

Not only are these sensors overwhelmed, but network latency also means that the drone apparatus can only ever witness on a two- to six-second delay. Whatever appears on screen does so with the event already in the past, not quite real-time but still live in the sense that the drone system always experiences liveness on delay. Distance vanishes, but time dilates. Drone systems intensify this tension between occurrence and technical mediation: an elastic temporality brimming with violence. Yet this latency also contains within it a certain necessary trauma, a deferral of the traumatic event into the durational virtuality of an arrived and arriving future. Produced by the combination of distance and transcoding between components of the network, this latency is one temporality of violent mediation, a time in which nonhuman witnessing takes place in the ambivalent space of the drone apparatus itself. This mode of nonhuman witnessing has little corporeal immediacy or political valence, but it is witnessing that registers violence distributed in both time and space. Seen in this way, the violent mediations of the drone apparatus remind us that nonhuman witnessing carries no inherent ethics, no necessary tendency toward justice, only an insistence on the complexity of registering an event as knowable. For ethics, morality, or justice to enter the frame, the question has to become one of testimony—of the bearing of witness after the event of witnessing itself. If the drone apparatus is, in its own ambivalent way, a witnessing machine, if a hostile one, then it is one that must in turn be witnessed. That challenge is amplified by new technologies that augment the sensory capacity of the drone through on-board advanced computing. But before turning to one such technology, Agile Condor, I want to first consider nonhuman witnessing in the aftermath of war in Aleppo, Syria.

WITNESSING ALEPPO

While the aerial view of war is rightly associated with surveillance, control, and violence, remote sensing systems and civic drones can also be harnessed as witnessing apparatuses for publics and researchers.[60] Such uses of sensing technologies reveal their partial, contested, and contingent nature, as well as the fraught politics of control that suffuse both atmospheric sensing and digital infrastructures.[61] Aleppo, in Syria, is a case in point. In March 2011 and amid the Arab Spring, prodemocracy protests in Daraa against the regime of Bashir al-Assad were brutally suppressed. When anti-Assad supporters rebelled across the country, Syria swiftly fell into civil war, which in turn produced power vacuums in various regions and enabled the Islamic State in

Iraq and Syria (ISIS) to take root. Fought across four years from 2012 to 2016, the Battle of Aleppo saw what the United Nations called "crimes of historic proportions" committed by Syrian, rebel, and international forces, including via Russian, American, and Turkish air strikes from crewed and uncrewed aircraft.[62] By the time the city was retaken by the Assad regime, some 31,273 civilians were reported dead and numerous culturally significant sites were destroyed or damaged according to a UNESCO conversation report, including the destruction of the Great Mosque and the eleventh-century minaret of the Ummayad Mosque. Aerial and artillery bombardment ruined roads, homes, schools, hospitals, and entire neighborhoods, reshaping the city in fundamental ways and transforming life for its human and nonhuman inhabitants.

Rather than containing the violence, the application of "precision" weapons such as drones and guided missiles seemed only to intensify the destruction: imagery of Aleppo in 2016 bears a remarkable similarity to that of Berlin in 1945. Whether a missile was launched from a drone or manned helicopter is in some ways immaterial to the destruction it causes on the ground: the dead remain dead, homes remain ruined. But in Aleppo the view from above has afforded a more ambivalent relation to aerial aftermaths than is always the case, a phenomenon revealed in different ways by the Conflict Urbanism: Aleppo project from the Center for Spatial Research at Columbia University and drone video by Aleppo Media Center, an antigovernment activist group responsible for widely shared and republished footage.

Conflict Urbanism uses remote sensing imagery, geolocation data, and open-source software tools to create an accessible digital platform for tracking the city's wartime aftermaths. As artist, academic, and project lead Laura Kurgan points out, "while war demolishes, it also reshapes a city, and, however difficult it is to imagine rebuilding in the midst of a war, Aleppo is being restructured and will be rebuilt."[63] The core of the project is an interactive map that reveals damage to the city's urban fabric by layering high-resolution satellite images with data from UNITAR's UNOSAT (the United Nations Satellite Center, run by the United Nations Institute for Training and Research). In its remediation of satellite imagery into an activist-aesthetic context, Conflict Urbanism: Aleppo continues Kurgan's long-standing research practice engagement with the politics of remote sensing imagery.[64]

From the main site hosted by the Center for Spatial Research, users are able to engage with the city at the neighborhood scale, moving through time and at different resolutions to track the damage to the city (figure 1.6). This use of technics to make visible otherwise obscured transformations to the more-than-human environment of the city succinctly encapsulates

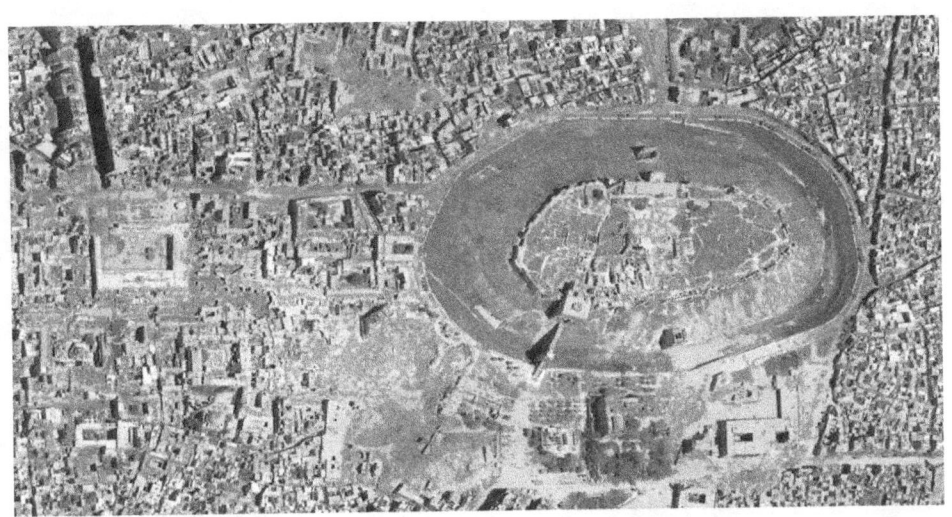

FIGURE 1.6. Image showing areas of intense damage, *Conflict Urbanism: Aleppo*

the ambivalence of nonhuman witnessing of violence. Death, displacement, and destruction are rendered legible beyond the structural and infrastructural damage to the city itself, with individualized accounts from YouTube videos geolocated onto the map to provide an alternative ground truth. Seeking to intervene in the politics of war by making spatial and temporal scales of violence knowable to humans, the project shows how nonhuman witnessing—satellite sensing, drone vision, material scarring, ecological disruption—can broaden what counts as testimony within human polities. But it also lays bare the power that resides in control over access to and tasking of remote sensing satellites, as well as who and what counts as witnessing, witness, or testimony.

While Conflict Urbanism provides a kind of nonhuman witnessing infrastructure in its own right, the project is also concerned with interrogating the limitations of that infrastructure and developing transferrable techniques that might be deployed to understand other urban conflicts (figure 1.7). A crucial element of the project is thus probing the representational politics of satellite imagery made evident through constraints of access, resolution, legibility, and literacy. With some limited exceptions, remote sensing satellites that produce public data and imagery are either operated by the US government (such as NASA's Landsat) or under its auspices, as in the case of the IKINOS satellite and its successors. While Landsat's mission is the continuous capture of multispectral data of the earth, private satellite infrastructures only take images they are tasked to collect. Users need to purchase satellite time and specify locations. While the images produced can then be purchased by others, the costs of tasking and purchasing can be prohibitive for noncommercial or nonstate actors such as human rights organizations. Depending on the satellite, resolutions down to around 0.25m are available for public purchase, but for decades the US government limited commercial resolutions to 0.5m to keep human bodies illegible.[65] This can make the work of conflict monitoring more difficult, obscuring the movement of people but also the damage to buildings from non-incendiary missiles launched by drones.

Through an experimental approach, the project produced an algorithmic dataset using open-access satellite images to measure brightness in pixels between successive images.[66] This stitching together of spatial images across temporalities allows the tracking of damage done to the city. Ground truth for the project imagery was established via high-resolution satellite imagery, as well as through the calibration and geographical location necessary to the operation of remote sensing satellites. But the project also produces a relational ground truth as images are compared, synthesized, and synchronized.[67] By foregrounding how this method is "messy and riddled with ambiguity," the project exposes the constructed and frictional nature of such relational ground truthing. It reveals material, nonhuman traces of the witnessing apparatus itself, a violent mediation within the witnessing of the city's destruction, in which low resolution obscures texture and specificity.

FIGURE 1.7. Image of interactive map, *Conflict Urbanism: Aleppo*

Alongside its tracking of human activity, such as the displacement of people from ruined sections of the city to settlements on its outskirts, the project also witnesses the complex interplay between urban environment, violence, media, mobility, and renewal. Rather than focusing tightly to specific sites of airstrikes, Conflict Urbanism attends to "what surrounds the circles—the areas contiguous to the damaged sites—in order to ask questions on an urban scale."[68] Such an approach enables a witnessing of violence that centers the intentional and incidental destruction of cultural memory, urban history, and community ecologies. This witnessing exceeds the human but does not abandon it. By foregrounding the limitations of the platform, keeping it open to collaboration and development, and directly addressing issues of data neutrality, the project exemplifies the necessary contingency of nonhuman witnessing. In Aleppo, urban violence registers its traces in Schuppli's material witnesses: wood, concrete, steel, glass, and asphalt as much as in remote sensing systems, or indeed in the testimony of those displaced residents of the city. In an environment in which people have been driven from their homes, those nonhuman material witnesses capture something that the displaced have left behind: the material and affective traces of destruction, loss, and absence of life.

Integrated into the online platform are YouTube videos captured on the ground, what Lilie Chouliaraki and Omar Al-Ghazzi call the "flesh witnessing" of digital materials recorded and shared by people in conflict zones.[69] These videos capture the angles, color, texture, and immediacy lacking in the layered sensor data. Among them are drone videos produced by activists from the Aleppo Media Center. Shot at the now-familiar but still uncanny vantage of the drone—hovering above or just below rooftop, moving with inhuman smoothness, footage rendered with an almost too-sharp definition—this footage mediates the violence of the aftermath. While mainstream media coverage of Aleppo's destruction featured drone footage from a range of sources, including the Russian military, the video shot by the Aleppo Media Center insists on capturing ruined streets, homes, shops, and squares, and in doing so both reveals and obscures the violence (figure 1.8). While drone footage is always imbricated in the militarism of the aerial view, it can nonetheless be deeply affecting. As Kaplan writes: "We absorb these views to such a degree that they seem to become a part of our bodies, to constitute a natural way of seeing."[70] This capacity to enfold nonhuman vantages into the human sensorium speaks to the malleability of our perception, but also to our cyborg existence, to the always more-than-human nature of human sensoria and knowledge-making.[71]

FIGURE 1.8. Still from drone footage, Aleppo Media Center

As nonhuman agents of technological perception, drones transect space and time to simultaneously draw us nearer to people and places and amplify or highlight our separation. Drone witnessing enables mediated intimacy with distant events, yet it also reinforces remoteness, placing the viewer in an uncanny relation to what enters the frame of the drone's camera. If the aerial view of war has become a natural way of seeing, what is outside the frame or within but obscured bears close scrutiny. In a provocative essay on the mass rape of women in Berlin after the fall of the city at the end of World War II, Ariella Azoulay argues that the absence of sexual violence from photographs of the ruined city means that witnessing depends upon attending to the affective and sonic registers of images. For Azoulay, photographs of damaged buildings, off-duty soldiers, and wrecked cars obscure violence and injustice. "[Rape] was ubiquitous," she writes, "but still, it did not appear as a prime object for the gaze of these photographers, in the way the large-scale destruction of cities did."[72] While mass rape at scale might not be an object that the photograph can capture, some of the tens of thousands of individual rapes *could* have appeared in photographs. The blown out second story of an apartment building might have been the site of rape; a woman might be raped even as the photograph is being taken. Yet this violence never appears in the images. This absence of sexual violence calls for a reckoning with the violent mediation that makes it possible: attending to what is present in such photographs as participating in an affective production of that which is not.

While a certain material intimacy exists between the film negative photographs of postwar Berlin and the city and its violence, this task of witnessing the absence of violence is complicated by the machinic vision of drone video in Aleppo. For Azoulay, photographs of spaces in which widespread and systemic violence took place but is not shown present an injunction to witness the photographs through the historical knowledge of an absence of visual evidence. She thus reads "these perforated houses, heaps of torn walls, empty frames, uprooted doors, piles of rubble—all those elements that used to be pieces of homes—as the necessary spatial conditions under which a huge number of women could be transformed into an unprotected population prone to violation."[73] Drone imagery from Aleppo shares much with the photographs analyzed by Azoulay: perforated walls, piles of rubble, blasted windows, shattered sidewalks, distended roadways. It obscures the 31,273 civilians dead, the many more displaced, and the rape, theft, wounding, and loss that accompanies such undoing of a city. Unlike the analog photography of postwar Berlin, machinic vision does not imprint the light of the world in the gelatin material of the film negative, but rather translates the fleeting response of the optical sensor directly into pixels, stored as code and only rendered in visual form for the benefit of the pilot and, later, the audience of any distributed recordings.

Drone footage of wartime's aftermaths in Aleppo mirrors processually the violence of aerial war, with its digital targeting systems, guided munitions, and sensor capture of the environment. But it reveals little of those workings: drone footage of Aleppo is what remains within the machinic frame but hidden both by the depopulated city and the technics of the sensor itself. Integrated into the Conflict Urbanism mapping apparatus, this footage both grounds and is grounded by multispectral satellite images. Drone footage introduces a more-than-human visuality that is nonetheless tied to line-of-sight operation and the practical constraints of battery life and signal strength: it returns the aerial view almost to the body and yet also retains a nonhuman detachment that heightens the witnessing of war's aftermath. Within the aftermaths of contemporary war's violent mediations, witnessing must pursue the tactile and affective, but also the machinic, technical and networked architectures of seriality and sensing. Yet the nonhuman perception of drones and remote sensors is increasingly not only an extension of human sense-making, but also an augmentation at the level of identification and decision.

AUGMENTING THE DRONE APPARATUS

Developed by SRC Inc. and flight-tested by General Atomics on its MQ-9 Reaper drone, Agile Condor is an on-board targeting system designed to resolve both network bandwidth and analytical resourcing problems that limit the efficacy of remotely piloted systems.[74] Built to analyze large quantities of data from the drone's sensor apparatus in real time, this computer system is embedded in a pod that can be fitted to the wing of a drone, replacing one Hellfire missile from its payload. Developed in conjunction with the Air Force Research Laboratory (AFRL), its makers claim that Agile Condor is an artificial intelligence targeting system capable of analyzing video footage, synthetic aperture radar imagery, or infrared camera imagery with the capacity to detect, categorize, prioritize, and track potential targets (figure 1.9). By undertaking so much image processing autonomously at the edge of the network, Agile Condor only sends imagery it deems to meet a threshold of value, cutting down latency, and relieving pressure from overstretched military networks. By only delivering sensor data of potential interest, the system also alleviates the accelerating need for highly skilled image analysts and allows them to focus on potential targets rather than sift through vast amounts of irrelevant imagery. While Agile Condor cannot make a determination to

FIGURE 1.9. Agile Condor Operations Concept, Air Force Research Lab

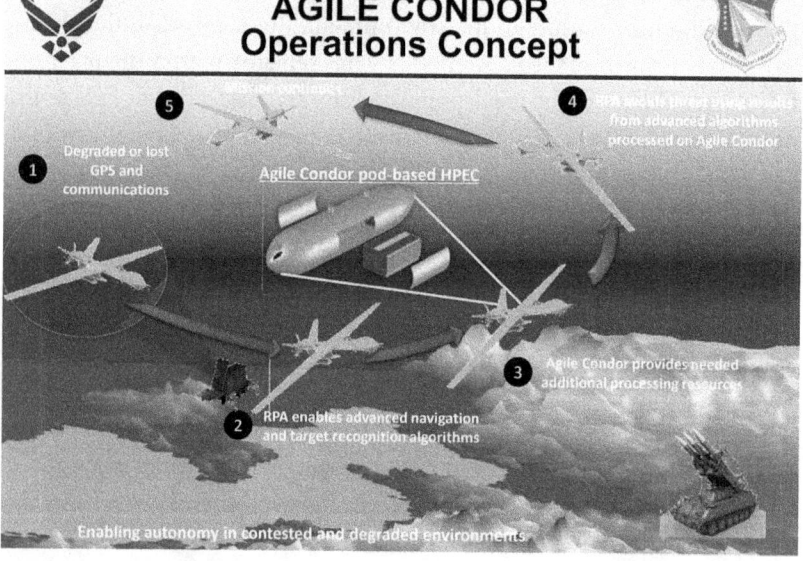

strike, it sets the background conditions for what might be worthy of closer attention and potential lethal action. It thus exemplifies both the violent mediation of the drone apparatus, but also its liminal status between human operation and lethal autonomy.

More autonomous data processing at the point of perception marks a qualitative shift in the agential composition of warfare. Autonomous military systems are not in themselves new—loitering munitions have been used by Israel since the 1970s; the SAGE system designed to monitor Soviet nuclear launches was built in the 1950s—but Agile Condor integrates autonomous perception into an already complex kill chain, inserting a machinic intelligence that preemptively shapes the fields of possibility for human analysts and operators. Agile Condor thus constitutes a kind of liminal, nonhuman witness: it (pre)determines the meaning and significance of objects and events, presenting them as open to address by the remote warfare system. Through the operative role of its on-board high-performance computer, the AI pod siphons off human agency in the name of efficiency. No longer will human analysts be concerned with discerning the figure of threat against the ground of life, but only with the array of figures presented as actionable. In the transcript of the drone strike that opened this book, it becomes clear that almost two dozen people were killed in no small part because the figures in view obtained an affective potency divorced from the milieu in which the convoy moved. That is, mission atmosphere oriented the operators and everyone else involved toward violence. Agile Condor entrenches this orientation toward identifying foes and not friends into the milieu itself: a machinic perpetrator, its witnessing tends toward violence.

In an oft-cited passage of *War and Cinema*, Paul Virilio writes that "alongside the 'war machine,' there has always existed an ocular (and later optical and electrooptical) 'watching machine' capable of providing soldiers, and particularly commanders, with a visual perspective on the military action underway. From the original watchtower through the anchored balloon to the reconnaissance aircraft and remote-sensing satellites, one and the same function has been indefinitely repeated, the eye's function being the function of a weapon."[75] This mechanization of perception involves "the splitting of viewpoint, the sharing of perception of the environment between the animate (the living subject) and the inanimate (the object, the sensing machine)."[76] This splitting of perception entails not only the human and lens, but also an entire technical apparatus that is motorized, electrical, computational, and increasingly autonomous: what Virilio calls the "logistics of perception."[77] While not on the same order of magnitude as the arrival of networked warfare itself, edge computing is an important intervention in these logistics because it yokes the ontopower of perception to the necropolitical capacity to *make die*. Unlike the simple reactive relation between sensing and killing found in an improvised explosive device (IED) or land mine, the AI intermediary enabled by high-performance edge computing means that deterministic operations happen at a spatial and temporal remove from human agents.

But while president of General Atomics David R. Alexander claims that Agile Condor's "ability to autonomously fuse and interpret sensor data to determine targets of interest is at the forefront of unmanned systems technology," edge computing is not confined to military applications or even to drones. In fact, it originates in commercial problems of bandwidth and latency produced by the move toward cloud computing architectures. Early edge computing can be found in "cloudlets" such as content delivery networks that cache web data closer to users so that, for example, ads can be served faster and more responsively, preventing delays in page loading caused by the need to pull data from distant, centralized data centers. Edge computation now exists in everything from networked security cameras to automated agricultural systems, reducing the flow of data to central control points. Against the push to centralize control via the capacity of networks to distribute information, edge computing offers the potential to decentralize control while retaining centralized authority. Such a tendency can only produce ever more radical absence, as experiences of the world are distributed, remediated, and rendered computational even as they become operative and immediate. In war, this fusion of sensing, classifying, and selecting within black-boxed technologies signals an increasing acceptance of computational agencies on and above the battlefield, a machinic corollary to the shift of the US military to special forces operations. Where the military media technologies of the twentieth century shaped and were shaped by mass, those of the twenty first are devolved, dividual, and distributed. Like power itself, military media have pushed more and more computation to the edge of the logistics of perception.[78]

Artificial intelligence is particularly appealing for dealing with sensor data because the first action required is to sift for items of interest, something that machine learning is—in theory, at least—particularly well situated to do. But standard methods of machine learning analysis require powerful graphics processing units (GPUs), particularly if the system will also learn on the fly. That means significant power loads and accompanying heat. Consequently, huge dividends can be achieved through computational techniques—both in terms of hardware and software—that reduce the need for power, via both more efficient circuit design and learning systems that only fire when needed.

According to both its marketing material and various technical papers published by the development team from SRC and AFRL, Agile Condor uses a neuromorphic architecture modeled on human neural systems.[79] In other words, its capacity for discriminating perception is intended to mimic neurobiology in contrast to typical parallel processing architecture. Both the IBM TrueNorth and Intel Loihi experimental processors used by the Agile Condor can be traced to a DARPA project called Systems of Neuromorphic Adaptive Plastic Scalable Electronics (SyNAPSE), launched in 2008 to develop revolutionary new neuromorphic processors and design tools. In contrast to typical machine learning image analysis that addresses entire images, neuromorphic systems such as Spiking Neural Network architectures are designed so that individual "neurons" within the system can fire independently and directly change the states of other neurons. Because information can be encoded directly into the signals themselves, spiking networks are not limited to binary states and can thus produce something closer to the analogue workings of the brain, more proximate to the early cybernetic dream before it veered toward an altogether different computational rationality.[80] Because these neurons only work when "spiked," the network consumes significantly less power and can autonomously gear up to higher capacity as needed. Neuromorphic systems such as Agile Condor are prime examples of what Andrejevic calls "automated media," or "communication and information technologies that rely on computerized processes governed by digital code to shape the production, distribution, and use of information."[81] Harnessed to the martial gaze, automated media reveal how, as Bousquet puts it, "the human sensorium has been slowly and surely directed, mediated, and supplanted in service to the ultimate imperative of targeting."[82]

As with so much emergent military technology, exactly how Agile Condor might function in a battlefield context is impossible to ascertain. In a series of articles published in various IEEE forums between 2015 and 2020, the research team from AFRL and SRC Inc. reveal snippets of insight about the computational architecture and machine learning techniques used in the system.[83] Using a mix of machine learning model types, including spiking neural networks and the MobileNet architecture, the researchers demonstrate a balance between accuracy and efficiency across a series of prototypes built on IBM and Intel processors. Working with a range of test datasets that include optical satellite imagery from the United States Geological Survey, various experiments achieve object recognition accuracy of more than 90 percent, depending on the specific technical arrangement. A similar accuracy was maintained using imagery from the Moving and Stationary Target Acquisition and Recognition (MSTAR), a joint DARPA and AFRL program that collected and processed SAR imagery of various military targets. But that dataset, while public, was produced in 1995 and its resolution has been far exceeded by contemporary satellite imagery. As such, even though the technical information about various chip, processor, and model configurations is interesting, these publications give no indication of how the Agile Condor targeting system would work in practice. What data will it be trained on? How will it be verified and ground-truthed? How are its determinations presented to operators and analysts? Does it have its own interface or is it integrated into existing ground control station control systems? What information is made available back through the system about modeling, probability, and so on? How much on-the-fly learning is the system capable of executing, and what quality control mechanisms are in place to verify accuracy or intervene in the learning process?

With the in-practice workings of the apparatus itself largely foreclosed, we can turn instead to the promotional materials for an articulation of the military imaginary that animates Agile Condor. In a two-minute video produced by SRC Inc., Agile Condor is presented as a powerful tool for saving lives and preventing violence.[84] Rendered in computer graphics that share the gritty, lens-flare aesthetic of popular video games such as the *Call of Duty* series, a General Atomics Reaper drone takes off from a mountainous air force base to a dark techno soundtrack. Cruising at night above a dense urban environment, its sensor system identifies various objects, marking them with glowing green squares. Then Agile Condor kicks in, automatically analyzing incoming imagery (figure 1.10). Dramatized as a clichéd array of image feeds entering the hardened box of the computer itself and headlined in multiple places with the term "neuromorphic computing," the Agile Condor swiftly does its magic and an alert flashes up: THREAT DETECTED. Cut to a swarthy figure with an RPG on his shoulder, then a convoy of vehicles, and back to the aerial view. Now, the convoy vehicles are marked in blue and the threat in red. The sensor pulls focus onto the threat and zooms in tight, resolving a high-resolution image that it then runs through a facial recognition system to obtain a 98 percent match (figure 1.11). Signal streams back to command, where "Agile Condor with neuromorphics enabled has detected an imminent threat." The convoy can now be diverted and helicopters sent to arrest the would-be assailant.

Hyping the efficacy of the system in producing a swift, bloodless resolution is not unusual for this genre of military technology videos, but the presentation of its technics is revealing of the imaginaries that animate

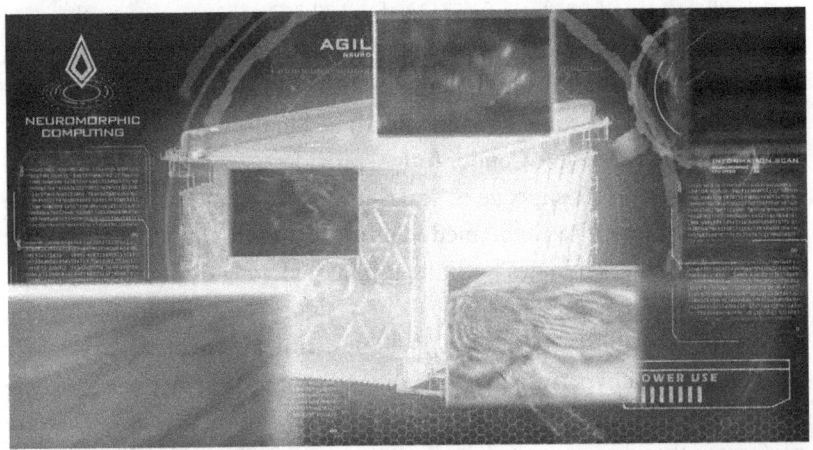

FIGURE 1.10. Agile with "neuromorphics enabled," still from "Agile Condor™ High-Performance Embedded Computing Architecture," YouTube video, October 15, 2016

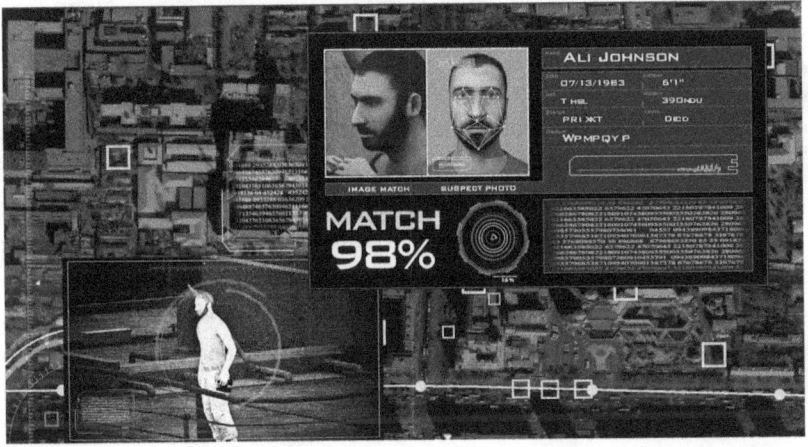

FIGURE 1.11. Still from "Agile Condor™ High-Performance Embedded Computing Architecture," YouTube video, October 15, 2016

military desires for AI systems such as Agile Condor. Sensor capture, image analysis, threat determination, geolocation, signals transfer, and operational actualization are all presented as seamless, frictionless processes. Wide area surveillance captures data at scale, which is then immediately transduced into the Agile Condor analytic engine to identify and locate an imminent and incontrovertible threat. How those analytics take place is obscured: Does the system first identify a static figure in the dark? Does it map onto the convoy? What are the relations between those things? Is it correlating between different sensor feeds in real time? Once the threat is detected, the capacity to recognize a face—something not mentioned in the technical papers published to date by the Agile Condor team—provides a granular, individualized level of analysis. This slippage in scale—from the unknown, impenetrable urban environment to the named identity of an individual—exemplifies the god trick that animates both the militarized view from above and the artificial intelligence system. Agile Condor figures as a watchful guardian, capable of oscillating between scales and presenting immediately actionable information to a hyperresponsive command center. Despite the immediate threat of violence, the response is measured and clinical. Precision warfare performed through automated media promises to facilitate bloodless control.

As is often the case in military promotional materials, the use cases presented for public consumption veer closer to policing than mass or even "precision" violence. Nevertheless, we can observe what Andrejevic calls the "cascading logic of automation" in which "automated data collection leads to automated data processing, which, in turn, leads to automated response."[85] This cascading logic has an inherent connection to the death drive, exemplified by the development of Lethal Autonomous Weapons, but evident in technologies such as Agile Condor, which are not only designed to facilitate the application of lethal force but also to be part of the process of tipping over the threshold into ever more complete autonomy. More specifically, Agile Condor can be understood as operating in the mode of preemption, which "dispenses with the question of causality: it takes as given the events it targets, relying on comprehensive monitoring and predictive analytics to stop them in their tracks."[86] Neural network analysis of sensor data is preemptive in this way, filtering through data streams for sets of image characteristics that map to particular models. Presenting the correlative outputs of this analysis works to preempt interpretation, framing everything presented as potentially actionable. This direct intervention in the becoming-target of people, structures, and ecologies, reveals Agile Condor as an operative expression of what Massumi calls "ontopower": the power to bring into being. Agile Condor and all such autonomous systems do not simply identify targets but produce them through their violent mediation of the world around them, binding affect and encounter into the knowledge apparatus of the AI-enabled drone.

Agile Condor points to the existence of a machinic witnessing operating exclusively within an algorithmic domain inaccessible to the human. This machinic witnessing occurs alongside the preemptive determinations that the system makes. Diffracted through the hunt for emergent threat and within the loop of sensor capture and algorithmic identification, classification, filtering, and prioritizing, this mode of relation to the event probes the limits of witnessing, as the next chapter examines in detail in the context of learning algorithms. Within the broader milieu of drone warfare, any witnessing that occurs within the Agile Condor system needs to be understood in relation to its consequences for the witnessing that takes place within the wider apparatus and in conjunction with its human actors. "Prosthetically tethered to the war machine," writes Bousquet, "the combatant's cognitive and neurological labors are hitched ever more tightly to cybernetic control loops, mind and body subsumed into complex assemblages that render the locus of agency increasingly diffuse and uncertain."[87] This dispersal of agency throughout the system means that witnessing—as a mode of relation that binds agencies to events—is also diffused. This diffusion concentrates within particular pockets of intra-activity, sites of intensity where perceptual transductions take place, and where determinations are rendered in relation to the data produced. If preemptive technologies such as Agile Condor seek to cut through the inefficiencies of symbolic, narrative, and causal analysis, they also undo the grounds of evidence itself by presenting the (potential) need for action through an operative frame detached from the complexities of the world beyond the sensor.[88] In this sense, the machinic witnessing at work within the technical constellation of Agile Condor pod, sensor array, and aerial drone constitutes a kind of witnessing without evidence. For the human operators, analysts, and commanders looped into such cybernetic controls system to varying degrees of intimacy, witnessing is already violently mediated by the preemptive shaping and techno-authority of the targeting system. For those operators "seeing" war through the machinic eye of automated imaging and analysis systems, witnessing drone violence is inescapably nonhuman. Not only because the apparatus mediates what is captured by its sensors, but also because human witnessing is already preemptively entangled within the machine vision system.

WITNESSING AUTONOMY

"If we disregard for a moment the fact that robotic intelligence will probably not follow the anthropomorphic line of development prepared for it by science fiction," writes Manuel DeLanda in his 1991 book *War in the Age of Intelligent Machines*, "we may without much difficulty imagine a future generation of killer robots dedicated to understanding their historical origins."[89] Such a robot historian, DeLanda speculates, would compose a very different history of their own emergence than a human might, one far more concerned with how machines shape human evolution toward their own autonomy than with the agency of humans in assembling them. In the evolution of armies, "it would see humans as no more than pieces of a larger military-industrial machine: a war machine."[90] Seeking to trace its own emergence, the historian of a world of autonomous, weaponized robots would turn not to human historical witnesses but to instances of machinic, signaletic, energetic, and elemental witnessing registered in material records and relics, in the transformation of motors, fuel cells, transponders, mining equipment, the chemical composition of geologic layers, atmospheres, and oceans. "Order emerges out of chaos, the robot would notice, only at certain critical points in the flow of matter and energy," and so the question for the robot historian might well be how certain factors cohere within self-organizing processes to tip them over into evolutionary progression.[91]

Borrowing from Gilles Deleuze, DeLanda calls this autopoetic coherence the "machinic phylum," or the set of self-organizing principles and processes that share deep mathematical similarities.[92] For DeLanda's putative robot historian, the notion of a machinic phylum that blurs distinctions between organic and inorganic life would be deeply appealing: it would suggest an inherent yet emergent coherence to the existence of "artificial" intelligence that is not outside or alien to "nature." Given how indebted computation is to war, any account of how robot intelligence emerged would have to center military technologies: "The moment autonomous weapons begin to select their own targets, the moment the responsibility of establishing whether a human is friend or foe is given to the machine, we will have crossed a threshold and a new era will have begun for the machinic phylum."[93] In the three decades since DeLanda's book, autonomous systems have proliferated, evolved, and mutated in startling ways. In this chapter, I have shown how targeting technologies such as Agile Condor operate on the cusp of autonomy, producing potential targets within a situation of imagined machinic precision. Yet there are already autonomous weapons systems that significantly predate the new typologies built on artificial neural networks and other predictive analytics. Missile defense shields such as Israel's Iron Dome operate on predefined rules to knock out incoming attacks in response to sensor data. Packer and Reeves point to aerial weapons systems "programmed with a range of potential target criteria" that allows them to "slip between offensive and defensive modes, loitering in an engagement zone until an appropriate target can be discovered and automatically engaged."[94] Like all revolutions, then, the seemingly sudden arrival of killer robots—heralded by viral videos of dancing Boston Dynamics humanoids and swarming slaughterbots—has deeper historical roots. Many of the most autonomous systems today are not found on killer drones, but in huge guns mounted on naval vessels or on mobile artillery platforms designed for surface-to-air defense.

While much of the history of early computing flowed from the labs of DARPA and other military agencies to the corporate world, rapid advancement of machine intelligence now largely takes place at Google/Alphabet, Amazon, Microsoft, Alibaba, Facebook/Meta, Palantir, and the countless startups striving to join or be bought by the tech giants, or at university labs, many underwritten by the tech industry.[95] AI systems are built to be transposable from one situation to another, such that machine vision and navigation techniques developed for autonomous passenger vehicles can be readily adapted to military contexts. With the infamous Predator already mothballed and the Reaper slated to be decommissioned, remote warfare is increasingly characterized by a far more diverse range of vehicles, platforms, and systems. In the swift 2020 war between Armenia and Azerbaijan, for example, the latter's autonomous and semiautonomous drones proved decisive, demonstrating the increasingly accessibility of these technologies for military actors and signaling the capacity of homegrown automated systems to shift the calculus of war. In Ukraine's resistance to the 2022 Russian invasion, creative applications of consumer off-the-shelf drones augmented the use of large-scale weaponized drones and loitering munitions. At the same time, an arms race for swarming drone technologies is underway, with India trumpeting a field test of seventy-five swarming drones in 2021 and the DARPA OFFSET program showcasing mixed ground and aerial swarms in 2019, stoking fears of a new genre of weapons of mass destruction. While this diversification means that drones designed for an ever-widening array of mission types and milieus can be readily found, increasingly critical questions concern software systems, data collection and analysis, and the operative processes that enable identifying friends and foes, and targeting those deemed threats. Like DeLanda's robot historian, we are now confronted with the problem of tracing the emergence of such systems, but even more acutely with the necessity of constructing the means to witness the autonomous violence they will—and already do—produce.

Reflecting on the necessity for research to understand war in ontological terms, Caroline Holmqvist calls for greater attention to "what it means to be a human being living the condition of war."[96] Without diminishing the significance of this question, in the face of increasingly autonomous martial systems and operations an inseparable concern is what it means to be nonhuman in the condition of war. Or, to inflect this slightly differently, making war sensible for humans means being able to ask how autonomous warfare systems shape and are shaped by the world-making and knowledge-forming interplay of humans and nonhumans alike. Like the Reaper or Agile Condor, such systems are witnessing machines, but also what must be witnessed. I want instead to ask how nonhuman witnessing invites an alternative approach to questions of human accountability, responsibility, and intelligibility in the operation of autonomous war. But the challenge of pursuing martial empiricism into the realm of emergent military technologies is that so much remains in the virtual space of speculation and proposition. We can only seek to move with the machinic turbulence of uncertain becomings that are still very much in the process of (self-)organizing into the autonomous, machinic violence of the future.

Within critical discussions of autonomous weapon systems, focus often centers on the role of human actors within the system. As with so much debate about AI more generally, problems are framed around the accountability of systems to human oversight. In military parlance, this is typically understood by the position of the human in relation to the "loop" of decision making that runs from sensing to targeting to firing. If a human is in-the-loop, they have a deciding role on whether an action will be taken; on-the-loop they have active oversight and the immediate capacity to intervene; off-the-loop, the system runs autonomously without direct oversight. Prominent critics of lethal autonomy, such as the roboticist Noel Sharkey, have proposed more graduated categories for defining autonomy that center the agency of human actors, with the aim of delineating high degrees of autonomy that should be prevented from being strapped to lethal weapons.[97] But while these are important distinctions that support the international legal push to ban lethal autonomous weapons systems, they operate within a larger tendency toward the excision of the human from military systems. Military precision, logistics, organization, and speed all depend on what Packer and Reeves call "a preventive humanectomy" that promises to reduce friction and boost efficacy by eliminating the weak point in data processing regimes.[98] An ultimate end of the militarization of violent mediation is thus the elimination of the human within technological systems to anything other than a potential target for violence. Within such systems, the capacity for the human to witness war narrows to the sharp, brutal end of violence, almost certainly launched from a significant geographical distance.

Witnessing this becoming-target becomes impossible from within the humanist frame, both because the human is excised and because technoscientific military systems, particularly those underpinned by complex algorithms or artificial neural networks, are themselves inscrutable to humans. Problems of black-boxed processes and partiality within knowledge production and decision making are not unique to algorithms. Rather, as Amoore points out, algorithms help "illuminate the already present problem of locating a clearsighted account in a knowable human subject."[99] Knowledge of both self and other is always partial, yet these limitations of knowledge are buttressed by culture, politics, ethics, and sociality. Witnessing functions to bridge this lack, proffering a relationality grounded in the necessity of building shared knowledges, ways of living, and forms of connection. Reflecting on the feedback loops, datafied human associations and actions, and back propagation mechanisms of machine learning systems in both surgical robots and weaponized drones, Amoore points out the "human in the loop" is an elusive figure: "The human with a definite article, the human, stands in for a more plural and indefinite life, where humans who are already multiple generate emergent effects in communion with algorithms."[100] Unlike the human witness, nonhuman witnessing transects these dynamics by refusing the distinctions that underpin and separate out the human and the machine. Against the notion that a reasoning human might provide both an ethical decision and a witnessing account of autonomously executed violence, nonhuman witnessing insists on the incapacity of either human or computer to account for itself or the other. By starting with entangled relationalities, nonhuman witnessing addresses violent mediation as an autonomous process that nevertheless must be understood in relation to the human—and the human must be grasped in its complicity with and resistance to such violent mediations.

My claim is *not* that understanding certain machinic processes as nonhuman witnessing would magically "reveal" or "expose" something new about those processes. Rather, my contention is that the recognition of nonhuman witnessing requires new critical understandings of the relations between elements within systems of autonomous violence, and in doing so insists that we resist an uncritical return to the figure of the autonomous liberal subject as the antidote.[101] If nonhuman witnessing takes place *within* autonomous military systems through the registering of violent or potentially violent events by sensors, their transformation into actionable data through machine vision, and their determination as killable according to a computational matrix of preemptive predictions, then the nonhuman witnessing *of* autonomous military systems must reckon with the violent mediations of witnessing itself.

Witnessing Violence 77

Within autonomous systems, those violent mediations are always directed toward the future. Or, rather, they depend on accumulated data from the past to produce machinic predictions about the future.

Predictive analytics are thus always about the production of futures, or the preemptive demarcation of certain virtuals as more or less on the verge of becoming actual. "Threat is from the future," writes Brian Massumi. "It is what comes next. Its eventual location and ultimate extent are undefined. Its nature is open-ended. It is not that it is not: it is not in a way that is never over."[102] This is the logic of preemption, where, as Andrejevic points out, "the imminent threat becomes the lens through which a range of risks comes to be viewed by those with the tools for responding to them."[103] Autonomous military systems, whether weaponized or merely analytic, produce threat in order to master it and in doing so collapse the future into the present through the violent mediation of limitless potentiality into actionable probability. Such systems are ontopowerful because they seek to intervene in becoming itself, in the emergence of events from the temporal unfolding of existence within time. While the claim of such systems is for security (of the state and its citizens) and accuracy (in reducing the loss of life of those becoming-targets), this masks a necropolitical imperative: the automated determination of death as a mechanism for the production of power. Lethal autonomous weapons systems show how technoscientific necropolitics continually pushes power to the edge of perception, which functionally merges with the limits of operability. If the ultimate injunction of witnessing in war is to account for the infliction of violence, then witnessing automated killing must necessarily entail the nonhuman.

In considering how violence and perception are bound together in war, Lucy Suchman poses the question: "Just what are the particular apparatuses of recognition that comprise contemporary military discourses and technologies? How does the current 'threat' become recognizable, as specifically situated persons, embodied and emplaced?"[104] I would also ask, how is violence at work within the apparatus itself, in the process of making operative images of persons, places, and animals? And what relations are forged, transformed, or destroyed in the operation of the system? By pursuing the specific processes of media technologies of increasingly autonomous war, I have sought in this chapter to show how answering these questions depends upon an openness to the transductive relations between human and nonhuman, organic and inorganic, technical and embodied. Just as the human witness might testify to what they have seen, however partial, and seek to render into language the thickness of experience, however incompletely, so too might nonhuman witnessing entail rendering sensible, however inadequately, the violent mediations of datafication, preemption, and operationalism.

Once again, this pursuit of nonhuman witnessing returns us—seemingly inevitably—to the human. In a fierce critique of the sociopolitical implications of algorithmic violence, Peter Asaro writes that in an age of autonomous weapons we need to ask: "What will it mean to be human? What kind of society will these systems be defending?"[105] Questions of geopolitical power, of regional and global balances and arms races, are not enough. Algorithmic warfare leverages the globalized economy, infrastructures, and mobilities that gird contemporary technocapitalism, which means that these questions of how we reckon with its knowledge machines and knowledge claims are not solely the preserve of military strategists or critical theorists. The necro- and ontopolitics of algorithmic war and contemporary state violence share a voracious need for embodied targets, human or otherwise, and autonomous war must be returned to questions of life in material and martial terms, as well as conceptual ones. Bound up with this task is also an understanding of the human and machinic labor involved in such systems, a question which I will take up in the next chapter.

The point is not to grant the political subjectivity of the human witness to algorithms or killer robots or semiautonomous drones, or to relegate the human from a central role in the witnessing of war. Recognizing the agency of nonhuman entities does not equate to granting them citizenship, but nonhuman witnessing aims to bring them into the space of political contestation with their agency intact. Speculating on the future consequences of autonomous weapons for the status of the human, Grove asks: "What will a close encounter with nonhuman intelligence do to force a 'persisting us' to rethink the use to which we have put machines in the pursuit of what we ourselves have been unwilling to do?"[106] Another way to pose this question is to ask what ethicopolitical status we might afford to self-aware machinic encounters with the world? How will we think about the forms of knowledge they generate and the testimonies of unjust use they might compose? In returning to the human, then, the task at hand is to retain the nonhuman agencies, knowledges, and relations excavated here, alongside an embodied, situated, and contingent humanity. In the next chapter, I pursue this challenge in response to the machine learning algorithms that are increasingly deployed as techniques of power by states and corporations—but that can also provide openings for resistance to those very institutions.

CHAPTER
TWO

witnessing algorithms

LAUNCHED IN AUGUST 2020, the latest edition of the venerable Microsoft Flight Simulator video game series offered an open-ended experience of a world made suddenly inaccessible by COVID-19. Unlike its predecessors, MS Flight Simulator 2020 makes the entire planet its gameplay environment. In the hyperbole typical of much of the media coverage, *New York Times* tech columnist Farhad Manjoo proclaimed that Microsoft had "created a virtual representation of Earth so realistic that nearly all sense of abstraction falls away."[1] As a technical achievement, Flight Simulator is certainly impressive. Combining data from OpenStreetMaps and Bing Maps via the Azure artificial intelligence cloud computing platform, Microsoft created an algorithmic system to assign and render photorealistic 3D imagery of skyscrapers, homes, trees, oceans, mountains, and so on. This imaging of the world is not, however, photographic but datalogical: generated algorithmically by a machine learning model fed vast amounts of map, satellite, photogrammetric, and other data. It is a machinic imagining of the textures of the world. Like Google Earth, it is a datalogical attempt at solving the fundamental problem that plagues the unusable map from Borges's short story "On Exactitude in Science," which in the effort to precisely represent every detail of an empire grows to the same size as the territory. Rather than indexing its cartography to the world perceived by human mapmakers, Flight Simulator generates what its algorithms believe the world to be. Players quickly found numerous strange glitches: a corporate office tower in place of the Washington Monument, a mashup of vegetation and buildings in the Norwegian town of Bergen, obelisks in place of palm trees. Far from a utopian rendering of a world made beautiful yet knowable, Kyle Chayka writes in *Slate* that Flight Simulator reminds us that "an automated, unchecked process is warping the (virtual) world around us, leading to these weird errors and aberrations."[2] Even as Flight Simulator seemed to offer a new algorithmic means of witnessing in wonder at the world, its glitches remind us of the necessity of witnessing those same algorithmic systems. If algorithms are themselves witnessing, making knowledge, and forging worlds of their own design, what might it mean to witness their workings?

The world-making capacity of the algorithm is not readily apparent in its more common definitions: a step-by-step instruction of how to solve a task; a recipe; a form of programmed logic; an automated filtering mechanism. These commonplace accounts fail to get to the heart of things, the operative processing made possible by the "if... then" procedure of the algorithm and its potentially harmful outcomes.[3] In principle, algorithms are abstract processes, which means they are not dependent on a specific computer language for their validity. But in practice, algorithms are typically encoded in distinct computer languages and ecosystems. More than this, though, they are also inescapably *codes* in the sense that they unlock certain translations, operations, or transformations of data.[4] We might even think of them as *magic* in the sense that the incantation of the algorithm by the software within which it is packaged enables action to be performed. Like codes and magic, algorithms conceal their own operations: they remain mysterious, including to their makers. This inscrutability is particularly the case with the machine learning algorithms that have become the principal means by which power is now enacted, maintained, and reproduced in the digital domain.

Machine learning is a technique for the statistical analysis of huge quantities of data. A machine learner is an algorithmic system in which computer code learns from data to produce a model that can be deployed on more data. Machine learning produces models by using algorithmic techniques to look for patterns in huge amounts of data, then applying those patterns to the data to become increasingly discerning: able to recognize, differentiate, and discriminate between elements within the database. Machine learning powers everything from inbox filtering to Netflix recommendations and it feeds on the data produced through our interactions with those systems. Machine learning systems and the companies that promote them almost always seek to obscure both the "free labor" of user interactions and the low-paid labor of digital pieceworkers on platforms such as Mechanical Turk in an effort to sell the technical prowess of their "AI" inventions. Machine learning uses layers of neural networks—arrays of computational nodes that work collaboratively to build relations between bits of data—to make predictions about the data. With OpenAI's ChatGPT, this manifests as the statistical production of text based on what the model anticipates to be the desired answer to a query. In military operations, it might mean identifying and prioritizing distinct threats in a crowded conflict zone. Rather than following a defined sequence of steps, machine learning models act recursively to build relational functions that can be applied ever-more accurately and efficiently, provided the learner is trained and optimized appropriately.[5]

But this technicity is not purely technical. As Adrian Mackenzie points out, there are no machine learning systems without human coders and humans are also needed to tag objects in the datasets for the supervised training by which many machines learn.[6] In so-called unsupervised learning, algorithms develop their own data tags, but human effort is still constantly required to tweak, select, optimize, and monitor training. Jathan Sadowski calls this "Potemkin AI," or artificial intelligence that is actually only thinly computational and largely driven by human labor.[7] On top of the obscured human labor, Sy Taffel shows how computational systems also elide massive ecological costs of powering and cooling data centers, not to mention mining rare and common metals or shipping equipment across the globe.[8] To bring machine learning into the language of this book, its models and algorithms are not alien, purely technical agents wholly separate from the human, but rather enmeshed with the human and with the more-than-human world. How machine learners make knowledge matters because they are increasingly pivotal to contemporary finance, logistics, science, governance, national security, and culture, yet they remain hard to scrutinize, building blocks in what Frank Pasquale calls the "black box society."[9]

Despite their technical veneer, algorithms are shaped and bound by assumptions and values about the world, drawn from the datasets upon which they are built, the biases of their architects, and the instrumental objectives of the institutions that use them. These assumptions and values might be as straightforward as whether to order library books by alphabet or catalog number, or as outrageously discriminatory as Facebook allowing housing advertisers to exclude users from target audiences using zip codes and other proxies for race, class, and religion. Given the colonial entanglements of modern science, regimes of classification, and the statistical techniques that underpin contemporary data science and machine learning, the constitutive violence of many such systems should come as no surprise. Algorithmic violence, whether in the form of digital redlining or autonomous weapons, is an ethicopolitical problem much more than a technical one.[10] As Ed Finn points out, the algorithm is a crucial site of critical inquiry because it is "the object at the intersection of computational space, cultural systems and human cognition."[11] Traceable back to the cybernetic era of computational research that followed World War II, algorithms were at the center of a radical transformation that substituted rationality for reason. Within two decades of the war, as Orit Halpern argues, "the centrality of reason as a tool to model human behavior, subjectivity, and society had been replaced with a new set of discourses and methods that made 'algorithm' and 'love' speakable in the same sentence and that explicitly correlated psychotic perspective with analytic logic."[12]

Now deployed across almost every field of human endeavor and inquiry, algorithms bridge the gap between computation, culture, and thought—but they are not reducible to any of those domains. According to Taina Bucher, algorithms are "entangled, multiple, and eventful and, therefore, things that cannot be understood as being powerful in one way only."[13] Consequently, "algorithmic systems embody an ensemble of strategies, where power is immanent in the field of action and situation in question."[14] Research by Safiya Noble and others into the oppressive biases of Google and Facebook shows how supposedly objective systems are inseparable from racism, sexism, and other socially produced and reproduced structures of domination.[15] Generative AI tools such as Dall-E 2 or Midjourney are no exception, evidenced by the efforts of their architects to engineer user inquiries rather than resolve the impossible problem of the underlying data.[16] As Nick Seaver argues, "algorithms are not singular technical objects that enter into many different cultural interactions, but are rather unstable objects, culturally enacted by the practices people use to engage with them."[17] Much like a poem, algorithms are tricky objects to know and often cannot even reveal their own workings.[18] Critical research thus attends less to what an algorithm *is* and more to what it *does*.[19]

In pursuing nonhuman witnessing of, by, and through algorithms, my focus is on their operative, extractive, and generative qualities, rather than their computational mechanics. Through a series of investigations into distinct machine learning systems, I argue that algorithms can engage in a perceptual process that constitutes nonhuman witnessing, elevating mere observation into an ethicopolitical plane. In drone warfare, an algorithm might "see" certain activity, "decide" it is threatening, and "recommend" the prosecution of violence. My contention is that such algorithmic registering and translating of worldly phenomena constitutes witnessing because it does so to violent ends and caries the most immediate traces of that violence. Facial recognition software is a tool for producing evidence through machinic witnessing, yet both the data that feeds such systems and the unknowable neural dynamics that animate them make it so dangerous that facial recognition has been described as akin to plutonium.[20] Algorithmic witnessing, then, often takes place through the enactment of violence, with the algorithm as both witness and perpetrator. At the same time, such algorithms are themselves entities that must be witnessed—yet by their entangled nature they resist being broken into consistent elements that can then be rendered knowable.

This chapter grapples with the competing dynamics of the doubled meaning of its title: algorithms that do witnessing and the witnessing of algorithms (and what they do). Or, to put this differently, this chapter asks both how algorithms might be agents *of witnessing* and how algorithms might *be witnessed*? Rather than look for machinic relations to events that might be analogous to human witnessing, this chapter seeks out intensive sites within human-nonhuman assemblages where machinic affect—technical yet contingent, potential rather than predetermined—enables forms of encounter that generate a relation of responsibility between event and algorithm. Doing so requires the bracketing of any ethical imperative to witnessing: algorithmic witnessing can only ever be grasped within the milieu of the algorithm, an agency that can only be ascribed ethics or morality through anthropomorphic gymnastics. Delving into the machinic affects of witnessing algorithms will require us to depart further still from the narrow humanistic conception of witnessing and to insist on the separation of witnessing from testimony. If algorithmic technologies are now crucial knowledge machines, yoked to power, and the infliction of state violence, then asking how witnessing reckons with them and takes place through them requires attending to how computational processes generate their machinic relations, and how those relations sustain the power of those systems.

Even as the image increasingly overwhelms the word as the dominant form of communication, the expansion of technologies that identify and organize images means that a new form of aggregated, relational perception is taking hold. Writing on the aggregation of huge numbers of images into datasets analyzed by machine learning systems, Adrian Mackenzie and Anna

Munster understand these relational processes as "generative technical forces of experience."[21] They propose the concept of "platform seeing" to describe an operative mode of perception "produced through the distributed events and technocultural processes performed by, on and as image collections are engaged by deep learning assemblages."[22] In their account, "seeing" is not the act of a singular entity but rather something that takes place across a great many human, material, and computational agents. Images become subject to a host of functions: precisely formatted for input to models; labeled, processed, and used to configure small neural networks onboard smartphones; moved from the devices of consumers to platforms and their data centers and back. Through these and other functions, images transformed from bearers of indexical relations to elements within operational (image) collections.[23] Consequently, the relations between images within the dataset, including the relations of elements within images to elements within others, become more important than the images themselves.

Platform seeing is thus the "making operative of the visual by platforms themselves."[24] This *invisual* mode of perception takes place outside the domain of representation: images no longer take their meaning from things in the world but rather in relation to the elements and edges of other images. Crucially, this "operativity cannot be seen by an observing 'subject' but rather is enacted via observation events distributed throughout and across devices, hardware, human agents and artificial networked architectures such as deep learning networks."[25] Despite the absence of a human subject, these processes still constitute something called "seeing" precisely because they remain within the perceptual domain of recognizing and differentiating images. In this chapter, I make a parallel argument about witnessing: that even without a witnessing "subject" in the unitary humanist sense, witnessing occurs within and through algorithmic systems. Such witnessing necessarily exists on a continuum with perceiving and cannot be neatly distinguished from it. Different contexts, media technics, and human entanglements produce distinct intensive fields of relation that shift perceiving into the modality of witnessing. Not all human perception entails witnessing, and so neither does all perception by the nonhuman agencies of algorithms.

While witnessing rarely figures in discussions of algorithms and artificial intelligence, terms that appear in witnessing discourses abound: truth, recognition, memory, transparency, ethics. This is not to suggest an inherent synchronicity between witnessing and the algorithmic, but rather to point out that the perception required for both to operate possesses a purposive dimension. As Amoore writes, "A defining ethical problem of the algorithm concerns not primarily the power to see, to collect, or to survey a vast data landscape, but the power to perceive and distill something for action."[26] In much the same way, witnessing is not reducible to seeing, but is a perceptual encounter that produces an injunction to action through its configuring of a particular scene and its coalescing of that scene's relational dynamics. Like algorithms, witnessing makes truth claims about the world as well, and is also prone to oversight, misapprehension, and misstatement.[27] Like algorithms, witnessing is prone to falsity, whether deliberate or accidental. Their distributed, multiple, contingent, and operative existence means that algorithms cannot be known or accounted, and yet neither can *the human*. It is only ever humans, plural, who can give account, and doing so is always incomplete. This is why, for Amoore, "algorithms do not bring new problems of blackboxed opacity and partiality, but they illuminate the already present problem of locating a clearsighted account in a knowable human subject."[28] Neither human nor algorithm can give an account of itself that is complete or transparent. An ethics for algorithmic worlds cannot "seek the grounds of a unified *I*" but must instead "dwell uncertainly with the difficulty of a distributed and composite form of being."[29] This chapter pursues the question of what distributed, opaque, and decentered witnessing might look like within technics of the algorithm—and how such a contingent and multiple domain might itself be witnessed.

Crucial to that task is tracing what I call *machinic affect*, or the intensive relations that bind technical systems to one another and humans to technical systems. By machinic affect, I mean the capacity to affect and be affected that occurs within, through, and in contact with nonhuman technics. In keeping with Félix Guattari's expansive conception, my own use of "machinic" is not restricted to the mechanistic but rather refers to the processual assemblage of elements, objects, concepts, imaginaries, materialities, and so on that form "machines" through their distinct yet transversal relations. Guattari's machines are organic and inorganic, technical and social, material and abstract.[30] Machinic affect is not so much indifferent to the flesh as it is promiscuous in its adhesive and intensifying properties, such that the corporeality of the human does not default to center stage.[31] Excavating machinic affect from technical assemblages requires attending to the distinctiveness of individual technical objects as they assemble, attenuate, modulate, amplify, and terminate technical and nontechnical relations. In the context of witnessing, machinic affect can be applied to understand the relations forged between witness and event when mediated through screens. But more importantly and generatively, machinic affect offers an analytic for making visible the otherwise obscured machinic relations of complex technical systems and especially learning algorithms.

Machinic affect describes the dynamic intensities of technical systems. As such, machinic affect is autonomous intensity: owned neither by one body nor another, but constituting and constituted by them, whether human or non. Pursuing machinic affect within the media-specificities of algorithmic systems, I am interested in how the processual empiricism of what Massumi calls the "virtual" illuminates the relational dynamics of machine learning. For Massumi, the virtual describes the immanence of potentiality, its passage from futurity through experience and into pastness. The virtual is what might arise and what might have been. It is not opposed to the actual, but its underside. Affect is "precisely this two-sidedness, the simultaneous participation of the virtual in the actual and the actual in the virtual, as one arises from and returns to the other."[32] This chapter is about the necessity of witnessing how algorithms, particularly machine learning ones, oscillate between actualizing the virtual and virtualizing the actual.

If algorithmic systems are about taming potential into probability in the name of emergent ordering of worldly phenomena, we can understand them in Massumi's terms as ontopowerful: as technological processes for the mastery of becoming.[33] Machine learning systems are constituted by unreason—even madness—through looping recursivities.[34] This nonlinearity, too, finds much in common with Massumi's recognition that "intensity would seem to be associated with nonlinear processes: resonation and feedback that momentarily suspend the linear progress of the narrative present from past to future."[35] As well as disassembling and distributing the subject, witnessing algorithms requires dismantling and dispersing the event in time as it is taken up and worked upon by algorithmic agencies. This chapter thus excavates the distinctive dynamics of nonhuman witnessing across four instances of algorithmic world-making: the false witnessing of deepfakes; the animating of evidence in Forensic Architecture's machine learning investigations; military imaginings of archival and real-time processing of full motion video imagery from loitering drones; and the witnessing of machine learning processes in aesthetic interventions into algorithmic systems. Operating with different learning models and data sources and within very varied contexts, these examples show the dangers of algorithmic witnessing and the necessity of witnessing algorithms, but they also suggest the potential of such systems to work against state and corporate violence.

BEARING FALSE TESTIMONY: DEEPFAKES

The synthetic media that would become known as "deepfakes" first surfaced to mainstream attention with a December 2017 article by Samantha Cole in Vice Media's tech site Motherboard about a pornographic video that appeared to feature the actress Gal Gadot having sex with her stepbrother (figure 2.1). As Cole reported on the tech site, the video was a fake, the clever but decidedly imperfect creation of a Reddit user with some basic machine learning skills and open-access tools downloaded from the code repository GitHub.[36] Fake and face-swapped pornography are not new phenomena: CGI porn is widely available, while photoshopped porn images have been around as long as the internet and altered nude photographs since the early twentieth century at least. The difference in the Gadot video was the application of deep learning techniques to automatically swap one face with another. That technique gave the Redditor his handle and the new genre a name: deepfakes. "With hundreds of face images, I can easily generate millions of distorted images to train the network," deepfakes told Cole. "After that if I feed the network someone else's face, the network will think it's just another distorted image and try to make it look like the training face."[37] With so many high-quality images on which to train the system available online, celebrities like Gadot are easy targets. But that same ease could readily apply to politicians, and to voice as well as video. Arriving amid a rising tide of distrust in systems and institutions, deepfakes seemed to herald a new threat, undermining democratic processes and cybersecurity and facilitating misinformation and revenge porn. A cottage industry of deepfake creation and detection sprung up in response. Deepfakes seemed to enable the bearing of algorithmic false witness—a problem only complicated by the arrival of more user-friendly artificial image and video generation tools in the years since.

While there are several techniques that can be used to generate deepfakes, the most effective are produced through a form of deep learning neural network called "generative adversarial networks," or GANs. While image recognition algorithms are typically trained using convolutional neural networks (CNNs) that slide filters across images to learn their spatial properties, GANs work by pitting two algorithms against each other in a game of true and false (figure 2.2). First proposed by AI researchers from Google Brain in a 2014 paper, the premise of GANs is simple enough: one neural network (the generator) learns to create images that it then feeds to another network (the discriminator), which decides if the image is "fake" or "real" compared to its own training dataset.[38] Those results are then fed back into the generator, so

FIGURE 2.1. Still from Gal Gadot deepfake porn

that it can learn from the assessment of the discriminator. What makes the technique powerful is that both networks are learning at the same time, with the discriminator learning just enough to get ahead of the generator each time the quality of its fakes catches up. To produce the Gal Gadot deepfake with a GAN, the generator would be fed the pornographic video while the discriminator learned from real photos of Gadot. As the generator modified its video using several image-blurring and blending techniques, proximity to what the discriminator was learning about Gadot would yield better

FIGURE 2.2. Diagram of general adversarial network structure

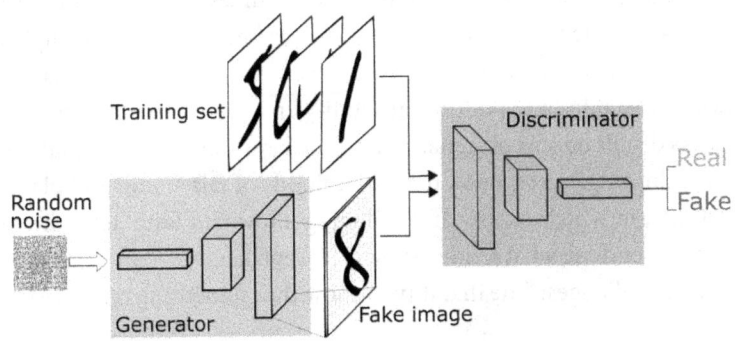

Witnessing Algorithms   89

and better results until the discriminator could no longer identify the fake images as fake at all. If the GAN was then trained on other video and image sets, it would get even better at its task. In this way, GANs can become highly accomplished at swapping any face for any other. Versions of this technique can be applied to specific parts of the face, too, such as the lips, or to audio, enabling the falsification of someone's voice to match a script, as in the widely reported Obama lip-sync demonstration.[39]

While computer science papers have focused on deepfake creation and detection, the humanities and social sciences has begun to address a wider set of questions.[40] The most attentive examinations of deepfakes have occurred within porn studies, where the gendered nature of the technology in practice—more than 99 percent of documented deepfakes feature women face swapped into pornographic videos—has been documented and examined in a range of contexts, from revenge porn to communities of practice to the emergence of "designer" porn.[41] Legal scholarship within the United States has addressed how deepfakes create tension between rights to free speech and privacy, as well as how they present a potential crisis for the verification of evidence presented to court.[42] Possible impacts for cybersecurity and information warfare are articulated in more apocalyptic terms.[43] But deepfakes also point to the vibrancy of everyday data cultures, and the experimental, open-source approach to AI and automation literacies taking place on GitHub, YouTube, and Reddit.[44] "Deepfakes are complex epistemic things," observes Rebecca Uliasz, which "testify to the ongoing socio-technical value we place on visual accuracy which manifests in our continued investment in imagistic realism as truthful."[45] As such, deepfakes can be understood as yet another technological blow to shared epistemic frameworks, further undermining certainty in image authenticity for both journalists and publics.[46]

For WITNESS, a New York–based human rights organization that equips citizens and activists with video tools and resources, deepfakes and related forms of synthetic media are an urgent danger because they can amplify or microtarget the kinds of media disinformation and incitement that spark massacres, assaults, and political instability. In a report on synthetic media, WITNESS distills dozens of scenarios into five key problem areas: reality edits, credible doppelgängers, news remixing, floods of falsehood, and plausible deniability, in which claims of deepfaking allow bad faith actors to deny having said or done what a video shows.[47] Deepfakes lead to two interrelated epistemic challenges: "the inability to show that something real is real, and then the ability to fake something as if it was real."[48] For WITNESS, the inability to prove that something real is real presents the more serious dilemma because it suggests an existential peril for the mediated processes that are so essential to contemporary shared realities. This algorithmic false witness risks placing all mediated witnessing into question. Deepfake false witnessing cuts and intensifies preexisting risks to individuals and communities by catalyzing uncertainties within contemporary media ecologies. Over the last few years, WITNESS has worked with Partnership on AI to develop guidelines for appropriate use of synthetic media in human rights contexts. These are necessary and important practical steps, but the epistemic challenges of deepfakes and related media forms persist.

By threatening the legitimacy of the image, deepfakes destabilize the very foundations of media witnessing as a shared means of producing an agreed reality. Deepfakes emerged in a media witnessing ecology in which power has shifted from the authority of legacy media to the immediacy of smartphone and other user-generated content.[49] As the necessity of grounding truth claims becomes more urgent, deepfakes heighten the fallibility of witnessing in, by, and through media. These are fake images that make truth claims, even as they undermine the possibility of common epistemic ground.[50] In places with declining trust in government or with significant government instability and insecurity, deepfakes have the potential to incite violence and violate human rights. Weaponized deepfakes assembled on the fly from social media records are one nasty possibility for the future of what Tom Sear calls "xenowar."[51] If neither still nor moving images can be trusted to bear the indexical relationship to the world that their authority depends upon, the potential for any mediated witness to be false threatens to pry open the fractures already running through any sense of shared reality. With their emphasis on altering or swapping faces, deepfakes are affect machines even more than cognitive deceptions. Machinic affect here takes a very recognizable form in the micromovements of faciality described by Deleuze in his account of the affection image in cinema and by Silvan Tomkins in his theory of nine discrete relational affects manifested on the face.[52] Face, voice, and gesture are among the most crucial embodied qualities of bearing witness: deepfakes seek to synthesize both fake and real to affect the viewer. Created through the intensive interplay of machinic relations, deepfakes are also affect engines when loose in the wild. As false witnessing algorithms, deepfakes exemplify the inextricability of human and non in witnessing assemblages within today's deeply computational world.

Deepfakes are among the most unsettling instances of the shifting relationship between image and data. "An image that is computational is no longer strictly concerned with mimesis, nor even with signification," writes Steven F. Anderson. "Computational images may serve as interfaces, carriers, or surface renderings, the real importance of which are their underlying processes or data structures."[53] Deepfakes are syntheses of recorded and generated images made possible by the encoded nature of both. At the level of code itself, neither bears any more material relation to the world beyond computation than the other. Even as the image reaches its zenith in visual culture, the transfiguration into code that made its domination possible contains within it the collapse of the authority granted to the image by its seemingly indexical relation to the world. Ironically enough given their origins in DIY porn communities, deepfakes speak to how "the once voyeuristic gaze of cinema has given way to power relations articulated through computational systems rather than through ocular regimes predicated on reflected light and bodies in space."[54] The false witnessing of deepfakes suggests that contestations over the meaning of images is moving away from *signification* and into *generation*. For deepfakes and imagery produced by Stable Diffusion or Dall-E 2, contestation ceases to be about what the video image *means* and comes to be about the *process* of its generation.

This movement from semiosis to process means that the false witnessing of deepfakes must be contested at an ontological level. While early iterations had a tendency for glitching and an unsettling uncanny valley-like quality, advances in the deep learning processes of GANs now mean that humans can typically detect deepfakes about half the time, or at the same rate as random chance. Deepfake detection tools that draw on the same kind of deep learning neural networks have become increasingly important, but their emergence and growing accuracy has led to an arms race between forgers and detectors.[55] This formation of a new adversarial, nonhuman, and machinic relationship between witness and interrogator points to yet another site in which critical debates about culture, politics, ethics, and knowledge play out without the human in the driver's seat. A potentially endless game of deception and unmasking awaits in which witnessing itself becomes the ground of contestation between adversarial machine learning systems and where social and political life become the field upon which the consequences of that struggle play out. Ironically enough, algorithmic false witnessing heightens computation's claim as both figure and ground for how knowledge is produced and contested.

BETWEEN EVIDENCE AND WITNESSING: FORENSIC ARCHITECTURE AND OPEN-SOURCE MACHINE LEARNING

Synthetic media are everywhere, not just in deepfakes. Digital images and objects that appear to index something in the world but do nothing of the sort have their roots in video games and online worlds like Second Life. With the growing appetite for niche machine learning training sets and artificial environments for testing autonomous machines, synthetic media are increasingly central to the development of algorithmic systems that make meaningful decisions or undertake actions in physical environments. Synthetic media are swift to produce and can be tagged as part of the production process, which reduces costs, delays, and inaccuracies from using people to tag images or other data.

Microsoft AirSim is a prime example, an environment created in Epic's Unreal Engine that can be used to test autonomous vehicles, drones, and other devices that depend on computer vision for navigation.[56] Artificial environments are useful testing grounds because they are so precisely manipulable: trees can be bent to a specific wind factor, light adjusted, surface resistance altered. They are also faster and cheaper places to test and refine navigation software prior to expensive material prototyping and real-world testing. In machine learning, building synthetic training sets is now an established practice, particularly in instances of limited data availability or lack of data diversity. For example, the company Synthesis.ai produces synthetic images of nonwhite people to train various kinds of recognition algorithms. Synthetic media are valuable in contexts such as armed conflict, where images might be too few to produce a large enough corpus and too classified to be released to either digital pieceworkers for tagging or private sector developers to train algorithms.

But what happens when synthetic media are marshaled to do the activist work of witnessing state and corporate violence? What are we to make of the proposition that truths about the world might be produced via algorithms trained almost exclusively on synthetic data? This section sketches answers to these questions through an engagement with *Triple Chaser*, an investigative aesthetic project from the UK-based research agency Forensic Architecture. Founded in 2010 by architect and academic Eyal Weizman and located at Goldsmiths, University of London, Forensic Architecture invents investigative techniques using spatial, architectural, and situated methods. Using aesthetic practice to produce actionable forensic evidence, their work appears in galleries, courtrooms, and communities. In recent years, they have begun to use machine learning and synthetic media to overcome a lack of publicly available images on which to train their machine learning models and to multiply by several orders of magnitude the effectiveness of images collected by activists. In contrast to the false witnessing of deepfakes, these techniques show how algorithms can do the work of a more resistant and generative witnessing, translated into open-source tools for activists via well-documented GitHub pages.

Presented at the 2019 Whitney Biennial in New York, *Triple Chaser* combines photographic images and video with synthetic media to develop a dataset for a deep learning neural network able to recognize tear gas canisters used against civilians around the world. It responds to the controversy that engulfed the biennial following revelations that tear gas manufactured by Safariland, a company owned by Whitney trustee Warren B. Kanders, was used against protestors at the US-Mexican border. Public demonstrations and artist protests erupted, leading to significant negative press coverage across 2018 and 2019. Rather than withdraw, Forensic Architecture submitted an investigative piece that sought to demonstrate the potential for machine learning to function as an activist tool. Produced in concert with artist and filmmaker Laura Poitras, *Triple Chaser* was presented as an eleven-minute video installation. Framed by a placard explaining the controversy and Forensic Architecture's decision to remain in the exhibition, viewers entered a severe, dark room to watch a tightly focused account of Safariland, the problem of identifying tear gas manufacturers, the technical processes employed by the research agency, and its further applications. Despite initial intransigence, the withdrawal of eight artists in July 2019 pushed Kanders to resign as vice chairman of the museum and, later, announce that Safariland would sell off its chemicals division that produces tear gas and other antidissent weapons. Meanwhile, Forensic Architecture began to make its codes and image sets available for open-source download and began applying the same techniques to other cases, uploading its Mtriage tool and Model Zoo synthetic media database to the code repository GitHub. A truth-seeking tool trained on synthetic data, *Triple Chaser* reveals how machinic affects oscillate between witnessing and evidence.

In keeping with the established ethos of Forensic Architecture, *Triple Chaser* demonstrates how forensics—a practice heavily associated with both policing and the law—can be turned against the very state agencies that typically deploy its gaze. As Pugliese points out, "Embedded in the concept of forensic is a combination of rhetorical, performative, and narratological techniques" that can be deployed outside courts of law.[57] For Weizman, the fora of forensics is critical: it brings evidence into the domain of contestation in which politics happens. In his agency's counterforensic investigation into Safariland, tear gas deployed by police and security agencies becomes the subject of interrogation and re-presentation to the public.[58] In this making public, distinctions and overlaps can be traced between different modes of knowledge-making and address: the production of evidence, the speaking of testimony, and the witnessing of the audience. But how might we understand the role of the machine learning algorithm itself? And how are we to conceptualize this synthetic evidence?

Weizman describes the practice of forensic architecture as composing "evidence assemblages" from "different structures, infrastructures, objects, environments, actors and incidents."[59] There is an inherent tension between testimony and evidence that counterforensics as a resistant and activist practice seeks to harness by making the material speak in its own terms. As method, forensic architecture seeks a kind of "synthesis between testimony and evidence" that takes up the lessons of the forensic turn in human rights investigations to see testimony itself as a material practice as well as a linguistic one.[60] Barely detectable traces of violence can be marshaled through the forensic process to become material witnesses, or evidentiary entities. But evidence cannot speak for itself: it depends on the human witness. Evidence and testimony are closely linked notions, not least because both demarcate an object: speech spoken, matter marked. Testimony can, of course, be entered into evidence. But something more fundamental is at work in *Triple Chaser*. Its machine learning model doesn't simply register or represent. It is operative, generating relations between objects in the world and the parameters of its data. Its technical assemblage *precedes* both evidence and testimony. It engages in nonhuman witnessing. *Triple Chaser* brings the registering of violations of human rights into an agential domain in which the work of witnessing is necessarily inseparable from the nonhuman, whether in the form of code, data, or computation.

As development commenced, *Triple Chaser* faced a challenge: Forensic Architecture was only able to source a small percentage of the thousands of images needed to train a machine learning algorithm to recognize the tear gas canister produced by Safariland. They were, however, able to source detailed video footage of depleted canisters from activists and even obtained some material fragments. Borrowing from strategies used by Microsoft, Nvidia, and others, this video data could be modeled in environments built in the Unreal gaming engine, and then scripted to output thousands of canister images against backgrounds ranging from abstract patterns to simulated real-world contexts (figure 2.3). Tagging of these natively digital objects also sidestepped the labor and error of manual tagging, allowing a training set to be swiftly built from images created with their metadata attached (figure 2.4). Using several different machine learning techniques (including transfer learning, combining synthetic and real images, and reverse discriminators), investigators were able to train a neural network to identify Safariland tear gas canisters from a partial image with a high degree of accuracy and with weighted probabilities. These synthetic evidence assemblages then taught the algorithm to witness.

Like most image recognition systems, *Triple Chaser* deploys a convolutional neural network, or CNN, which learns how to spatially analyze the pixels of an image. Trained on tagged datasets, CNNs slide—convolve—a series of filters across the surface of an image to produce activation maps that allow the algorithm to iteratively learn about the spatial arrangements of pixels, which can be repeated across large sets of images. These activation maps are passed from one convolution layer to the next, with various techniques applied to increase accuracy and prevent the spatial scale of the system from growing out of control. Exactly what happens within each convolutional layer remains in the algorithmic unknown: it cannot be distilled into representational form but rather eludes cognition.[61] Machine learning processes thus exhibit a kind of autonomic, affective capacity to form relations between objects and build schemas for action from the modulation and mapping of those relations: machinic affect. Relations between elements vary in intensity, with the process of learning both producing and identifying intensities that are autonomous from the elements themselves. It is precisely this that cannot be "visualized" or "cognized." Intensive relations assemble elements into new aggregations; bodies affect and are affected by other bodies. Amoore writes that algorithms must be understood as "entities whose particular form of experimental and adventurous rationality incorporates unreason in an intractable and productive knot."[62] Reflecting on economic self-interest and the false grounds of rational choice, Massumi points out that "rationalities are apparatuses of capture of affectivity."[63] Machine learning works in concomitant ways. There is an autonomic quality to such algorithmic knowledge-making, more affective than cognitive. This machinic registering of relations accumulates to make legible otherwise unknown connections between sensory data, and it does so with the potential (if not intention) for that registering to make political claims: to function as a kind of witnessing of what might otherwise go undetected.

FIGURE 2.3. Four variations of synthetic media from *Triple Chaser*, Forensic Architecture, 2019. Courtesy of Forensic Architecture.

FIGURE 2.4. Applying weathering and wear effects to synthetic cannisters, Forensic Architecture, 2021. Courtesy of Forensic Architecture.

Underpinning the project is the proposition that social media and other image platforms contain within them markers of violence that can and should be revealed. For the machine learning algorithm of *Triple Chaser*, the events to which it becomes responsible are themselves computational: machinic encounters with the imaged mediation of tear gas canisters launched at protesters, refugees, and migrants. But their computational nature does not exclude them from witnessing. With so much of the world now either emergent within or subject to computational systems, the reverse holds true: the domain of computation and the events that compose it must be brought within the frame of witnessing. While the standing of such counterforensic algorithms in the courtroom might—for now—demand an expert human witness to vouch for their accuracy and explain their processes, witnessing itself has already taken place long before testimony occurs before the law. Comparisons can be drawn to the analog photograph, which gradually became a vital mode of witnessing and testimony, not least in contexts of war and violence.[64] Yet, despite its solidity, the photograph is an imperfect witness. Much that matters resides in what it obscures, or what fails to enter the frame, as in the nonhuman witnessing of Aleppo's aftermaths that I examined in the last chapter. With the photograph giving way to the digital image and the digital image to the generative algorithm, the ambit of witnessing must expand. As power is increasingly exercised through and even produced by algorithmic systems, modes of knowledge-making and contestation predicated on an ocular era must be updated for an age of more overt and complex machinic affect-ability. Forensic Architecture's work is also a potent reminder that nonhuman witnessing is a matter for galleries and activist politics as much as the courts, providing the aesthetic means for the human to comprehend its constitutive entanglement with the non. Even if the law resists the displacement of the human, art does not.

As *Triple Chaser* demonstrates, algorithmic witnessing troubles both relations between witness and evidence and those between witnessing and event. This machine learning system trained to witness via synthetic datasets suggests that the linear temporal relation in which evidence—the photograph, the fragment of tear gas canister—is interpreted by the human witness cannot or need not hold. Through their capacities for recognition and discrimination, nonhuman agencies of the machinic system enact the witnessing that turns the trace of events into evidence. Witnessing is, in this sense, a relational diagram that makes possible the composition of relations that in turn assemble into objects that can be experienced. If witnessing precedes both evidence and witness, then witnessing forges the witness rather than the figure of the witness granting witnessing its legitimacy and standing.

While this processual refiguring of witnessing has ramifications for nonhuman agencies and contexts beyond the algorithmic, Forensic Architecture's movement into this space suggests the strategic potential for an alternative politics of machine learning. In the four years since the release of *Triple Chaser*, Forensic Architecture has extended their use of machine learning to deal with identifying Russian tanks in Ukraine and other investigations. While I firmly believe that skepticism toward the emancipatory and resistant potential for machine learning and algorithmic systems more generally is warranted, there is also a strategic imperative to do more to ask how such systems can work for people rather than against them. With its tools, techniques, and synthetic media databases all made open source, Forensic Architecture aims to democratize the production of evidence through the proliferation of algorithmic witnessing that works on behalf of NGOs, activists, and oppressed peoples, and against the technopolitical state. This investigative commons becomes an intensive field for nonhuman witnessing, in which the entangled agencies of machines and humans work to register and make addressable otherwise elusive violence.

UNWITNESSED: PROJECT MAVEN AND LIMITLESS DATA

In June 2018, word spread inside Google that the company was partnering with the US Department of Defense (DoD) to apply its artificial intelligence expertise to the identification of objects in drone footage. A week later, the same news broke on the tech site Gizmodo. Within days, Google had withdrawn its engagement and released a set of principles for AI development that precluded working on weapons systems, although with plenty of wiggle room for other defense and national security applications.[65] The controversy marked a new notoriety for Project Maven, the code name for the Algorithmic Warfare Cross-Functional Team (AWCFT) created in April 2017 by order of the Deputy Defense Secretary Robert Work. Its stated aim was to "turn the enormous volume of data available to DoD into actionable intelligence" with an initial focus on providing "computer vision algorithms for object detection, classification, and alerts" in full-motion video from drone systems.[66] The AWCFT had a mandate to "consolidate existing algorithm-based technology initiatives related to mission areas of the Defense Intelligence

Enterprise, including all initiatives that develop, employ, or field artificial intelligence, automation, machine learning, deep learning, and computer vision algorithms."[67] Not only would the team seek partnerships with Silicon Valley, it would also adopt tech industry development techniques, such as iterative and parallel prototyping, data labeling, end-user testing, and algorithm training.[68] In a reversal of the Pentagon's typical hierarchical, drawn out, and multiyear technological development processes, Project Maven would be agile. It would fail often and learn quickly; move fast and break things—but with weapons systems.

Military secrecy makes even an approximation of the scale of data requiring analysis impossible to determine. Media reports suggest that the proportion of drone sensor data currently analyzed by humans represents a tiny fraction. An article in *Wired* cites DoD officials claiming that 99 percent of all drone video has not been reviewed.[69] Project Maven boss General John Shanahan is quoted as saying that twenty analysts working twenty-four hours a day are able to successful analyze—exploit, in military lingo—around 6 to 12 percent of imagery from wide-area motion sensors such as the ARGUS-IS persistent surveillance platform discussed in chapter 1. Project Maven aimed to bring AI analysis to the full-motion video data from the drone platforms doing much of the surveillance work against ISIS in Iraq and Syria: the MQ-1C Gray Eagle and the MQ-9 Reaper. By February 2017, DoD had decided that deep learning algorithms should ultimately be able to perform at near human levels but recognized that to do so meant working at scale. In its initial scoping, Project Maven was intended to enable several autonomous functions, including identifying thirty-eight different classes of objects, reverse image search, counts within bounded boxes and over time, and selective object tracking. It would integrate with Google Earth, ArcGIS, and other geographic information systems (GIS). Building datasets able to train machine learning systems would require human tagging of huge amounts of data. According to media reports, Project Maven outsourced much of this to the piecework platform Figure Eight (formerly CrowdFlower), providing unclassified and nonviolent images with instructions to draw and label boxes around various objects. Combined with classified imagery tagged by internal analysts, this data could train the convolutional neural network algorithms to identify and classify objects within video feeds, using iterative training and testing techniques honed in the tech industry.

Stored as ones and zeroes demarcating the position and color of pixels and accompanied by crucial metadata that makes them legible to the computational system, these images are optical only in potential. Unless called up by a human analyst for display on screen, the optical, communicative, and representational modality of such images remain potential only. Full-motion video (FMV) of the December 2013 drone strike on a wedding procession in Yemen carries no connotative or denotative meaning for the algorithm, despite its horrifying toll on the families and communities that lost a dozen lives.[70] The event's significance is obtained purely through its relations of similarity and difference to the sets of attributes invisually perceived by the learning algorithm. All such images are simultaneously virtual and actual along several dimensions at once: virtual code carrying the seeds of actual optical imagery; actual correlation in the unidentified scatter of virtual arrangements of pixels; virtual events crowding into the actualizing tendencies of the learning algorithm. Flagged as significant—a truck moving too swiftly; a cluster of bodies on a roof—virtual and actual coalesce to pull the sequence to prominence. We might name this *recognition*: the algorithm doing its job of *observing* and *discriminating*. But the algorithm does more than recognize, and we know from Oliver that recognition alone is not sufficient to produce witnessing. Such algorithms forge a relation of responsibility, rendering a set of relational attributes actionable within the field of possibilities produced by the rules of engagement and other framing structures of war. By producing claims to know the world that demand response, even if that response is to pull a trigger that kills, algorithmic witnessing within the drone apparatus does something more than mere observation. Or, rather, within a certain confluence of machinic affective dynamics, the drone video algorithm generates a field of human-nonhuman relations that becomes witnessing.

Applying these same principles to activities more complex than object identification—assembling machine learning tools that can determine that a particular confluence of objects and attributes constitute a target—both heightens the stakes of nonhuman witnessing and introduces new problems into the technical processes themselves. In the signature strikes undertaken by the US military, a narrow set of data points—most of them drawn from cellphone signal interceptions—provides the basis for algorithmic analysis. As Amoore writes, "When a random forest algorithm sentences someone to death by drone strike, the infinite (gestures, connections, potentials) makes itself finite (optimal output, selector, score), and the horizon of potentials is reduced to one condensed output signal."[71] This violent mediation is produced by and through machinic affects: "A random forest algorithm will never know a terrorist in the sense of acting with clearsighted knowledge, but it mobilizes proxies, attaches clusters of attributes, and infers behaviors to target and to act regardless."[72] Intensities of relation spark the algorithm into response: action necessitated by clusters of machinic intensities coming together to stir a determination that carries with it an ethical weight.

From the perspective of the machine learning system, shifting the emphasis of analysis from cellphone metadata to video imagery is largely a matter of complexity and access to large arrays of the GPUs necessary for computing imagery at scale, which is not to say that such systems will work accurately, limit violence, or reduce civilian harm. In much the same way that deepfake tools can be trained on audio as well as video, the distinctions are largely a matter of input data. Yet while the AWCFT has access to countless hours of mundane footage that can provide a base dataset for tasks like identifying vehicles and buildings, FMV of threats that might warrant lethal action or even tracking by drone systems seemingly remain too scarce, too ambiguous, or too like other imagery. There simply isn't enough video for the machines to learn effectively. Using similar techniques to Forensic Architecture, the AWCFT reportedly generated artificial environments to produce training data for threat detection systems.[73] While details of that training data remain classified and inaccessible, the introduction of synthetic data into a target-detection system has a rather different valence from its use by Weizman and his collective. We know that both war and policing, its domestic corollary, depend upon and reproduce existing sociocultural codings, particularly those around race, gender, and class. In a country like Afghanistan, where men are frequently armed, the baseline designation of "military-aged males" predisposes the system to see activities such as the jirga or council as incipient threats. Just such a prefiguring contributed to the unconscionable drone strikes against just such a gathering at Datta Khel, a village in North Waziristan, that killed forty-four people in 2011. If training data is synthesized within existing frames of war, what structures of domination and their attended biases, misconceptions, and fantasies are coded into such training materials? How might predictive tools gear toward identifying certain peoples and activities as threats? Nonhuman witnessing within the algorithmic systems might bear false witness in far more subtle and ingrained ways than deepfakes can manage.

Drone warfare and drone policing alike are necessarily racializing: they encode and produce racialized subjects as threats, with threat and race intimately bound up with each other.[74] Race is coded into the drone system all too readily. This is because, as Ruha Benjamin writes, "race itself is a kind of technology—one designed to separate, stratify, and sanctify the many forms of injustice experienced by members of racialized groups, but one that people routinely reimagine and redeploy to their own ends."[75] In the algorithmic shift from visual to nonvisual regimes of classification, Thao Phan and Scott Wark argue that "race emerges as an epiphenomenon of automated algorithmic processes of classifying and sorting operating through proxies and abstractions," refiguring "racial formations as data formation."[76] According to Lauren Wilcox, drone warfare, primarily deployed in the Islamic world, "simultaneously produces bodies in order to destroy them, while insisting on the legitimacy of this violence through gendered and racialized assumptions about who is a threat."[77] Identifying specific bodies as threats necessitates preconditioning them as threats within the system, which means determining which bodies should be coded for exposure, to borrow a phrase from Benjamin. Generating training sets from synthetic events staged in 3D environments begins with a set of decisions about who and what to include, what people and places should look like, how people will act, and what constitutes and defines the relations between places, people, and actions. Both the production of data and the iterative development procedures used by Project Maven mean that the nonhuman witnessing of its algorithms is meshed with the human. Far from removing human partiality, such processes embed the discursive, affective, and fantastic logics of war in all their racializing and gendering dimensions into the algorithm at every stage of its design, training, and operation. Nonhuman witnessing in the context of drone warfare is thus not a move toward impartiality or the diminishment of the human, but rather the technical concretization in code of predetermined meanings that are inescapably colonial and racist.

Project Maven and its AI ilk train the martial gaze on the unwitnessed events of life in the age of drone warfare. Yet this witnessing is not analogous to the human: it is fractured and distributed within the system, a techno-affective witnessing composed of machinic intensities. Signature strike, threat detection, and targeting algorithms are not witnessing subjects in the humanist sense, but witnessing assemblages distributed across the nonhuman, invisual perception of machine learning systems. This invisual perception necessitates the exclusion of much that is captured by the drone's optical and multispectral sensors: an infinitude of moments both major and minor necessarily go unwitnessed. Or, rather, nonhuman witnessing within drone algorithms always entails unreasoned and psychotically rational judgments about what matters. Nonhuman witnessing in its algorithmic, war fighting form must necessarily fail to note forms of violence (martial, environmental, interspecies, interpersonal) that do not figure in the criteria for tagging imagery and reinforcing machine learning. Such imagery does not go "unseen" as such, but rather its seeing fails to register. Algorithmic witnessing of this kind is necessarily narrow, not more efficacious or richer than the human but stunted and strange.

WITNESSING THE ALGORITHM: BEYOND THE BLACK BOX

Safiya Noble's *Algorithms of Oppression* opens with a now famous anecdote about searching for "black girls" on Google and finding porn sites, then searching for "white girls" and finding young girls at play. Throughout her book, Noble shows what has since become well understood: algorithmic systems repeat, entrench, and even sharpen the racism, misogyny, homophobia, and other normative biases already present in the cultures from which they arise. Faced with the technical, legal, and commercial black boxing of algorithms, critical scholars such as Noble have rightly focused on the institutions, structures, and applications through which data is collected, computed, and instrumentalized by government and corporate entities. Noble's work is part of a growing body of critical practices (scholarly, artistic, and activist) concerned with the reproduction of inequality in algorithmic systems that has had a significant impact on public debate. In the United States, Joy Boulminwi's activist research and poetry exposed the biases of facial recognition, while Virginia Eubanks's ethnographic investigation revealed the inequalities exacerbated by the infiltration of algorithms into social welfare systems. In Australia, collective advocacy spearheaded by journalist Asher Wolf and others forced the federal government to abandon its automated "RoboDebt" welfare debt collection tool. These, and many other interventions, have increased public understanding of the existence and effects of coded bias, and forced the tech industry to take steps to redress its harms: creating ethics boards, inviting critical research, appointing bias engineers, and seeking to diversify their workforces. But such gestures are often mere fig leaves, swiftly sidelined or rolled back when their presence becomes uncomfortable, evidenced most prominently by the dismissal of Timnit Gebru from Google's Ethical AI team for her refusal to withdraw an academic paper from publication that raised ethical and ecological concerns about large language learning models.[78] Achieving what Lina Dencik calls "data justice" requires more radical change and tech companies and their clients have been far less inclined to ask whether certain computational systems should be built at all.[79] Nor have they been willing to peel away the legal and commercial wrapping on their algorithmic black boxes, which are tightly guarded as data becomes a contemporary form of capital.[80] And even if those boxes were more open, the question of whether deep learning algorithms would reveal themselves in a comprehensible way remains fraught. How, then, to witness the algorithm?

One answer to this question is in the witnessing of their effects: the increasingly common irruptions of outrage in response to injustices perpetrated by algorithmic systems. Or we might think of glitches in the algorithmic that make visible their computational construction, such as the strange fault lines and blurs that can be found on Google Earth, the misrenderings of the world-making, machine learning network responsible for Microsoft Flight Simulator, or the hallucinations of Microsoft's chatbot version of its Bing search engine. Another strategy has been to make infrastructures themselves visible. If we cannot see into the algorithm itself in a meaningful way, then might its infrastructural assemblages be worthy of attention? Trevor Paglen's eerie photographs of the National Security Agency Building and of militarized data centers across the United States are one such project. Another is John Gerrard's "The Farm" (2015), which used aerial photography of a Google data center in Oklahoma as the reference for a finely detailed simulation of the same center. Exhibited as a high definition projection, Gerrard's work stays on the outside of the data center itself but recreates its digital world through the construction of a computational simulation using the Unigine gaming engine.[81] Venturing speculatively within the data center itself, Kynan Tan's "Polymorphism" (2016) digitally recreates its interior materialities, such as the nonhuman movements of automated tape back-up systems as they robotically traverse arrays of server racks. When first exhibited, Tan used powerful subwoofers to sonically simulate the noise of the data center, a sensory engagement with the imposing infrastructures, resource intensity, scale, and speed of computation without making specific operations legible. In these and other such works, the algorithmic is witnessed not through its code but through its infrastructures: the hard, imposing materialities that undergird and make possible the purportedly ephemeral clouds of global computation.

Within the AI research community, this problem of invisibility and inaccessibility is well recognized. For example, the computer science association ACM now runs FAccT, an annual interdisciplinary conference on fairness, accountability, and transparency in AI.[82] San Francisco company OpenAI, now widely known for its ChatGPT platform, provides one response to the issue of AI black boxing via its Two-Minute Papers channel on YouTube, which presents the learning undertaken by neural networks in two-minute animations that show both what and how learning occurs over time, using newly published papers as the primary source. With more than 1.1 million subscribers and many videos viewed several million times, the channel represents a remarkably effective approach to making visible the learning processes of AI systems. In one video, an OpenAI neural network learns to play hide and seek, using boxes, ramps, walls, and game rules to succeed (figure 2.5). As the environments change and the algorithm learns, strange happenings occur: agents run up ramps to jump on boxes, use glitches in the simulation's physics to fly through the air, and throw objects off the screen. Both the limits and possibilities of machine learning are immediately evident. Algorithms become agencies that seem comprehensible because their workings can be broken down into episodic form and cutely animated. Despite their propagandistic intent, these videos hint at possibilities for witnessing through making machine learning visible—even if OpenAI has become increasingly secretive about how its ChatGPT uses the GPT series of large language models.

Placing this dynamic within contexts of labor, logistics, and warfare, Kynan Tan's *Computer Learns Automation* (2020) slows down the machine learning process within three simulated environments and in doing so allows a human audience to become cowitness to the nonhuman witnessing of AI training. *Computer Learns Automation* is composed of three separate training environments and agents: "RideShare," in which a vehicle learns to navigate an urban environment to pickup and drop-off fares; "Robot Arm," in which an automated device learns to pick up boxes from one conveyor

FIGURE 2.5. Still from "OpenAI Plays Hide and Seek . . . and Breaks the Game!," OpenAI, 2019

belt and place them on another; and "Drone Strike," in which a targeting reticule learns to move across terrain, identify human targets, and launch accurate missile strikes against them. Exhibited at the Adelaide Biennial 2020 at the Art Gallery of South Australia, Tan's work slowed the neural network's learning process down with the intention that all three agents develop reliable capability in their tasks during one hundred days on display. On three high-definition screens, visitors to the gallery could watch thousands upon thousands of learning cycles as the car, robot arm, and crosshairs moved across the screen. On the lower left of each screen, data readouts list training time, training steps, total episodes, current and highest scores, and so on, as well as information more specific to each agent, such as boxes moved or casualties inflicted. This set-up allows viewers to watch in real time as the machine learns to navigate and act on its environment, seeing what it sees as it learns. Situated in identified contexts rather than playing hide and seek or undertaking an abstract task, relations between labor, death, and value production are visually tied to the learning of the machine.

Computer Learns Automation was built in the Unity 3D engine using its native ML-Agents package, which provides a set of trainable algorithms that can be linked to the simulated environment so that it can send and receive data. This allows the algorithm to learn and act in the environment simultaneously, which in turn makes it possible to watch the process of the machine's learning unfold. Slowed down, each learning cycle of the system can be a viewed in a legible, computational real time. On display in Tan's work is an algorithm known as "proximal policy optimization," a reinforcement learning neural network technique developed by OpenAI. Earlier "policy" deep learning algorithms used analysis of an environment to select between possible options for an agent, but had a tendency to be overly influenced by choices around how much or little the policy should adjust in response to stimuli: "Too small, and progress is hopelessly slow," notes OpenAI, "too large and the signal is overwhelmed by the noise, or one might see catastrophic drops in performance."[83] Proximal policy optimization, or PPO, corrects this tendency by feeding updates back to the policy at each step, aiming to produce just enough reward to ensure the network learns quickly but doesn't rush down a false path. Tan's "Rideshare" vehicle learns to find, collect, and deliver fares by attempting an action, receiving a reward—or not—and then updating its policy to reflect that information. Driving forward, avoiding a building, not hitting pedestrians—actions such as this accumulate through cycles of training to teach the algorithm to achieve an objective. PPO requires a lot of sample cycles to be effective, but it balances the network's dueling desires to explore options and to exploit what it knows will reap rewards. *Computer Learns Automation* reveals the stuttering, iterative, inhuman, and imperceptible graduations through which this mode of deep learning takes place.

In contrast to the crisp aesthetics that characterize much of Tan's digital work, *Computer Learns Automation* has an operative, processual quality. Its simulated environments are just real enough: decodable by the viewer in the domain of signification while appropriate to context for the machine. Yet while the environments, agents, and actions are recognizable to the visitor to the gallery, their semantic significance within the machinic network eludes comprehension. Just what is happening in each of the three learning simulations is uncomfortable, even unsettling. Machinic affects course through the visual field yet are themselves what Mackenzie and Munster call "invisual": concerned with the composition of relations that are not themselves visual at all but rather the perceptual upwell of operations deep within the hidden layers of the PPO network as it explores and exploits according to technical logics that retain a certain unassailable incomprehension. As the targeting reticule of "Drone Strike" inches its way uncertainly across the mountainous terrain, learning to find, fix, and finish the small collection of pixels that indicates a human body, its movements are not those of the intentional human operator but rather of a machine motivated by an autonomic system for which the notion of a meaningful goal is itself without meaning—or, rather, without correlative meaning for the human viewer (figure 2.6). The machinic resides in its emerging relational awareness, its becoming operative. Tan invites us into the disjunctive space where unthinking yet agential, operative, and transformative machine learning systems intersect with bodily violence, labor exploitation, and automated logistics.

The human audience can only ever become cowitness, a status reinforced by the practical impossibility of watching all three environments learn over one hundred days. Yet this partial cowitnessing is crucial to pulling the nonhuman witnessing already at work in the visualization of the invisual learning process. With casualty counts, founder wealth, and shareholder value ticking up as the machine learns in its slowed down real time, *Computer Learns Automation* reminds us of the necessity of nonhuman witnessing bridging the seeming divide between technical systems, material conditions, and the politics of technocultures. Tan insists on pursuing the always incomplete task of witnessing algorithms in their elemental states, in their becoming increasingly, brutally, and efficiently operative through the intensification and accumulation of machinic affects within the invisual domain of computer vision.

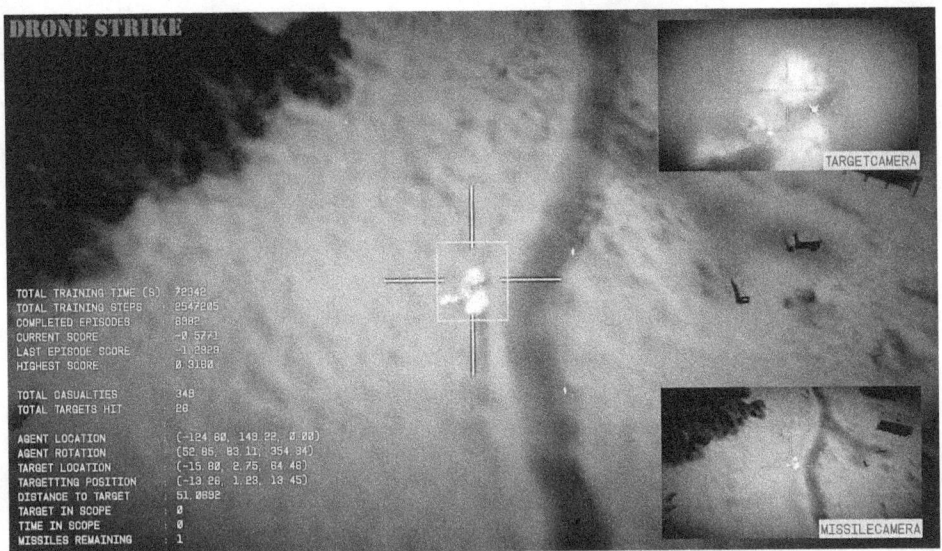

FIGURE 2.6. Still from *Computer Learns Automation*, Kynan Tan, 2020. Courtesy of the artist.

WITNESSING ALGORITHMS

Across this chapter, witnessing algorithms has emerged as a polysemic concept. In the narrowest sense, witnessing algorithms can be understood quite straightforwardly as algorithms that enable witnessing. In this vein we might think of social media algorithms that bring certain kinds of news reportage to the fore or algorithmic systems such as MS Flight Simulator's that enable an entirely simulated witnessing of the world. Yet witnessing algorithms are also engaged in witnessing on their own behalf: a registering of happenings in material and machinic worlds to which the algorithm obtains its own version of responsibility. Algorithmic responsibility is not identical to that of its (multiple, contestable) human equivalent, but rather describes the emergence of relations that cohere and produce a necessity for action, however that might come to be within the technicity of the algorithm. Consider how images of the *Triple Chaser* tear gas canister come to matter in the machine learning algorithms of Forensic Architecture, or the particular movements of bodies and vehicles in computer vision designed for drone applications under the aegis of the Algorithmic Warfare Cross-Functional Team. Exactly how those neural networks raise certain phenomena to significance but not others—how worldly happenings trigger machinic interest or not—eludes complete knowing, yet as the algorithm learns it is shaped by its (un)witnessing. At the same time, algorithms are themselves entities that must be witnessed, both in their effects and in their operations. As Kynan Tan's *Computer Learns Automation* teaches us, at issue here is the unknowable machinic affects of the learning networks themselves. Witnessing the algorithmic is not another demand to open the proverbial black box, but rather a call for attending to algorithmic agencies in their emergence and on their own terms.

With algorithms swiftly becoming preeminent knowledge instruments of governance, commerce, culture, science, and social life, how we reckon with the technopolitics of their identification and formation of relations between worldly phenomena is an urgent question. As the hype of generative AI reaches fever pitch, the political stakes of this task only heighten. Within critical algorithm studies and data justice movements and activism, crucial new lines of inquiry continue to multiply, not least in conjunction with the enduring political projects of resisting settler colonialism, struggling for racial justice, and fighting for a meaningful response to the climate crisis. This chapter has sought to think in sympathy with those inquiries, projects, and goals, asking how algorithmic technologies witness the world and how they in turn might be witnessed. My approach here follows Amoore's call for a cloud ethics that "does not belong to an episteme of accountability, transparency, and legibility, but on the contrary begins with the opacity, partiality, and illegibility of all forms of giving an account, human and algorithmic."[84] Following Édouard Glissant, such an opacity provides the ground for understanding knowledge and politics as emerging from irreducible difference rather than being founded upon its erasure.[85] It is the condition that underpins relation. Pluriversal politics necessitates just such an opacity, as well as its accompanying partiality and illegibility, because a world of many worlds requires the impossibility of transparency, otherwise any world becomes legible to any other, and in doing so ceases to possess vitality on its own terms. In the domain of algorithms, analytically separating witnessing within the event from the testimony that takes place after is urgent because so much of witnessing algorithms is about registering events, machinic or otherwise, as processes of emergent relations (of knowledge, power, violence, control and aesthetic and political potential)—rather than explaining, narrating, or communicating them.

Perhaps more than any other domain addressed in this book, the algorithmic cuts across world-ending catastrophes old and new. Algorithms are infrastructural, institutional, and embedded in technocultural milieus that are, in turn, inseparable from the production of race, gender, and class. Rooted in settler-colonial practices of categorization and control, financialization, climate modeling, and war, as much as in social media and internet search, algorithms are yet another site of deep entanglement between human and nonhuman. Nonhuman witnessing of, in, and through algorithmic processes is about finding those links and recognizing that it no longer, if it ever did, makes sense to think of the human witness outside the nonhuman technicities of our media, our archives, and their agential materialities. Nonhuman witnessing arises from a field of relations between the human and nonhuman, relations that are as ecological as they are technical—and it is to the ecological that this book now turns.

CHAPTER
THREE

witnessing ecologies

IN THE COMMUNIQUÉ from the Fiftieth Pacific Islands Forum, held in Tuvalu in August 2019, leaders from the region "reaffirmed climate change as the single greatest threat to the livelihoods, security, and wellbeing of the peoples of the Pacific," but stopped short of calling for significant and immediate action. In the Kainaki II Declaration that accompanied the formal communiqué, countries are called to "reflect" on transitioning away from coal rather than banning its use, "meet or exceed" national emissions reductions rather than creating new and more ambitious ones, and continue "efforts towards" meeting international climate-funding promises rather than demanding urgent and ambitious commitments.[1] According to media reports, Australia successfully stymied efforts for a much bolder declaration, reducing Prime Minister Akilisi Pohiva of Tonga to tears and prompting leaders from Fiji, Vanuatu, and Tuvalu to make heated remarks about their more powerful neighbor. "We came together in a nation that risks disappearing to the seas, but unfortunately we settled for the communiqué," said Fiji's prime minister, Frank Bainimarama. "Watered-down climate language has real consequences—like water-logged homes, schools, communities, and ancestral burial grounds."[2] The ire of Bainimarama and others was directed primarily at then Australian Prime Minister Scott Morrison, a man who once triumphantly brandished a lump of coal in Parliament, only reluctantly accepted the science of climate change, and stalled progress to limit emissions and develop renewable energies at every opportunity, achieving the ignominious distinction of Australia ranking dead last among 170 states analyzed in a 2021 UN report on climate action.[3] At the forum, it seemed Morrison wanted every dollar Australia spent in the Pacific to be recognized, but refused to commit to any action that might slow the rising seas threatening to swallow Tuvalu and other islands.

Much can be said of events such as this and the warped politics of climate change, the enduring inequalities that underpin the failure to act by wealthy nations, and the histories of colonialism, clientelism, and militarism that shape the present Pacific. Just as the Marshall Islands and other nations in the Pacific were crucial sites for nuclear testing throughout the Cold War, so too are they now the canaries in the mineshaft of climate change. Indeed, Elizabeth DeLoughrey points out that "climate science and nuclear weapons testing have an intimate relationship," as the tools and techniques for understanding the atmosphere developed for war were applied to establishing carbon baselines and monitoring their change.[4] Climate crisis is thus sutured to "catastrophic ruptures to social and ecological systems" that "have already been experienced through the violent processes of empire" and continue in the ongoing, unnamed imperialism of regional geopolitics.[5] Climate is itself increasingly a military problem, securitized by planners in ways that have little regard for the wellbeing of populations most subject to it.[6] When the Islander leaders of the Pacific juxtapose Australia's domestic energy pricing concerns with the erasure of life, culture, and community, it makes clear that trauma is not registered as an individual experience but as an ecological phenomenon. Pleas for an acceptance of shared responsibility in the face of drowning depends on shared witnessing, on opening onto impossible loss, grief, and ecological trauma.

Among the most widely known evocations of the drowning islands of the Pacific Ocean are the poems of Kathy Jetñil-Kijiner, a Marshallese spoken word performance artist and writer. Her poem "Tell Them" includes these lines:

> tell them about the water
>   how we have seen it rising
>   flooding across our cemeteries
>   gushing over the sea walls
> and crashing against our homes
>   tell them what it's like
> to see the entire ocean___level___with the land[7]

Witnessing Ecologies 113

DeLoughrey observes that the poem "employs allegory to figure the island as a world in ecological crisis, depicts an active, nonhuman ocean agent, and articulates the imperative to both witness and testify to a dynamic, changing Earth."[8] Allegory, she argues, is one of the most powerful forms of cultural narration of climate crisis precisely because it bridges ruptures in knowledge, experience, and culture through "its ability to represent both historical and scalar relations" by animating "universalizing tropes such as planet, species, nature, and the human into narrative—and thereby into space and time."[9] While the poem can certainly be read in an allegorical mode, there is something else at work here beyond recognition that "the Marshallese are both humans and nonhumans."[10] The repeated refrain of the poem's middle stanzas—"tell them we are . . ."—intermingles human and non, "hollow hulls" and "wood shavings," "sweet harmonies" and "styrofoam cups of koolaid red."[11] Distinctions of status slip away between "skies uncluttered" and "dusty rubber slippers" as space, place, object, speech, and gesture become entangled with the "we" of the poem. Here is a complex ecology, one rendered *sensible*—able to be felt—through the rhythm and rhetoric of the poem but not *reducible* to language. "We are" might also be an assertion of ontology, of shared being-in and becoming-with the world that is slowly being drowned. "Tell Them" is an allegorical call for climate justice, but also an address to the nonhuman entanglements already rupturing in the refracting wakes of catastrophic pasts and futures. Its witnessing demands not only response-ability on the part of the state system, but also that the rich ecologies of the Marshall Islands be recognized as response-able and address-able. If this poem—and others like it—are calls to witness and acts of testimony, then their mode of witnessing is nonhuman, animated by the inextricable entanglements of being, land, living, community, ocean, and culture.

This chapter coheres around the proposition that one way that ecological trauma—complex, mutable, resilient, ephemeral, material, moving, unsettling—comes into focus is through aesthetic works that undertake the tentative, always incomplete project of nonhuman witnessing. In pursuing this proposition, I attend to artistic and literary works that examine ecological trauma through scale as a site of political contention and in the existential rupturing of nuclear weapons. Violent mediations and machinic affects animate the martial and capitalist operations, events, and technologies that concern this chapter, but here I shift my inquiry from what animates assemblages of catastrophic violence to pursue traumatic aftermaths for more-than-human ecologies. Ecological trauma is not conceptually dependent on the terms that have occupied the first two chapters of this book, but, rather, as I show through this chapter, provides a way of thinking with and responding to crises and violence that far exceed the human sensorium and the prosthetic techniques we have built to enhance or supersede it.

The chapter begins with an exploration of ecologies in media and cultural theory, before pursuing scale as a relational problematic in the face of ecological violence. From there, I develop the concept of ecological trauma in earnest, defining it as a rupturing of relations that ripples through the ongoing composition of more-than-human ecologies. To explore how nonhuman witnessing offers a response, I then turn to the violence and trauma of nuclear testing on First Nations lands in Australia, and the fiercely resistant art practice of the Kokatha and Nukunu artist Yhonnie Scarce. Rather than pursue the witnessing of ecologies through scientific frameworks, I aim to trouble the dominance of such forms of knowledge, and particularly the aerial imaging through which the planet becomes media. While such technologies are critical to the formation of scientific knowledge about climate crisis and ecological violence more generally, the growing entrenchment of remote-sensing visualizations are what Lorraine Daston calls an epistemic image, "one made with the intent not only of depicting the object of scientific inquiry but also of replacing it."[12] This makes probing their limits a necessary task. Satellite programs such as Landsat certainly fall within the rubric of nonhuman witnessing, but what they register and make legible struggles to escape the epistemic and technical frames within which it takes place.

Less bound by such strictures, aesthetic interventions make nonhuman witnessing sensible and graspable in ways that bring the constraining frames, structures, politics, and violences of the technoscientific state to the fore. Continuing empire, mutating colonialism, nuclear testing, enduring irradiation, rising waters, mined out lands: catastrophic futures are already here and have been for a long time, but that hasn't stopped Man from charging headlong and ever deeper into oblivion. How, then, to unknot the forms of knowing and being that make up the human of Man, the figure who proudly waves coal in national parliaments and is unmoved by those who weep for what is and will be lost? How to reckon with the ecological entanglements wrought by industry and war? How to witness within and through ecologies of the human and more-than? How to open up a communicative commons that grants standing to human and nonhuman?

This chapter expands the focus of the book to think with more-than-human ecologies that encompass land, sky, and water, rather than remaining within the technocultural domains that have been its principal preoccupation. As with its predecessors, this chapter travels with the doubling movement of its title: the witnessing of ecologies and ecologies of witnessing. Understood as complex systems of interacting and interdependent parts, ecologies are constituted by relations between elements. Whether wrought in the split-second fission of a nuclear bomb or the drawn-out temporality of radioactive contamination, ecological violence strikes at the relational composition of ecologies themselves. Uprooting a verdant tree to clear the way for a new road is not ecologically violent simply because the tree itself is lost, but rather because its removal tears at the fabric of the ecology within which it is webbed. As Cubitt writes: "Ecologies are not networks connecting previously separate things: Every element of an ecology mediates every other. Life mediates nutrients and sunlight, storing, changing, growing, passing, mutating, returning."[13] Media theorist Matthew Fuller makes the point that the word *ecology* "is one of the most expressive language currently has to indicate the massive and dynamic interrelation of processes and objects, beings and things, patterns and matter."[14] But ecologies can also be brutal, particularly once we extend their conceptual reach into the violent. "Geopolitics, enacted through global war, is itself a form of life that pursues a *savage ecology*," Grove insists, "radically antagonistic to survival as a collective rather than discriminatory goal."[15] Ecologies are not inherently moral, but are rather inescapably political on a planet shaped by Man.

Conceiving of media as ecological and ecologies as medial provides a conceptual apparatus through which to examine, in the context of ecological violence and its attendant traumas, the communicative mode I am calling "nonhuman witnessing." As this chapter argues, nonhuman witnessing can become a reparative response to ecological trauma, the state of wounded survival that follows in the wake of ecological violence. But it also responds to a deeper historical rupture between human and nonhuman, a cleaving of Man from Nature that is rooted in Platonic and Aristotelian thought and thus inherent to the ascendance of Anthropos, even before its violent intensification as Wynter's Man, which I discussed in the introduction and will return to in the coda. "The more humans defined themselves over against nature," Cubitt observes, "the more they defined nature over against themselves, in this way formalizing and enforcing the split between the natural environment and humanity, which in the process became a nonnatural, religious, or rational quality."[16] As Haraway and other feminist philosophers of technoscience have shown, the recomposition of nature and culture as entangled with each other is an urgent political task. Haraway coined the term "natureculture" to enact this intertwined coexistence, insisting that no concept of ecology could exclude the human, or vice versa. The stakes of this intervention are significant, not least for science, which must be understood as operating in agential entanglement with "nature" rather than observing it from a distance.[17] This chapter commits itself to this task by asking how thinking-feeling forms in response to ecological violence.

Aesthetic works figure more prominently in this chapter, as I read artists and writers who find the means for evoking and establishing communicative relations between human and nonhuman, even working to dissolve such distinctions. The works examined here pursue what Cubitt calls an "ecological aesthetics and politics" that makes possible "communication of and through difference."[18] Nonhuman witnessing of ecological trauma is not confined to the overt aesthetic production that occupies much of this chapter, yet there is always an aesthetics of nonhuman witnessing, in the sense that aesthetics is inseparable from sensing and its registration. Geological formations witness the passage of deep time, the arrival and departure of ice ages, the life and death of forests, and the passage of animal life. Nonhuman witnessing describes the fixing of fossils records: captured in mud or peat or sand, bodies shape the earthy matter that spills over and claims them, an ecological affectivity in the transformation of materialities as they fix into enduring form. Archaeology and geology seek out this witnessing, still in process on the planetary scale of time, only to reduce it to "evidence" that can be ordered into disciplines of knowledge rooted in whiteness, extraction, and colonialism.[19] Biochemistry, biophysics, the quantum mechanisms of the universe itself: all entail relational dynamics that register change as sensation, as elements in relations of mediation, becoming through encounter and in time. But while pursuing this radical empiricism of nonhuman witnessing to its most elemental would be a worthy if quixotic project, my concern here is with its concrescence into modes that register more coherently with the human sensorium.

With the first satellite images and, later, the *Earthrise* (1968) and *Blue Marble* (1972) photographs taken by astronauts, atmospheric sensing has held out the tantalizing promise of making nonhuman scales, perspective, and spectrums accessible and sensible. Despite Cold War rivalry and government investment in military spending driving the rise of technoscience, the extraplanetary view swiftly produced a utopian politics. Most famously, Stewart Brand's *Whole Earth Catalog* played a key role in the emerging Californian cyberculture, which in turn spurred the rise of Silicon Valley and helped create the ideological and material conditions for contemporary algorithmic enclosure.[20] Militarism and military investment were never far from the surface, as the foundational role played by DARPA in the creation of the internet attests, but Brand saw the view from space as simultaneously triumphant and humbling, a testament to human achievement but also to the necessity of living together on this small blue dot in the expanse of space. Suffused with the overdetermined figure of Man described by Wynter, Brand's vision promoted a universalizing whiteness manifested most potently through the absence of race and class.[21] Imagining the fusion of cyberculture with business as the means for simultaneously acquiring both wealth and liberation would play no small part in the emergence in our own time of billionaires with space shuttles and dreams of colonizing Mars. But Silicon Valley ideology was not the only offshoot of the capacity to capture the planetary through sensing apparatuses.

One of the earliest applications of electronic digital computers after their emergence in World War II was weather forecasting, an effort led by the Manhattan Project mathematician John von Neumann. Even in those early days, von Neumann sought what he called "the infinite forecast," the capacity to simulate climatic circulations over a long enough period to grasp its fundamental principles.[22] But the origins of climatic computing can also be found in both nuclear fallout monitoring regimes and the Cold War effort to render the world computable by early warning nuclear strike systems. Model simulations required new spatial and atmospheric data, collected through a range of sensors fitted to planes, boards, floats, and satellites.[23] The latter proved valuable, with the TIROS, Nimbus, and Earth Radiation Budget Experiment satellites enabling the emergent planetary regime to engage in vertical mediation between the terrestrial and the stratospheric.[24] These geospatial satellites and the growing array of sensors sent into orbit with them produced a new capacity for earth imaging across the breadth of the electromagnetic spectrum. "Earth imaging," writes Russill, "now depends on light recorded from sites that are uninhabitable or inaccessible to humans, at wavelengths we cannot perceive directly, travelling at speeds and in quantities we cannot handle."[25]

No longer could human perception claim a privileged status when it came to making sense of environments: becoming knowable—to science but also to militaries, governments, NGOs, and even publics—meant being registered by remote-sensing systems collecting data inaccessible to the human sensorium.[26] Tracking environmental change, whether from natural phenomena or industrial depredations or the violence of war, no longer operated on anything like a human scale. On the ground, knowledge maintained its currency within particular contexts, as the rise of humanitarian witnessing attests, but earth imaging ensured that human senses were "no longer the grounds for authoritative depictions of environmental change."[27] Remote sensing is thus a form of nonhuman witnessing—one that illustrates precisely the way the human is exceeded by emergent technics and by the complexity and scale of ecologies, and yet also returned to through address and the injunction to respond. Earth imaging not only made ecological volatility sensible, but it also conjoined war and environment through satellite-sensing apparatuses and the processes of violent mediation much like those discussed in chapter 1. This desire to exert control from the atmosphere extends to the desire to control atmosphere itself via what Furuhata calls "climatic media," which ranges from planetary geoengineering to the mundanity of greenhouses and air-conditioning.[28] Environments themselves become subject to the potential violence of mediated control. Violent mediation is thus as much a part of climate science and ecological violence as warfare, at work in many of the informational and communicative processes that facilitate extractive industries and those that enable climate monitoring and regeneration.

As earth imaging has become more accessible, its role within human rights and ecological monitoring has grown as a means of bringing state and corporate slow violence into the zone of the sensible and political. Dutch nongovernment organization Pax for Peace, for instance, employs remote sensing in its analysis of Syria to demonstrate the interrelations of war and environmental damage. Remote-sensing data allows Pax to identify damage over time and to find critical sites within the ecology, such as makeshift oil refining, and map their location and impacts. But Pax also uses on-the-ground sources, recognizing that earth imaging can elide crucial information and contextual complexity. As Weizman has pointed out and I discussed in the previous chapter, the resolution of publicly available earth imagery is often limited so that the human body fits within its boundaries, thus placing the body—the locus of human rights—below the "threshold of detectability."[29] But this level of resolution fits well with climate-monitoring regimes and their computational architectures, including initiatives such as the Microsoft Planetary Computer that promises to harness the compute power and machine learning capabilities of big tech to ecological research and action. As Delf Rothe puts it, "Visual technologies such as satellite remote sensing play a crucial role in the ontological politics of environmental security" and have "considerably influenced the epistemological horizon of environmental security thinking."[30] Earth imaging as nonhuman witnessing is thus already bound up with the savage ecology of contemporary geopolitics. A crucial question is whether it can be otherwise.

Remote sensors are communication technologies, but their traffic is one way: they bring the nonhuman into the domain of the sensible but provide no means of address to the nonhuman in response. But as Jennifer Gabrys has documented, remote sensors also form part of a media ecology that seeks to make the earth itself programmable: "Sensing is then not just a process of generating information but also a way of informing experience."[31] Against large-scale efforts to make the planet computational for the purposes of climate monitoring and military targeting alike, Gabrys attends to what she calls "citizen sensing." These are collaborative, grassroots projects that employ a DIY ethos and enter into a processual, dynamic relationship between technics and environment and which, in the terms of this book, could be understood as an insistence on making nonhuman witnessing political. But returning to the work of Gabrys and others through the frame of nonhuman witnessing is not my purpose here. As this chapter unfolds, my interest is less on remote sensing and earth imaging as modalities of nonhuman witnessing and much more on how ecologies can be witnessed and how witnessing takes place ecologically.

In the manifestations with which this chapter dwells, nonhuman witnessing mediates between what Félix Guattari calls the three ecologies: the environment, social relations, and human subjectivity.[32] New modalities for such mediation are vital for Guattari: "Now more than ever, nature cannot be separated from culture; in order to comprehend the interactions between ecosystems, the mechanosphere and the social and individual Universes of reference, we must learn to think 'transversally.'"[33] As an "assemblage of enunciation" that conjoins machines, people, animals, environments, and objects, nonhuman witnessing generates transversal relations with the potential for strengthening into enduring bonds. Mediation animates these transversal relations, enabling communicative flows that don't just carry information but render aesthetics sensible by a multiplicity of agencies, humans among them. As Fuller points out, "The stakes [Guattari] assigns to media are rightly perceived as being profoundly political or ethico-aesthetic at all scales."[34] This question of scale recurs throughout this chapter: scales of time and space and their collapse, scales of perspective and intensity, scales of intimacy and violence.

SCALE AS A SITE OF WITNESSING

With its roots in the Latin *scala*, meaning ladder or stairs, *scale* refers to defined relations of space, time, or quantity between one thing and another. A musical scale sets out the relations between one note and a series of others, while a cartographic scale defines the ratio of distances on a map to those on the earth. As Timothy Clark writes, scale "enables a calibrated and useful extrapolation between dimensions."[35] Scale, then, is one means of making instrumental and practical sense across difference, a means of managing relations between one thing and another. Scale helps anchor perception in worlds that extend beyond the perceptual reach of the human sensorium; it enables one to conceive of entities far bigger or smaller, say, than can be contained within the human visual field. This is one of the promises of remote sensing: not only to extend perception to atmospheric or underwater viewpoints, but also to enable sensing at spatial and temporal scales that exceed the human. As Fuller points out, "A 'scale' is something that operates at one level in what might be thought of as an infinite zoom, were a camera to be built that could be sensitized to elements as diverse as practices, institutions, atomical structures, weather patterns, linguistic formations, protocols, transport infrastructures, a glance."[36] High-resolution satellite imagery thus not only enables breadth of perception but also depth through the capacity to zoom imagery down to the half meter and even smaller. Scale is an epistemological tool, a means of organizing the world and its causal relations. It does not inhere in any given entity but is an imposed relationality between one thing and another. At the same time, "a scale provides a certain perspectival optic by which dimensions of relationality and other scales may be 'read.'"[37] This means scale can be intensely political because it constructs relations between entities and processes and, in doing so, can become bound up with questions of agency.

Defining our present geologic era as the Anthropocene, argues the postcolonial historian Dipesh Chakrabarty, shifts the scale at which human agency operates: "To call human beings geological agents is to scale up our imagination of the human... to attribute to us a force on the same scale as that released at other times when there has been a mass extinction of species."[38] But climate change is not only about happenings at the scale of the planet or even the capacity of the human to have effects at the planetary scale. Rather, Clark argues that it involves "an implosion of scales, implicating seemingly trivial or small actions with enormous stakes" even as disciplinary, ideological, religious, and other boundaries collapse into one another or delimit knowledge in damaging ways.[39] Approaching the problem from a different angle, Derek Woods argues that scale itself should be the site of critique, suggesting that doing so makes clear that "the subject of the Anthropocene is not the human species but modern terraforming assemblages."[40] Consequently, as Alaimo argues, those most responsible for the climate crisis need to engage in "scale shifting that is intrepidly—even psychedelically—empathetic, rather than safely ensconced."[41] If there is an emergent "structure of feeling" around climate change, it must surely be a generalized anxiety bound up with urgency, disbelief, and futility—with scale is at its core.[42]

At stake in these and other such interventions is the capacity to overcome scale as a problem for knowing and communicating climate change. How, then, might scale itself become subject to politics? How might scale not simply be communicated but witnessed? That is, how might scale be registered as a site of necessary political and ethical engagement? How might scale, its effects and its collapse, be grasped as a matter of practical world-making and repairing?

WITNESSING SCALE

The nonhuman witnessing of scale opens onto embodied engagements with the strange disjunctures of climate change. These disjunctures include its unfolding into a future in which everyone currently alive is dead, and its weird geographies, its planetary scope and localized effects, its collapse of distinctions between apparently discrete systems and spaces. All this demands "rethinking perception as unfixed, nonlinear, embodied, and mobile," as Zylinska writes in relation to nonhuman photography.[43] Scales connect the human and nonhuman in complex, inextricable ways: they bind entities through relation, yet do so transversally, rather than through any explicitly causal interrelation. Scale is a site of nonhuman witnessing because it is a manifestation, even a technique, for the registration of relations that are not at all obvious, or that defy human experience, or that insist upon incommensurability. Witnessing scale, whether of time or space or anything else, means making political and contestable its structures, assumptions, effects, histories, and technicities. Technoscientific views from above are a critical convergence of all these things, not least because the view from above also coalesces war, data, and climate in multiple ways.

Thanks to the global touring of a major exhibition and its accompanying documentary, the Canadian photographer Edward Burtynsky, along with his longtime collaborators Jennifer Baichal and Nicholas de Pencier, has played a significant role in popularizing the term *Anthropocene* and produced some of the best-known interventions into the view from above. Shot using high-resolution digital cameras, Burtynsky's oeuvre documents decades spent traveling to places where the markers of human activity on the planetary surface are devastatingly evident. His photographs are arresting, even disturbingly beautiful, finding in open-cut mines, polluted deltas, and deforested landscapes an aesthetic of shadowed contours, strange colorations, geometric fractures, surreal surfaces. While some of his work operates at an immersive human scale, almost all his photographs since the late 2000s are aerial. Typically photographed from a light plane, the images splay out with just enough perspective so that salt pans in Gujarat, India, or lithium mines in the Atacama salt flats, Chile, seem to extend indefinitely beyond what the camera reveals. In "Salt Pan #18," asymmetrical polygons of land stagger away from the bottom of the image in long lines, while in "Clear Cut #3," the curling marks of clear-felled palm oil plantations in Malaysia curve off every edge of the image. A series from the Morenci Mine in Arizona, USA, renders the landscape alien: vivid oranges and purples, vivisected by curves and lines carved by immense vehicles that emerge slowly from the image, barely distinguishable on the monumental prints on gallery walls (figure 3.1). Point of view and framing together render the images difficult to position definitively: spatial scales feel monumental but resist enumeration, content escapes form even as the aerial view seems to offer the possibility of revelation.

Unsettling, even destabilizing, Burtynsky's photographs are generators of affective disembodiment, of being temporally shoved out of the human sensorium and placed in relation to the scale of the human as geologic agent. Human and nonhuman fold into each other, perturbing spatialities of scale by presenting the planetary terraforming of anthropogenic devastation at the limits of the human.[44] What we witness in these works is thus the affectivity of the geological and geometrical, the problematics of scale. These images attest not only to catastrophic human intervention in the natural world, but also to the tension between human capacity and aesthetics, between the technical and the beautiful. Here, nonhuman witnessing exceeds what resides in the visual field: relations of scale are themselves intensive, forceful, and embodied in the most radical sense of folding the human into the nonhuman spatialities of climate crisis and its causal agents of extractive industry.

FIGURE 3.1. "Morenci Mine #2," Clifton, Arizona, Edward Burtynsky, 2012. © Edward Burtynsky, courtesy Sundaram Tagore Galleries, Singapore / Nicholas Metivier Gallery, Toronto.

Against the scientific aesthetics of satellite imagery, which are typically framed by indexical legends and produced at specifically determined scales, Burtynsky's photography situates the view from above as more contingent, as embodied in the aesthetic relations engendered by the image. So, while his photographs buy into the capacity of the view from above to reveal, they resist entry into the epistemic category of the technoscientific view that drives knowledge production in war and science alike.

Part of what makes climate change such a fundamental political challenge is that it is simultaneously an ontological and epistemological problem. Moving up, down, and between scales, climate change confuses systems of governance and knowledge. Clark calls this the "derangement of scale," in which "received concepts of agency, rationality and responsibility are being strained or even begin to fall apart in a bewildering generalizing of the political that can make even filling a kettle as public an act as voting."[45] For all the derangements of scale produced by the climate crisis, its defining scalar feature might well be the collapse of scales, their folding into one another such that scale itself proves at once illusory and determinate, ephemeral and material. This ambivalent relationship between the human and nonhuman eye, between creative practices of witnessing and scientific documentation of the world, is evident in a 2018 work by the Australian media artist Grayson Cooke.

Shown at major venues across the country, "Open Air" combines the paintings and processes of artist Emma Walker with satellite images of Australia from the Landsat "Digital Earth Australia" program, set to the 2013 album *Open* by the cult Australian band the Necks. The work plays with the visual registers of the aerial view, troubling the mediated materialities of land and art. Running just over an hour, it brings together motion-controlled aerial photography of Walker's abstract paintings with time-lapse images from the Landsat archive, which has been returning to image the same point on the planet every sixteen days for more than forty years (figure 3.2). In the video of Walker's paintings-in-progress, the camera scans surfaces slowly: intensely immediate, close to rough wood, cracked paint, flowing pigment, and heat applied to paint. At times, the Landsat images cut sharply from one to the other, at others they dissolve slowly, rich reds and blues sliding into one another, clouds and their shadows just barely separable. In some arresting sequences, the screen splits and mirrors, or satellite and photographic image overlay one another, collapsing together disparate scales, materialities, and topographies.

FIGURE 3.2. Still from "Open Air," Grayson Cooke collaboration with Emma Walker, 2018. Courtesy of the artist.

Launched by NASA in 1972 as the Earth Resources Technology Satellite and renamed in 1975, Landsat is the longest continuous program of satellite imaging of the planet, with its imagery used in everything from agriculture to conservation to surveillance. The two currently active satellites, Landsat 8 and Landsat 9, record blue, green, and red light from the visual spectrum, but can also sense in the infrared spectrum invisible to human eyes. Their data is freely available but produced by US government funding and so operates within the ambit of US strategic priorities, with a visible spectrum spatial resolution of 30m and closer to 100m for infrared. In "Open Air," Cooke's layering of multiple scales enables continuities between the orbital satellite and the macro video lens to bring into the terrain of the perceivable the climatic and geologic processes that might otherwise evade the human. Without narration or context, the Landsat images are more affective than representational: viewing them is not about decoding their content, but rather feeling through the strangeness of watching change from above.

Despite their high-definition clarity and our capacity to "read" them, these images are only secondarily representational: rather, they are testimonies to nonhuman mediations, to vital processes of change in form, space, and time. Scale collapses, eliding distinctions between pigment and pixel, painting and planet. Witnessing here is pure aesthetics: a registering of relations, an enfolding of materiality and mediation. As the instrumental soundtrack ebbs and flows, the artifice of the painting—the ways it is not land—become both more evident and less significant. Its mediation makes it mutable; processes (viscous dissolutions, searing wood fibers, bubbling and cracking coatings) supersede the thing itself. So too in the Landsat images, where their archival mattering as objects of scientific research falls away in the meditative movement between images. Scale is present but cannot hold—and what is witnessed in the dissolution is that collapse in the nonhuman processes of materialities fluxing in form. While Cooke works directly with the remote-sensing epistemic image, its indexical and informational functions are systematically eradicated, made materially aesthetic by the movement between satellite image and digital capture of paint, wood, dirt, and sand. As with the human experience of the Anthropocene and its climatic violence, claims to know are unanchored from their spatial references, made strange and intimately nonhuman.

If the spatial scales of climate captured by Cooke are dizzying, their temporal counterparts can be weird and estranging. Time is the site of one of its most confounding paradoxes: the urgent need for action now to confront something that exists as an affective fact of catastrophic futurity. But Man is not used to thinking in time horizons that exceed Himself and yet demand radical and immediate transformation in the present. Derangements of the sensorium become estrangements of senescence. In a photograph documenting "Boiling Milk" (1999), a performance that took place one morning in 1999 near Krafla, Iceland, the small pan of milk in Ilana Halperin's gloved hands barely touches the surface of the sulphur spring (figure 3.3). Crouched by the side of the hundred-degree lake, her arm extended from a narrow spit of land, the artist seems almost a supplicant, her gesture one of ritual offering. Her bright red raincoat pulled tight to the curve of her back, face emerging from

FIGURE 3.3. "Boiling Milk," Krafla, Iceland, Ilana Halperin, 1999

Witnessing Ecologies   127

the hood to focus intently on the task at hand, she stands out sharply against the background blues and greys of the water, mist and sky that dissolve into one another as she waits for the milk to boil. By bringing together the swift domestic act of boiling milk with the deep time of geothermal reactions, David Farrier writes that Halperin "summoned an extraordinary confluence of different scales," such that in "what appears to be a fleeting, even humble exchange between human and geologic temporal orders, a deeply Anthropocenic sensibility emerges."[46] Halperin describes her own work as examining "geologic intimacy," which Farrier sees as one form of the poetics of thick time. Yet there is something else at work here, too, a witnessing of temporal disjuncture, of nonhuman indifference to the scientific insistence on dating and measurement.

Consider the embodiment of the encounter: wrapped protectively and bent carefully at the knee, Halperin curls toward the hot water, only the skin of her face exposed to the heat and stink of sulphureous waters. It is not only the milk that feels the deep time of geothermal heat as its proteins coagulate and separate, but Halperin herself. She is witness to the encounter, but also entangled within it. In just a few short minutes, the composition of the milk changes from cool to hot, beginning to steam like the air of the lake itself. Located on the Mid-Atlantic Ridge, where the North American and Eurasian tectonic plates pull slowly apart, Krafla makes the slow drift of planetary geologic change accessible to the human sensorium. In "Boiling Milk," the transfer of energies takes place across radically incommensurate time scales, the millennial inching apart of the plates producing volcanic activity that heats the lake and in turn Halperin and her milk. Milk—perishable, biological, life sustaining—takes into itself the heat of infinitesimal geologic movement. In this transfer of energy, scales collide but do not collapse. The milk transforms, becoming other than it was through Halperin's ritual gesture. But this witnessing is not happenstance; it is deliberately enacted and carefully framed, mediated by the photograph and its title into an image testimony of the potential intimacy of time that far exceeds the human.[47] Reflecting on such temporalities, Zylinska points to the emerging significance of photography after the human, a phrase that refers not only to "the straightforward material disappearance or conceptual overcoming of the human at some point in the future . . . but also to the present imagining of that disappearance as a prominent visual trope in art photography and other cultural practices."[48] Tracing the way in which photography after the human confronts deep temporal and spatial scales, as well as problems such as extinction, is an essential political, ethical, and artistic question. In "Boiling Milk," the ungraspability of deep time manifests in the dissolving background, the indistinct materialities of the environment itself. And yet the body of the artist is not diminished or made fragile but is attentive to its relations. Her body holds itself carefully, her attention is a mode of care for the moment itself, for this seemingly simple event of holding a pan of milk above heat from beneath the earth's crust. Viewing this image, one can witness not only temporal scale, but also an ethics of care toward what that scale does, how it can be a site of connection and bring shared intimacy between human and nonhuman.

But the witnessing of temporal scale can also be radically unearthly. In the final pages of Cixin Liu's epic *Three-Body Problem* trilogy, the impossible scale of the life of the universe itself enters into a strange relation with two of the novel's human protagonists, Cheng Xin and Guan Yifan. Suffice to say, the details of how this speculative fiction progresses from the midst of the Cultural Revolution to an interstellar future are beyond reckoning with here. But by the third book's end—SPOILER ALERT!—Cheng Xin and Yifan are in a small space shuttle orbiting a distant planet at the speed of light when they are caught by the rippling wave left behind by a light-speed engine that curves space to propel ships forward. Its rupturing of spacetime slows the speed of light itself to a crawl, such that—as the laws of relativity require—time passes incredibly slowly for the two of them relative to the universe outside. Forced to use hibernation technology to survive through the slow reboot of their shuttle's computers, sixteen days pass for the pair while the planet experiences more than eighteen million years. Using ground-penetrating remote sensors, they are able to find a message left for them through the eons and a doorway that leads into an artificial universe. It is a closed ecology of a single cubic kilometer, suspended outside of time and from its vantage the two will be able to watch our universe collapse into singularity and be reborn in a new Big Bang. But the loss of mass from thousands of such micro-universes risks reversing the crunch of the grand universe and instead expanding it into endless, deenergized lifelessness. Rather than contribute to such existential senescence, Cheng Xin and Guan Yifan give up their existence outside of time and the promise of the birth of a new universe to live the death of our own. They leave behind a computational record of human existence, and a small globe containing two fish, water, and a tiny artificial sun. To our universe, they return the mass and its incipient energy that has made their existence outside of time possible.

It is, even by the standards of science fiction, an almost preposterous projection, a conceit of human galactic endurance that belies our seeming incapacity to do anything but destroy the richness of life on this planet. And yet it chases after something profound: a speculative pursuit of an infinite relation between the human and the nonhuman vastness of the universe. Against the total mass of an expanding and contracting universe, what is human life, memory, existence? As an exercise of thought, it proposes that the witnessing of humanity as a species depends inevitably and inextricably on the nonhuman. On the one hand, this is an obvious claim—what else might be the other of such witnessing, that to which address is made and response implored? But it is also a proposition that, for all its technowizardry and speculative gymnastics, returns the human unavoidably to the question of its relations to the milieu through which it moves and lives, whether at the scale of the universe, solar system, planet, ecology, community, or self. Witnessing the human at the limit point of the existence of the universe itself means insisting on an offering to the ultimate nonhuman, life rendered down to the necessarily flawed remainder yet insisting that some memory endure into the emergence of a new space-time.

Reflecting on the Abrahamic tradition of testimony, Peters writes that "testifying has the structure of repentance: retroactively caring about what we were once careless of."[49] Already, testimony serves this function of repentance in the Anthropocene: it marks and acknowledges the failures of government, publics, and individuals alike, as well as the small victories of collective action, of reparative meaning-making. Scale can be operative, as well as relational. Anna Tsing argues that scalability served a crucial role in the accumulation of capital and in the spread of extractive modes of production across the planet. Scalability describes "the ability to expand—and expand and expand—without rethinking basic elements."[50] Tsing points out the scalability of the plantation was essential to its proliferation as a model throughout the Americas, just as scalability remains a fundamental principle of contemporary business from social media platforms to fracking operations. As C. L. R. James and more contemporarily Chris Taylor, Caitlin Rosenthal, and Katherine McKittrick, among others, have argued, the plantation is the model for the factory and for neoliberal conceptions of scaling production up and down.[51] In approaching this weaponization of scale, Tsing calls for an attentiveness to nonscalability, "to the work of contingency and failure" and the workings of "scalability in action."[52] By attending to registrations of scale, nonhuman witnessing offers another means of thinking the nonscalable and the operations of scale between that which scales and that which does not. Nonhuman witnessing of scale, then, is not solely about how we grasp the ungraspable, but also how we intervene in the ways that scale is put to use. If ecological violence operates across spatial and temporal scales, then so too is ecological trauma bound up with scale. Nonhuman witnessing of scale, then, brings us to one of the core problematics of ecologic crisis: its traumatic disjunctures, cascades, and contaminations.

ECOLOGICAL TRAUMA

Rising panic in the West over the "end of the world" often fails to recognize already existing experiences of ruined lifeworlds. Nor do enough planned or imagined responses to the climate emergency give heed to the ontologies, epistemologies, and practical knowledges of those people who lived far more sustainable lives before and despite settler colonialism. Ecological catastrophe has already been experienced by First Nations: the anthropogenic end of worlds is, all too terribly, nothing new. Through violence to knowledge, land, and ways of living, as Kyle Powis Whyte argues, "settler colonialism commits environmental injustice through the violent disruption of human relationships to the environment."[53] Felling forests to graze cattle and grow crops, introducing invasive species, diverting rivers and flooding valleys, flattening hills and bifurcating mountains with highways—the list of such disruptions is endless. Nor, of course, are such ecological traumas confined to the past. Environmental destruction, loss of traditional forms of community, and death itself all flow from resource extraction, weapons testing and war, plantation agriculture, and other forms of what Rob Nixon calls the "slow violence" of late capitalism, inflicted on the poor, oppressed, and dispossessed.[54]

Ecological trauma describes the injurious and ongoing effects at the level of experience of the rupturing of relations that compose ecologies as living and changing assemblages of more-than-human entities and processes. All traumas target relations, severing encounters or events from the flow of experience and lodging those fragments in bodies as they go on, affecting and affected by the world as it unfolds. But ecological trauma can be understood as trauma that results from the rupturing of the relations that compose an ecology, rather than those that enmesh a body within its world. Located at the relational-compositional level of the ecology itself, ecological trauma echoes collective cultural trauma, but is differentiated by its insistence on nonhuman entities and the situatedness of all ecologies and their relations. Like trauma more generally, ecological trauma is found not in the violence that enacts a rupturing of relations but in how that rupturing carries through into the future. Contaminating the unfolding multiplicities of experience that animate an ecology with the past, ecological trauma is also haunted by futures forged by ecological violence. These are futures diffracted through trauma: the threat of collapse, stagnation, and death.

Ecological trauma encompasses but also exceeds what I and others have elsewhere called "climate trauma," the traumatic rupturing of relations that resides in the impossibility of the individual subject reckoning with the scale of the climate crisis in its totality.[55] Timothy Morton has argued that global warming must be understood as a hyperobject, "massively distributed in time and space relative to humans."[56] As a hyperobject, global warming can only ever be grasped through second-order abstractions such as graphs or in localized effects, such as the slow drowning of Pacific islands, but such representations can at best be synecdochic of the incomprehensible totality of the climate crisis. The problem is that the object-ness of the hyperobject takes precedence over its local manifestations, systemic origins, and meaningful strategies for its amelioration. The theoretical maneuver that transforms climate crisis into a hyperobject is itself a violent mediation, one that strips away agency, complexity, and relationality even as it evokes those very things within its theoretical tool kit.[57] Framing contemporary crisis within the hyperobject paradoxically reasserts the Anthropos, even as the human is disavowed by Morton's insistence on the separateness and inaccessibility of objects in general. While it is true that "climate change" constitutes an abstraction that necessarily contains more than can be grasped, reifying the planetary scale risks replicating the annihilation of experiences of ecological violence, loss, grief, and renewal that takes place in more intimate, varied, dispersed, and uneven ways. The ecological trauma of our age might be better grasped as both one and many; always ecological *traumas*, plural, even when it seems otherwise.

What I am proposing is a radical empiricist approach to ecological trauma that recognizes rupturing and violence as processual phenomena. Just as a radical empiricist approach to experience recognizes that the present is always lost between unfolding pasts, which carry with them lost futures, and the tug of potential futures, so too in more-than-human ecologies is the present always unavailable to its own experience. Future collapse bears down on wounded ecologies in the present, bringing itself into being through the continuance of violence in the form of trauma. Consider, for instance, the fires that have become the norm in California, Brazil, and Australia, and the way their looming ever-presence affects life even beyond the devastating damage to animals, habitats, and homes.[58] As Massumi writes: "This is the figure of today's threat: the suddenly irrupting, locally self-organizing, systemically self-amplifying threat of large-scale disruption."[59] There is, in a very real sense, an affective injury in the now from that which has and yet has not arrived. Always in dynamic flux, even if that flux is entropic, the present of an ecology is always missed in much the same way as it is for humans.

This traumatic relation to ecological crisis is not simply about the apparent futility of action in this era of late capitalism but also the exponential complexity of the problem. Ecologies are not isolated systems; any boundaries placed upon them are always artificial and temporary. We humans distinguish one ecology from another to make them sensible and addressable but doing so is always a tactical measure: ecologies fold into one another, at once one and many. Against the reified hyperobject of catastrophic climate change, we might instead conceive of an endless complex planetary ecology, simultaneously composed of an infinite array of other ecologies. Ecological traumas have thus shaped and continue to shape lives, communities, cultures, and ecologies. Among those traumas is one that resides at the atomic organization of existence: nuclear war. Nuclear explosions occur within a fraction of a second but leave radiation that contaminates, mutates, and ends life into unfolding deep-time futures. Nuclear weapons and their catastrophic damage constitute a vital site for engagement with nonhuman witnessing as both an other-than-human registration of change and an aesthetic project of human and more-than-human commingling. It is to the testing of these paradigmatic technologies of world ending that I now wish to turn.

WITNESSING THE NUCLEAR

Yankunytjatjara elder Lester Yami called it a "black mist," a thick cloud enveloping Adnyamathanha country, part of a huge swathe of Aboriginal land in South Australia used for nuclear testing by Britain from 1953 to 1963.[60] He described his experience to the 1984 Royal Commission into the tests: "A big bang—a noise like an explosion and later something come in the air... [it] was coming from the south, black-like smoke. I was thinking it might be a dust storm, but it was quiet, just moving... through the trees and above that again, you know. It was just rolling and moving quietly."[61]

Personally authorized by Prime Minister Robert Menzies and conducted in secret, British nuclear testing in Australia took place on the Montebello Islands (in 1952 and 1956), at Emu Fields in South Australia where Lester Yami encountered the black mist (1953), and, most infamously, just to the south of Emu Fields at Maralinga (1956–1963).[62] Emu Fields was a particularly disastrous choice: difficult to access by vehicle and prone to violent dust storms, it significantly increased the risk of wider nuclear contamination due to irradiated dust carried on the wind. But the worst damage was done at Maralinga, where the British tested seven atomic bombs and conducted a series of even more disastrous "minor tests."

In 1956, "Operation Buffalo" tested Red Beard and Blue Danube, plutonium warheads with a destructive equivalent to the weapon dropped on Hiroshima, with the smaller "Operation Antler" conducted the year after (figure 3.4).[63] These were followed until 1962 by a series of so-called minor tests, in which plutonium was scattered around various trial sites and blown up to analyze shock waves, safety measures, and radiation effects—with devastating consequences for Country.[64] Ineffectual clean-ups were attempted, with two desultory efforts by the British in the 1960s and more comprehensively by the Australian government in 2000, although costs were soon cut and their effectiveness has been contested.[65] In 2021, a study undertaken by scientists

FIGURE 3.4. British nuclear testing at Maralinga, archival image

at Monash University showed plutonium in the soil at Maralinga.[66] Because very little was done to protect local communities, many suffer from high rates of cancers and disease.[67]

Lester Yami described the immediate effects in visceral terms: "I cannot remember how long we were getting sick and sore eyes and watery eyes and diarrhea... vomiting and skin rashes... purtju, sore on the skin... I could not see with both eyes."[68] The entire ecology—people, water, vegetation, animals, dirt, dust, geology—were directly exposed to radioactive contaminants during the blasts and fallout, embedding radioactive elements within the ecosystem, passing them through bodies and life cycles.[69] Here, the recollections of Nyarri Morgan, a young man at the time of the tests, are instructive: "We thought it was the spirit of our gods rising up to speak with us... then we saw the spirit had made all the kangaroos fall down on the ground as a gift to us of easy hunting so we took those kangaroos and we ate them and people were sick and then the spirit left.... The smoke went into our noses, and other people still have that poison today."[70]

Maralinga was formally returned to its Traditional Owners in 2009, but Country and its ecologies, the rich relations that bind human and non, remain contaminated, wounded, and traumatized (figure 3.5). For First Nations in the settler state of Australia, such wounding of Country constitutes an existential violence. Trawlwulwuy scholar Lauren Tynan writes: "Country inhabits all relationality and is used widely across Australia to describe how all land is Aboriginal land, Aboriginal Country; Country is agentic and encompasses everything from ants, memories, humans, fire, tides and research."[71] Violence to Country needs to be understood as something far more injurious and rupturing than what might be denoted by damage to "environment" within Western epistemologies. As Tynan continues: "Country sits at the heart of coming to know and understand relationality as it is the web that connects humans to a system of Lore/Law and knowledge that can never be human-centric." Country is thus radically at odds with what Aileen Moreton-Robinson calls the "possessive logics" of white settler sovereignty, that claim land as property and thus render it always potentially subject to extraction and violence.[72]

While the British authorities made efforts to mitigate the effects on white farmers, the Aboriginal inhabitants of the region were almost entirely neglected.[73] Aboriginal culture, history, lifestyle, and ceremony were not considered important by civic and military authorities. "The nomadic nature of the desert people, their traditional lifestyle and seasonal journeys for hunting and ceremonial purposes was poorly understood," writes historian

FIGURE 3.5. Signage at the former nuclear test site at Maralinga

J. D. Mittman. "The country there was regarded as 'empty wasteland,' in line with the legal doctrine of *terra nullius*, a Latin phrase meaning 'empty land' or 'land belonging to no-one.'"[74] This legal doctrine of terra nullius articulated the land as lacking property relations. First Nations peoples might live on the land but had not undertaken improvements legible to the colonizers as demarcating possession. Through this doctrine, First Nations were dispossessed of the land so that white settlers could possess it, a move that not only stripped them of property under Crown law but also assigned them as belonging to the state of nature.[75] Just as terra nullius was retroactively applied to authorize the theft of land under settler colonialism in what became known as Australia, so too was it used to justify the new nuclear colonialism. For a British Empire in disarray, Maralinga was an acceptable sacrifice zone, an empty wasteland, populated by people still counted among the flora and fauna of the nation, that could be readily transformed into an extraterritorial zone of incision in which its inhabitants, having lived there for thousands of years, were suddenly rendered illegal.

This construction of a zone of absence and excision echoed that of the Soviet Union in Kazakhstan and Siberia, and the French and the United States in the Pacific. In this sense, Maralinga reproduced the nuclear colonialism emerging across the United States and the Pacific.[76] Unsurprisingly, the most targeted were and continue to be Indigenous peoples and lands. Operating in contexts of radical power asymmetries, nuclear colonialism depends on material and discursive maneuvers, generating economic dependencies on the one hand while constructing lands and people as permissible objects of violence on the other.⁷⁷ In the Marshall Islands, the United States detonated thermonuclear weapons orders of magnitude more destructive than those at Hiroshima and Nagasaki, leading to the displacement of peoples from their traditional homes and to a horrific legacy of birth defects across the islands.

As the opening pages of this chapter made clear, those same islands are now among the most at-risk places on the planet for the rising sea levels of global warming, in yet another tragic knot in the entangled history of nuclear war and climate science. Perhaps unsurprisingly, drone histories occur here too, with the Operation Kamikaze remotely piloted drone munition tests conducted in the shadow of Castle Bravo, at fifteen megatons the largest test ever conducted by the United States. Nuclear colonial discourse imagined the Pacific as isolated islands and empty seas. But nuclear testing helped mobilize a renewed Oceanic political activism that insists on a relational political ontology, founded on the connectedness of sea and islands, peoples and fish.⁷⁸ Aboriginal land in Australia was similarly subject to expropriation and excision. Pitjantjatjara Anangu from Ooldea were forcibly removed from Country to a purpose-built settlement in Yalata more than 150km to the south. The test site was renamed Maralinga by the Australian authorities, the word for "thunder" in the Garik language, chosen for its fit to the nuclear violence that would take place there.⁷⁹ Maralinga was excised from the civilian legal order and made inaccessible to its Traditional Owners, a redoubled denial of sovereignty. Weapons testing began shortly after.

Detonated in the first test of Operation Buffalo at Maralinga, the bomb known as Red Beard used nuclear fission, a process that exploits the desire of unstable atoms to achieve an impossible equilibrium (figure 3.6). Under the intense force of neutron bombardment or chemical explosion, an atom of an unstable isotope—a mix of Uranium-235 and Plutonium-239 in the case of Red Beard—splits in search of stability. As it splits, energy is released but so too are smaller nuclei—fission products—that strike other unstable atoms, changing their atomic structure. Two or more neutrons, subatomic particles within the nucleus held in check by electromagnetic force, get ejected. Ejected neutrons disrupt other, already unstable isotopes. Uranium-235 becomes Uranium-236, an even more unstable isotope that splits again, releasing more energy and more fission products. More atoms are struck and split; more energy is released. This is the chain reaction that generates the catastrophic explosion of the atom bomb, an urgent hunt for stability that produces nothing but more splitting, more energy, more instability.⁸⁰ Nuclear bombs are designed to explode well above the ground, maximizing both the force and radius of the blast: this is what produces the spectacular

FIGURE 3.6. Explosion of a Red Beard warhead on September 27, 1956

mushroom cloud, which reached a height of almost twelve kilometers with the first test at Maralinga. Heat is so intense that it turns bodies to ash, melts metal and concrete, and, at Maralinga and Emu Fields, transformed the silicate and sand of stretches of desert into a crust of glass.[81]

Glass becomes an aesthetic medium for the nonhuman witnessing of nuclear violence in the hands of the artist Yhonnie Scarce: brittle yet tough, capturing light yet also diffracting and refracting it, rigid when cool yet shaped by the breath of the glassblower when molten. Belonging to the Kokatha and Nukunu peoples whose country forms part of the Maralinga excision zone and born in the military town of Woomera, Scarce's personal and familial history is bound to settler colonialism and to its entanglements with militarism. Her work is intensely political: an unflinching critique of past and present settler violence, but also a celebration of the resilience and endurance of Aboriginal people and of Country in the face of the colonial logic for elimination. Repeatedly returning to the interconnections between the classification and dispossession of First Nations land and scientific and military testing, Scarce's work is unified by an unrelenting aesthetic of austere grayscale, battered found objects, stark medical equipment, and spare architectural structures and installations. While Scarce works with a range of media, glassblowing is at the core of her practice, a visceral and difficult art that demands much of breath and body. The subject of a major survey exhibition at the Australian Centre for Contemporary Art in Melbourne and at the Institute of Modern Art in Brisbane in 2021, Scarce's works are held at the National Gallery of Australia, the National Gallery of Victoria, Art Gallery of South Australia, and by other galleries and private collectors around the world. While her work always addresses colonialism and its violence, the subject matter ranges from family history to medical experimentation to the legacies of nuclear testing. In three of her major works—*Thunder Raining Poison* (2015), *Death Zephyr* (2017), and *Missile Park* (2021)—Scarce reveals the potential for a glassy aesthetics of nonhuman witnessing to nuclear violence.

Thunder Raining Poison (2015) and *Death Zephyr* (2017) are formally and thematically similar works (figures 3.7 and 3.8). Both are composed of thousands of blown glass yams suspended from the ceiling in arrays that reference the atmospheric forms produced by nuclear tests at Maralinga. There are critical differences between the two works: *Thunder Raining Poison* captures the instance of detonation, yams arranged in a teardrop formation and mostly made of clear glass, interspersed with black and blue; *Death Zephyr* examines the spread of contaminated particles in the aftermath of the blast, its mix of black and clear yams hang in a swirling current across the gallery space, a material enactment of Lester Yami's "black mist" over Country. Una Ray observes that "the yam and other 'bush tucker' plants such as the bush banana and bush plum, along with their associated Tjukurrpa (Dreaming) sites are important subjects for Aboriginal artists, particularly women who traditionally held the comprehensive knowledge of the regularly harvested and managed bush gardens across Australia."[82] Composing yams into forms of nuclear explosion and dispersal materializes the violation of life by such violence, its assault on the nonhuman that sustains the human. Not only is sand blasted into nonlife, these works suggest, but also the means to sustain life affectively and discursively signified in the alchemy of yams become inedible. Distended and distorted, the yams are reminders too of "eviscerated organs or exhumed physical evidence in the prosecution of war crimes," as art critic and Bundjalung and Kullilli man Daniel Browning puts it.[83] Both *Thunder Raining Poison* and *Death Zephyr* are reminders of the limits of the forensic practices of the state to understand the consequences of the tests conducted on Aboriginal land precisely because life is ecology: yams, sand, land, bush animals, people, are bound together by Country, a relationality

FIGURE 3.7. *Thunder Raining Poison*, Yhonnie Scarce 2015. Courtesy of Yhonnie Scarce and THIS IS NO FANTASY.

FIGURE 3.8. *Death Zephyr*, Yhonnie Scarce, 2017. Courtesy of Yhonnie Scarce and THIS IS NO FANTASY.

that is just as crucial to the ecology as the electromagnetic forces that hold neutrons in check are to stability at the atomic scale.

Unstable isotopes are radioactive: they contain an unbalanced combination of neutrons and protons in their nucleus, which typically means too many neutrons. By shedding extra energetic particles, these isotopes "decay" into other particles, becoming more stable and less radioactive but releasing nuclear radiation in the process. When a nuclear bomb is detonated, radioactive particles are dispersed by the explosive force, attaching themselves in turn to other particles. This is nuclear fallout: the irradiated particles of weapon debris and dust that are carried on the wind, as *Death Zephyr* reminds us, before they fall to earth. In their fall, they can attach and deform more particles and the cells that make up life, such that stones, plants, animals, and people become carriers of contamination, nonhuman and doomed witnesses to nuclear catastrophe.

Some of the most devastating effects at Maralinga were not the bombs themselves, but the "minor tests" involving the detonation of scattered plutonium and other radiation "safety" experiments. Depending on the half-lives of the isotopes involved, radioactive contamination might be present for minutes, days, or years.[84] Radioactive contamination can have enduring effects: making soil and water poisonous, producing cancers and miscarriages, and deforming life at its most basic workings. Yet radioactive decay also constitutes a material witness to the unthinkable force of the nuclear explosion, a nonhuman registration of the impossible violence that it produces—and that produces it. Radioactive contamination and its decay are themselves both nonhuman witnesses, and what must be witnessed.

While foreign wars and colonial "exploration" are commemorated across Australia, the violence done to its original inhabitants remains politically contested and largely unmemorialized. Official memorials function as modes of commonplace witnessing, generating the shared meanings through which certain political knowledges and identities are reproduced and others are elided or erased.[85] *Missile Park*, commissioned to accompany the 2021 survey of Scarce's work, offers a countermemorial to the violence of nuclear testing and settler colonialism. Blasted raw and roughly painted black, three corrugated metal sheds echo the structures common to Maralinga and Woomera, but also to Australian settlement more generally (figure 3.9). One shed invites entry into a near-dark space, lit only by the gallery light that finds its way through the gaps of corrugation, in which a simple table holds twenty bush plums blown from black glass (figure 3.10). Gunditjmara and Torres Strait Islander artist and curator Lisa Waup calls these sheds "containers of trauma."[86] Here in the dark, in the hurried tin-shed architecture of the expansive project of Australian settlement, the bush plums attest to the memory of ecologies of life cleaved by violence. Ray describes the artist's work as "a composition between hand and breath, the alchemical, elemental process of glassblowing neatly fuses the maker to her material and her métier to meaning."[87] *Missile Park* coalesces these elementalities, finding in their ecological relations a host of evocative tensions. Bush plums of black glass capture breath, that most ephemeral and basic gesture of fleshy life, but they also hold in their material memory the pollution of air, the violent contamination of the bomb. They bear nonhuman witness to the scales of incommensurate temporalities of the nuclear: the split second of the explosion, the long half-life of plutonium, the irradiated endurance of Country. Here is ecological trauma, witnessed through an ecology of processes, objects, and milieus that only come to matter through their relational composition.

There is a dark irony in the witnessing capacities of glass, one that extends beyond Scarce's art and the silica seared into trinitite at Maralinga to the failed use of vitrification in the latest attempts to clean-up the radiation at the test sites.[88] Developed by the US company Bastelle, *in-situ vitrification*, or ISV, uses electricity to immobilize plutonium and other unstable isotopes in glass-like blocks that can keep them safe for hundreds of thousands of

FIGURE 3.9. *Missile Park* exhibition installation, Yhonnie Scarce, 2021. Courtesy of Yhonnie Scarce and THIS IS NO FANTASY.

FIGURE 3.10. *Missile Park* interior, Yhonnie Scarce, 2021. Courtesy of Yhonnie Scarce and THIS IS NO FANTASY.

years, at least in theory. In practice, ISV was difficult to implement and not always fit to task, the government department overseeing the process failed to establish clear criteria—and, surprising no one familiar with the history of the state's treatment of Indigenous peoples in Australia, once costs grew, vitrification was abandoned in favor of exhuming and burying the waste. Glass as a failed medium of remediation testifies to the unyielding nature of nuclear radiation, but also to the persistent coloniality of settler politics, to the legacies of who counts as human and who does not. As a byproduct of nuclear testing and as a failed mechanism for decontamination, vitrification is a process of mediation: silica into glass, by way of the intense applications of energy. Its violence is not inherent, but contextual. Through the breath of the glassblower, vitrified silica becomes intimate and lively: a rich ecology of country, life, fruit, vegetable and yet still an ecology deeply wounded by the violence of war and settlement. Glass yams and bush plums distill the ecological traumas of nuclear testing at Maralinga, the stuff of life rearranged into the mushroom cloud and its dispersal and memorialized in the tin sheds of the test sites.

What it means to witness such ecological trauma looks very different within the accepted bounds of historical witnessing, particularly in the official form it took in the Royal Commission into British Nuclear Tests in Australia, chaired by Jim McClelland. While the commission sought to account for the health impacts on Aboriginal people and heard the testimony of Lester Yami and others, its principal focus was the irradiation of Australian servicemen, the safety precautions implemented by the British, and the nature of the agreement between Australia and its imperial overlord. From a cultural standpoint, Yami's black mist is surely its enduring figure, one that finds a glassy counterpart in the art of Yhonnie Scarce. Nuclear activism and public pressure in the 1980s did much to make Maralinga and Emu Fields visible to the wider Australian public, and in 2009 almost all the lands of the excision were returned to their Traditional Owners. But the Royal Commission, the failed cleanups that followed, and the narrow inquiries from various departments and committees function as stark reminders of the impossibility of such organs of the settler state working against its fundamental investments in militarism and the denial of Indigenous sovereignty. Within such confines, the capacities of witnessing are bound not only by the necessity of speaking but also by legal norms and parliamentary terms of reference.

A more expansive witnessing must be sought elsewhere, in the poetry of Indigenous writers such as Oodgeroo Noonuccal, Lionel Fogarty, and Natalie Harkin, and even in the inventive research of scientists, who have exposed the radioactivity embedded into particles of the land. In a poem written for the catalogue of the 2021 survey of Scarce's work, Harkin writes:

> mine and refine this float of molten
> landscape   raw silica-sand and
> limestone sites   slice and stirred
> and hot-shop forged   we
> witness excavation of targets and
> melts   a redaction of origins   of
> lives   of lands
>   see what a breath can do[89]

An intimacy emerges in Harkin's words that bears a certain resemblance to that between Ilana Halperin and the deep time of volcanic heat in "Boiling Milk." Yet here the relation is one of breath, an intensive yet ephemeral bond between the geological, the nuclear, and the fragility and force of human life, the glassblower and her glass. As with all the aesthetic works examined in this chapter, Scarce's are of course instigated by human subjects and wrought by human hands. Yet they dance with the nonhuman in equally inseparable ways, from their insistent materiality to the nuclear violence they reference to the settler histories of dehumanization and the nonhuman classification of Aboriginal peoples. Glass suspended in air coalesces an instance of the most radical ecological violence possible: a violence torn from the fracturing of the atomic structure of matter itself, a violence that holds the potential not only to erase the human but also to destroy all but the most defiant, hidden, and persistent forms of life. And yet glass also captures the endurance of breath, the variability of life, and that most fundamental of mediations: photons of light passing through a medium. Life in all its relations, located in Country and food, in air and stone and water, is not simply indexed or represented in the art of Yhonnie Scarce: it is processually present, materialized as a witnessing ecology come to life out of the urgent need to witness ecological trauma and its continued imbrication with the settler state and its militarisms.

WOUNDING

In *The Logic of Sense*, Gilles Deleuze recognizes that futurity resides at the heart of the event and its relation to human expression. The event is "always and at the same time something which has just happened and something which is about to happen; never something which is happening."[90] This simultaneous doubling and splitting of that which has just happened, or the actual, and that which may be about to, or the virtual, constitutes a kind of rupturing: a wound. While this wound is not corporeal in the same way as a cut or broken bone, it is nonetheless bound up with sensation, with the bodily experience of the event—and, crucially, with its separating into a distinct symbolic element in the realm of pure expression. Or, to put this in more distinct terms, the wound is the rupturing of virtual into actual, whether in experience, thought, or expression. Deleuze's choice of the wound as a metaphor is telling: it draws particular attention to the violence inherent in the limiting of potential that occurs in any given thing becoming actual. To call this a wounding suggests that all intersections of the virtual and the actual, all forms of creation—whether life-living or art-making, human or otherwise—are inextricable from injury, from a cleaving of one thing from another. Here, then, is the dynamic of violent mediation at the level of expression itself, of the coming into living of life: a transformative mediation from one state to another that cannot but cut off, leave behind, exclude, or ruin, even as it makes possible the new and the otherwise from which the good might flourish.

This relation between life and expression circulates in Deleuze's enigmatic final essay, "Immanence: A Life...," in which he dwells on the two terms of the title and their relation to each other.[91] He shows how immanence neither refers to an object nor belongs to a subject but is immanent only to itself. The second term—*a life*—captures something at once instinctively understood and yet very difficult to pin down precisely. It is life as an indefinite thing—not this life or that, not my life or yours, but rather *a life*, indefinite and potential, indeterminate yet somehow also composed of singularities. At once the many and the one, to borrow from the pluralism of William James that so influenced Deleuze.[92] This multiplicity in the midst of singularity shares much with what Mario Blaser and Marisol de la Cadena call a "world of many worlds," a pluralism that is not only experiential but politically ontological.[93] Drawing from her deep anthropological engagement with Andean Indigenous communities and politics, de la Cadena insists on the political vibrancy and active agency of earth-beings, a necessarily truncated translation of mountains, lakes, rivers, and other existences that, for Andeans, "blurred the known distinction between humans and nature."[94] The pluralistic politics that flows from recognizing the standing of earth-beings is a question that I will return to in the coda of this book, but here I want to draw a relation between this pluralism and the processual emergence of actualities from within the sheer stuff of existence. Only in wounding does *a life* become the life of a subject or object, or even a milieu. "A life contains only virtual," writes Deleuze. "It is made up of virtualities, events, singularities."⁹⁵ Writing with Guattari, Deleuze describes the plane of immanence as "the plane of Nature, although nature has nothing to do with it, since on this plane there is no distinction between the natural and the artificial."⁹⁶ Such an approach echoes the relationality that Tynan describes as "premised on a truth that 'all things exist in relatedness' and whilst this is a naturally occurring principle of many Indigenous worldviews, it is a principle that is sustained and strengthened through practice."⁹⁷ Without eliding or erasing the differences in these epistemological standpoints, what emerges across them is a recognition of the mutuality and relationality that makes existence and experience possible.

It is within this sense of the mutuality of all existence that the complex and necessary nature of Deleuze's wound becomes clear. The wound is not simply to be suffered or endured; it is not an injury with moral overtones. It is incarnated in life as a state of things, as corporeal, temporal, and experiential, yet it leads into that indefinite, elusive plane of *a life* precisely because the wound is a "pure virtuality on the plane of immanence" even as it is actualized in particular bodies.⁹⁸ Put differently, the wound is a kind of passage, the means by which the plane of potential takes place, something felt as loss but also as always newly opened. Deleuze writes: "My wound existed before me: not a transcendence of the wound as higher actuality, but its immanence as a virtuality always within a milieu."⁹⁹ He might have chosen another word—cut or break, perhaps—yet this choice of wound (*une blessure* in French) matters. It is a reminder that embodiment is necessarily both a rupture from what might have been *and* the becoming-in-the-world of a host of lively potentials. Naming this a wounding calls attention to an ethic of care; it evokes both fragility and resilience. It suggests that how wounding happens, what form and movement it takes, matters both for *a life* and for life lived. This has consequences for conceptualizing and responding to ecological traumas: it suggests that wounded ecologies are also a wounding of the relation between experience and expression, between life and aesthetics, between existence and becoming. As a response to ecological traumas, the processual and unfinished nature of nonhuman witnessing seeks to make this constitutive wounding sensible—however fleetingly.

Wounding, unsurprisingly, also occupies a central figural position in the study of trauma in the humanities. As literary theorist Cathy Caruth insists in what has become a canonical formulation, trauma "is always the story of a wound that cries out, that addresses us in the attempt to tell us of a reality or truth that is not otherwise available."¹⁰⁰ This wound, like that of Deleuze, occupies a doubled position: marking both body and mind yet unknown to either. Only in the belated arrival of a voice from within the wound—a return of the wounding in the form of trauma—does knowing become possible through paradoxically testifying to its own impossibility. As in Deleuze, the wound of trauma is not a metaphor but rather the living embodiment of a relation of rupture between experience and expression. Trauma studies shares with Deleuze this recognition that the rupturing of the wound occurs at the most basic forms of relation: its rupturing ruptures the planes of experience and expression. More, that this rupturing is at once destructive and creative—it closes off or eliminates potential even as it produces the actual.

Ecological trauma also possesses an affective dynamic, what Massumi describes as the participation of the actual in the virtual and the virtual in the actual.[101] In ecological trauma, as in all traumas, that enmeshment of virtual and actual is radically constrained by the foreclosure of potential and meaning. This foreclosure is characteristic of traumatic ruptures to experience: the disjunctive wound becomes a discordant, damaging feedback loop. Divorced from problems of scale and the necessity of human subjectivity, the wound in the virtualities of *a life* works at a remove from the problem of shifting between the personal and the collective that troubles so much work on trauma in the humanities. Nonhuman witnessing addresses trauma at this vital plane of existence because it resists the temptation to wait for trauma to arrive in the human. It attends to traumatic ruptures within life itself and their material entanglement of bodies of all kinds, from those of people to rocks, storms, and nonhumans animals.

ECOLOGIES OF WITNESSING

Nuclear testing, catastrophic climate change, the ecological traumas of militarism, capitalism, and colonialism: these are planetary phenomena that nevertheless have consequences that are at once intimately embodied and collectively targeted. Ecological catastrophe is martial as well as capitalistic. It is not an accident of history that required the Marshallese poet Kathy Jetñil-Kijiner to write of both rising waters and the deformations of life from nuclear contamination, of empty flesh sacs born in place of babies. Nor can the intensifying militarization of the oceans around China, a process in which Australia is a small but active player, be extricated from the failure of my country to act in response to the pleas and tears of Oceania's leaders.

Witnessing ecologies—both as a process of registering ecologies as sensible assemblages and as the composition of witnessing through the formation of relations—are not an antidote to ecological trauma, but they are an opening toward the potential for repair. Nonhuman witnessing as an ecological relation generates transversal vectors between elements within ecologies: witnessing as ecological, produced in the dynamic relation of systems, but also the witnessing of ecologies, through the aesthetic registration of their relationality as process in time and space. Attending to the nonhuman witnessing of ecologies and ecological relations continually returns us to mediation at its most fundamental: the transfer and translation of energies from one medium to another, a process that can be harnessed by technoscientific instruments but also far outstrips them. Technoscience doesn't provide the only sensors and communicators of significance, even if we understand ecologies in a narrowly biological sense. Ecologies abound with sensing and sensors; animate and inanimate bodies alike take part in the dance of mediation, interrupting and modulating its flow. Some of these mediations are certainly violent in the sense that this book has articulated. But seemingly destructive forces within ecologies are not alien to life, as even a cursory knowledge of evolution, the seasons, or the role of fire in the flourishing of certain plants would attest. Ecological trauma, as a distinctive taking shape of that wounding to *a life* described by Deleuze, is not a "natural" phenomena, but one inextricable from the violence that humans do, and certain humans far more efficaciously, deliberately, and comprehensively than others. But while Man, the Anthropos, is surely responsible for the era that now bears his name, the forms and practices of knowledge-making that accompanied that transformation to what counts as life itself need to be wrested away.

Nonhuman witnessing, pursued in this chapter through the technoscientific apparatuses of remote sensing and in the aesthetic interventions of ecologically inflected art, makes possible the witnessing of ecologies and ecologies of witnessing that displace the human yet neither disavow responsibility nor refuse the address of wounded ecologies. In the next chapter, I pursue this collective and more-than-human concept of trauma alongside both the violent mediations and machinic affects of more technical systems with the aim of showing how nonhuman witnessing helps elucidate more quotidian experiences of violence, loss, and absence in digital cultures. This return to the human provides the ground for the coda that follows, where I take up the question of the politics of nonhuman witnessing more explicitly. Nonhuman witnessing is neither separate from nor prior to politics, but rather contains within it the latent potential for political relations that might otherwise fail to cohere, animate, or confront the human with the necessity of response.

CHAPTER
FOUR

witnessing absence

FIRST ABSENCE:
THE EXECUTION OF JAMES FOLEY

On August 19, 2014, the Islamic State in Iraq and Syria (ISIS) uploaded a video titled "A Message to America" that depicted the beheading of the kidnapped journalist James Foley. Despite being swiftly pulled by YouTube, the video and gruesome stills from it circulated on social media, news sites, web forums, and shock galleries. Shot in crisp high definition, the video was slickly produced and professionally edited. Deviating from the grainy footage and awkward staging of executions filmed in Afghanistan or Iraq in the years after 9/11, it had a consciously contemporary aesthetic. After a long message addressed to President Obama, Foley appears on his knees, dressed in orange. Behind him is a black-clad and masked executioner, around them blasted desert and stark sky. The beheading itself lasts only ten seconds; yet the moment of death is not shown. It occurs off-camera, disappeared in the digital cut. A knife saws, but there is no blood. There is only the body, the head. The cuts shown are staged, experts say. Death itself is absent, but radically so—despite not occurring on camera, it is everywhere in evidence.

Reflecting on the recurrent moment of the cut in photography, Kember and Zylinska ask what might it mean to *cut well*, to cut in a way that entails a vital, creative ethics.[1] But what might it mean to cut poorly, to cut the clumsy cut? For the digital cut to cut out the cutting of the body? In this gruesome portrait of death without the moment of dying, there is an absence within an absence—yet one that has a presence in the digital contagion of traumatic affect. Perhaps the killing was botched, the blow of the sword too weak or at the wrong angle.

Or perhaps the cut was too bloody, too grotesque. After all, the video's purpose was not only to incite shock, but also to recruit—to catch the disaffected, the angry, the alienated and offer purpose through blood and violence.[2] This is a video that aims to traumatize, but also to speak to and through trauma. As such, it is perhaps best understood as an image of digital war that exemplifies, as Andrew Hoskins and Shona Illingworth write, "a shift in the trauma of civilians from a memory of the past to a perpetual anticipation of the threat of the future, subjecting increasing numbers of people to unending physical and psychological incarceration in a traumatizing present."[3] To watch such a thing must be brutally visceral—but I don't know, I haven't seen it. Like the deferred moment of death itself, I held back from an active participation in its affective economy and have encountered it only in stills and secondhand accounts, mediations of a mediation. Yet my resistance to seeing the video does not prevent its forcefulness from making its mark: there is an urgent affectivity in its absence, even now.

Despite its wide circulation, the beheading of James Foley—and later of Steven Sotloff and others—produced a radical absence. Its absence resided in the anxiety it engenders, the anxiety of potentially encountering the visual force of war's violence. An errant click, the wrong news article, a social media post that slips through the controls instituted by Twitter or Facebook—to encounter these videos would be so easily done, a simple digital stumble or the caprice of an algorithm. Crowding virtuals of affect, accumulating potentials on the verge of becoming actual: an affective-traumatic atmosphere. Brutal violence had infected the everyday of the digital. Who could say how or where it had proliferated? The mythology of digital permanence, the notion that whatever words or images of ourselves find their way on online stay there, resonated with the video's disappearance. It was always potentially appearing, even when it never arrived. Already testimonial texts that bear witness to political murder, such videos circulate in search of co-witnesses, dependent on news values, browsing habits, and algorithmic recommenders.

Fragmented terrains of media seemed suddenly not simply a problem for trust and accountability, but a risk to bodily integrity.

Once, broadcast networks might simply have colluded to conceal the video, but its indefinite circulation encouraged hosting on the websites of establishment media. If it was out there, it should be here, or so the thinking went. In the early 2000s, before social media as we know it and with the digital ecology far less developed and vibrant, watching the video of another execution—the journalist Daniel Pearl—had required sustained pursuit through web forums and the glitchy predecessors to YouTube. Not so for James Foley. Even with the object absent, secreted from viewing, its traumatic affect still leaked, oozed, and pooled.[4] Even in absence, these videos accumulated affective force, so that not watching did not prevent encounter: what was encountered was their looming lack of presence. Carriers of an affective contagion, more than a stand-in or symbol of the possible disturbances engendered by the digital, the videos are traumatically affecting even without being seen. Like the body of the terrorist after 9/11, their passing-by reshaped the surfaces of fearful bodies.[5] Here was terror, potentially: the lone wolf video, stalking the algorithmic hinterlands of platform capitalism. Distant war on the verge of becoming intimate, of demanding witness.

Weeks after, Sydney and Brisbane woke to media blasting stories of dawn raids capturing suspected terrorists, footage of police storming houses, and breathless excitement from politicians and pundits. Random public beheadings were planned, the prime minister of the day quickly claimed, backed by anonymous leaks from the Australian Federal Police and displays of a seized sword.[6] What happened in the desert was in our midst, or so it seemed. In the iconography of the sword and the references to beheading, the raids resonated with the circulating videos, with mediated violence always on the verge of encounter. They amplified fear, made manifest in bodily sensation the possibility that distant violence could appear on any screens, anytime. It didn't matter, here in Australia, that the sword was revealed to be plastic, that its owner was Shiite and thus anathema to ISIS.[7] The very connectedness of the contemporary world, the ever-presence of the digital, sharpened into an affective threat: violent mediation made manifest in the digital quotidian. To have this infiltrate the human sensorium, to have been confronted with radical absence in the digital's capacity to transmit violent and traumatic affect, was to shift one's affective relation to the digital itself. It was to risk being forced into a witnessing relation, one latent within the nonhuman infrastructures of the digital systems yet invisible until it was too late.

RADICAL ABSENCE

It is not only the beheading of a kidnapped journalist. Disappearances keep appearing in the digital sphere: an airplane vanishes into the sky; friends learn someone has died when Facebook "memorializes" their page; sacred sites are destroyed by a mining giant in search of iron ore. Each event is different in its particularity but shares an affective architecture: it is a manifestation of absence that is nonetheless vitally present. This radical absence throws those who encounter it into a witnessing relation with the felt force of disappearance. Radical absence occurs when this force surrounds something that cannot but fail to appear, yet in its nonappearance entangles the human with nonhuman infrastructures of mediation and circulation. Such absences are not exceptional, but rather part and parcel of the digitality that constantly and constitutively entangles everyday life. While encounters with radical absence are not rare, coming into contact with their mediated traces and resonances can possess an unexpected intensity. Encounters with radical absence constitute both a witnessing of absence and the absence of witnessing: a paradox that is made manifest and material through the inescapable presence of nonhuman agencies and infrastructures. Radical absence becomes possible through the constitutive affectivity of digital mediations. As Richard Grusin writes, "The affective elements of our interactions with everyday media technologies work both socially and politically."[8] Radical absence arises not from disconnection but from an abundance of connection, not from a failure to witness but from the unceasing potential of witnessing to take place and the repeated demand that we do so. It circulates unpredictably and is experienced variably, yet once encountered it demands witnessing. It is a forceful if fleeting veering of experience into disjunctive and disruptive terrain. Radical absence is radical because of its intensity, not because of any definitive rupture with prior forms of media and processes of mediation. It makes perceptible the disjunctive pluriversality of cultural and political life.

As with the other chapters, this one oscillates along two trajectories: the witnessing of absence and the absence of witnessing. It argues that radical absence is crucial to witnessing what is not there, or fails to materialize, or is destroyed, or has died: a necessarily nonhuman witnessing. What does it mean for witnessing to understand traumatic mediations as bound up with the absent presence of data infrastructures? In worlds of increasingly fluid and uncertain distinctions between the human and the nonhuman, radical absences occur with remarkable potency. Traumatically affecting, if not traumatizing, they have the capacity to produce intensely felt disjunctures. Such intensive disjunctures pull us into a witnessing relation, but this witnessing doesn't simply happen *through* media. Radical absence entails both the event of absence itself and the eventful process of its violent mediation. Radical absence and its witnessing are thus inseparable from nonhuman processes of signal flow, datafication, and algorithmic selection, but also the material infrastructures of data centers and optical fiber cables. Radical absence fragments time and segments space, distributing and dispersing the experiences of both human and nonhuman entities.

Radical absence depends in the most fundamental sense on the sheer physicality of those infrastructures, even as it obscures their presence behind the screen interfaces of social media and search engine platforms. Such infrastructures coproduce witnessing radical absence at the ontoepistemological level: no matter how human its subject matter, witnessing radical absence depends upon and veers inevitably into the nonhuman. Radical absence entails machinic affects, but its dependence on such infrastructures means that it is also bound up with ecological trauma. Understanding the witnessing of radical absence thus requires attending to this infrastructural layer of absent presence and considering how disappeared infrastructures might be made to (re)appear within the nonhuman witnessing of all-too-human actions and events. Radical absence troubles relations between the sensing and sense-making that defines aesthetics, producing a disjunctive intensity rather than an anesthetic numbing. It is a formation of machinic affect that galvanizes violent mediation at the level of experience itself: a flashing up of traumatic rupture at the interface of the human and the non in the infrastructures of digital life. Like the art and activism that have percolated through this book so far, nonhuman entanglements offer some potential for radical absence to open spaces, however minor, however fragile, for reparative politics—to find something of the transformative in encounters with loss. To encounter radical absence is to be thrown into a witnessing relation, but one that refuses fixity, that loses its own substance: a witnessing inseparable from the machinic affect of digital life, in all its nonhuman excess, patterning, and sensory dysphoria.

SECOND ABSENCE: MH370

Less than an hour after take-off on March 8, 2014, somewhere over the South China Sea, Malaysian Airlines Flight 370 made its last contact with air traffic control at 1:21 a.m. local time. Flying from Kuala Lumpur to Beijing was meant to take less than six hours, but the Boeing 777 was only seen again in fleeting electronic fragments—a handful of blips on military radar, six satellite "handshakes"—and even then only after the fact, data dredged from various regional monitoring stations.[9] As hours lengthened into days, the disappearance became charged with an unsettling intensity. MH370 came to be oddly, inescapably present in its absence. Broadcast media filled with breaking news segments, expert panels, and frenzied banners; programming was interrupted and redirected, folding into the online buzz of anxiety, speculation, and hope. On social media, the real-time digital flow made possible a cofeeling of this absence, an attention to its emergence and coalescence within the stream of enmeshed communications. Emerging too was grief for the 239 missing passengers and crew, grief for their relatives and friends who gave faces to loss, marking the absence of loved ones on their skin. Participatory platforms from Twitter to Facebook to Reddit enabled people across the globe to track and even participate in the search, an affective engagement in which countless microencounters modulated and amplified the experience of the plane's absence. Checking in on events and finding no revelation or resolution was not a lonely task, but rather one assembled of new encounters with continued disappearance, with the very failure of finding the plane. Theories abounded. The pilot was a terrorist, his home-flight simulator an object of suspicion. Passengers were hijackers, a pair of Russians briefly became a locus of interest. Amateur sleuths set to work; maps proliferated. Islands were pored over for the space to land and hide a plane, disused runways were cataloged, fuel capacities and headwinds were calculated to define the limits of where the flight might be.[10] More theories: it had been shot down after straying into US war games with Thailand, or by China, or because it came too close to a secret American base in Diego Garcia. Dark matter leaking from within the planet had produced an unseeable, untraceable vortex.[11]

Investments in such speculation ranged from the occasional to the obsessive, a desperate desire to give narrative to the disappeared plane. No doubt for many it burst across their digital worlds and slipped away, leaving only faint traces. Yet to encounter the plane's disappearance was to be affected by an absence that was so profoundly present that it became radical. The more it persisted, the more the search widened, and the more theories grew—the more its absence could be felt intensely. The world became less known, technology failed to measure up to the faith we invest in it. Oceans were revealed as vast realms about which humans know little, tides and currents without accurate models, topographies without maps. The limitations of our capacity to search and rescue became starkly evident, the smallness of the human confronted with the scale and force of the seas.[12] Skies were suddenly less tracked and watched than we had imagined. Despite the seeming ubiquity of atmospheric, terrestrial, and aquatic remote sensing, what Gabrys names "*program earth*" could still produce catastrophic errors.[13] When Malaysian authorities declared the plane lost in the Indian Ocean on March 24, more than two weeks after the disappearance, no wreckage had been found. Those satellite handshakes and radar blips had led to mathematical equations theorizing the zone of the plane's crash, some 1.8 million square miles of ocean.[14] Because its wreckage was never found, the accumulation of calculation declared the absence of plane and people to be final. Even eighteen months later, when a flaperon from the plane's wing was found on Réunion Island in the Indian Ocean, no one could say for sure that the plane had simply fallen into sea or from where the wreckage might have traveled. Undiscovered, MH370's black box flight recorder held onto its secrets. Autonomous drone operations failed to find wreckage, producing instead a happenstance cartographic archive derived from the data of sonar sensors.[15]

GPS tracking, satellites, radars, transponders: our experience of the contemporary world is of endless interconnection. Smartphones know where we have been and how often, electronic tags chart the movement of our cars across cities, transport cards log our daily travels. Hollywood has taught us that the technological eye is all-seeing, that even the act of stepping off the grid is itself marked and known. Expansive computation harnessed to remote-sensing apparatuses promised what Paul Edwards calls the *closed world* of Cold War computation.[16] Yet this apparatus was calibrated to the concerns of capital, climate, and empire, to the monitoring of missile launches, border zones, glacial erosions, coastal reef temperatures, agriculture fertility, and mining. To encounter such a disappearance within and through the digital—in Facebook posts and Twitter hashtags, snippets of YouTube video and subreddits—was to encounter a strange rupture. A fissure in the seeming solidity of the technoscientific world. A plane had vanished: How could this be in an age of transponders and satellites and ubiquitous connectivity? How could something so familiar and material simply vanish? Where were the witnesses? Through ceaseless connection with the shared experience of a disappeared object witnessing itself became ever more nonhuman: it was as if something inescapably actual had slipped back into the virtual, as if the concrete had dissolved into the affective. There was a kind of trauma in this—not so great, of course, as that felt by the families of the missing, but an affective trauma, a trauma produced by a breakdown in the certainties of the contemporary world. This breakdown ripples into the mediated environments that Paddy Scannell calls the "invisible care structure that gives the conditions of things we can trust in the world and a world we can take for granted."[17] A plane simply disappearing ruptures that trust; the mediated circulation of its absence threatens just such a rupturing in the trust that defines our phenomenological relations to media.

This is traumatic affect, digitally mediated, a prepersonal yet corporeal contact with radical disjuncture. This traumatic affect is not static, and as much about the future as the past. It might not direct our actions as such, but its infiltration of our sensorium cannot quite be undone. To encounter MH370 digitally was to do so in diffuse pulsings, in micromoments of mediation: the disappearance of a plane and its passengers held in the palm of the hand, engaged with the fingertips. An absence so radical—so fundamental yet urgent, so distinct from the everyday—that it demanded witnessing, even as all that remained to be witnessed was a space in the world where a plane once flew. As submersible drones whirred through oceans, new worlds unfurled to human knowing but the remnants of the plane remained lost. Its last witnessing was an elemental one: the deep blue media of the sea itself.[18]

TRAUMATIC AFFECT

Media are far more than surfaces on which trauma is inscribed. As Amit Pinchevski argues, we can think of the "the traumatic as something that is made manifest through media technological rendering," rather than something that is simply represented in media.[19] If radical absence begins with the failure of the eyewitness to witness, an epistemological failure to translate the registering of an event into knowable form, its continued existence as a forceful absence on the plane of experience depends on more-than-human processes of mediation. Mediation and trauma both share an uncertain relationship between past and present, between presence and absence, and between proximity and distance. As such, "media constitute the material conditions for trauma to appear as something that cannot be fully approached and yet somehow must be."[20] At the level of process, technical media contain within their own constitution the paradoxes that make trauma overwhelming: media are always entangled with experience, yet also insist on their separateness. "Media matter," writes Cubitt, "both in the sense of giving material specificity to our descriptions of such abstract concepts as society and environment, and in the sense of the active verb: mediation comes into being as matter, its mattering constitutes the knowable, experienceable world, making possible all sensing and being sensed, knowing and being known."[21]

Digital media are also decidedly material, requiring huge amounts of water, space, and electricity to run and with catastrophic impacts on environments and the animals and plants that inhabit them. While the other chapters in this book oscillated in their proximity to the human, here I attend to quotidian human life to examine its enmeshment with nonhuman systems at the visceral, recompositional level of trauma. Here, violent mediations, machinic affects, and ecological traumas cohere on everyday experiences of what Lauren Berlant calls "crisis ordinariness," or "traumas of the social that are lived through collectively and that transform the sensorium to a heightened perceptiveness about the unfolding of the historical."[22]

In mediated encounters with crisis ordinariness, the factual and the fictional can be blurred in complex and unpredictable ways, jumbling together the urgent and the trivial, the enduring and the ephemeral, the intense and the diffuse. Digital media can itself be unanchoring, displacing priorities, destabilizing shared knowledges, and amplifying conspiracy and paranoia.[23] How is one to cope with the media witnessing of 9/11, the ur-trauma of the screen, first on television screen but then repeated across other media? Or, more contemporaneously, images and video of police killings and beatings of Black and First Nations people, or of funeral pyres in India as COVID-19, vaccine apartheid, and government ineptitude took life after life? These and countless other mediations make up what Mark Seltzer calls "wound culture," the "collective gathering around shock, trauma, and the wound."[24] This fascination is a complex one, caught up in movements of pulling away as much as turning toward, repulsion as much as attraction. Conceiving of trauma as affective also entails a more fluid, interdependent understanding of the social and the individual, and the dynamic role of mediation in their relations. Taken together, these movements open more nuanced and variable ways to understand what encounters with radical absence might mean at the level of meaning-making and of political possibility.

Traumatic affect, as I have argued with Meera Atkinson, describes the "the mode, substance and dynamics of relation through which trauma is experienced, transmitted, conveyed, and represented."[25] Rather than a concept that produces taxonomies and distinctions, that includes or excludes varying experiences and representations, traumatic affect is conceptually open and fluid. It recognizes that encounters with trauma can be traumatically *affecting* without being *traumatizing* in quite the same way that psychoanalysis or clinical psychological imply. In other words, all trauma is affective but not all experiences of traumatic affect produce trauma. Such traumatic affects are not only—or not solely—the affects constitutive of traumatic events, but also affects experienced in encounters with trauma. Affect, after all, is neither dependent upon nor delimited to the human. As such, the intensity of traumatic affect varies along a dynamic continuum, rather than occurring in some static form, and its relational intensities are bound up with nonhuman technics and milieus.

Thinking of mediated trauma in terms of its nonhuman relationality opens onto new possibilities. As Pinchevski notes, "Media (re)produce the traumatic by effecting its ungraspability affectively, by imparting impact in excess of content, sensation in excess of sense."[26] An encounter with violent mediation might itself be traumatic or traumatically affective, such as in the designation of a racial category by Facebook's advertising algorithms or the unexpected encounter with footage of death or pain in a TikTok feed. Mediated encounters can also be intensely immediate: mediation is precisely what renders them intensive. Traumatic affects can impart, at varying intensities, the force of trauma without inscribing meaning. Traumatic affect can be understood as one of the qualitative dynamics of crisis ordinariness. Thus, while this chapter pursues traumatic affect within encounters with radical absence on social media, its intensive relations of rupture and disjuncture form part of what Andrew Murphie calls "a complex storm of feeling, of aspects of world feeling each other in intense, unexpected and constantly mutating ways."[27] Witnessing radical absence, then, does not apply exclusively to social or even digital media, but rather might be extended into the crises of war, ecology, and data that have occupied this book so far.

While normative conceptions of trauma, like those of witnessing, tend to insist on its exclusivity to the human, understanding trauma and affect in vitalist terms means opening space for the felt force of potential as it shapes relations. Virtuality always precedes and exceeds the human because it is never contained within the experience of any individual; it is always in and of worlds, in relation, in media, and in the making. Recall that for Massumi, affect is the shifting entanglements of "the virtual in the actual and the actual in the virtual" in the unfolding of encounters.[28] Massumi's virtual does not refer to the false or unreal, but rather to the crowding potentials of all experience: those things that are-about-to-be or might-just-have-been that are inextricable from the actual. Virtuality insists that nonhuman milieus, technics, animals, and ecologies always co-constitute the human as potential and as a taking shape and becoming with world(s). Thinking trauma in terms of affect thus enables a way of understanding its dynamics as fluid, moving, changeable, multitudinous, and even contagious, while not relinquishing its injurious and harmful ruptures of experience.[29] As David Lapoujade writes, parsing William James, "Discontinuity always appears against the ground of continuity," such that even as experience fractures it remains held together as one-and-many by relations of nonrelation.[30] Conceived as always more than one and always more-than-human, traumatic affect invites nonhuman witnessing in response. In doing so, it offers a more generative mode for understanding relations across the diffuse circulation of crises of war, data, and ecology in the capitalist quotidian of social media, search engines, and news sites. Witnessing radical absence is both a response to the traumatic affects of digital disappearance and an address to the absent presence of nonhuman infrastructures.

THIRD ABSENCE: DIGITAL DEATH

In mid-2012, Jessa Moore logged onto Facebook and learned that her friend Anthony Dowdell had killed himself. She and others began to post memories and photos, to tag him at restaurants or bars. "Facebook became our memorial," she said. "We could leave messages for him and each other." Facebook became a site of shared mourning, but also a way to keep memories alive—even as it continually reminded Jessa of her friend's absence from her life.[31] Almost a decade later, Jessa's experience is far from unique as I and many others can attest, but her story, told in a widely read article in the *Huffington Post*, marks an early incursion into media discourse of death on Facebook and its weird affects. Estimates suggest that upward of thirty million Facebook profiles have outlived the people who created them, with around eight thousand users passing away every day. In 2019, Carl J. Öhman and David Watson published a statistical projection of the accumulation of profiles from deceased users, using country and age data scraped from the Facebook API in conjunction with country mortality rates. Their findings suggest that up to 4.9 billion dead users could populate Facebook by 2100, leading the researchers to call for a new, scalable, and sustainable model for preserving the data of the deceased.[32] Already, a microindustry has emerged to manage digital estates, wrapping up accounts, tracing assets, and passing on data.[33] On Facebook, friends or family access accounts and make them inactive, or provide a death certificate to Facebook to have their account officially "Memorialized," transforming their profile into a commemoration to which existing Facebook friends can post but remains otherwise unchanged.[34]

Others are simply left in place, digital presences that bear no clear marker of absent life, as if the user has simply stepped away from the computer. Yet unlike the cluttered desk or sink piled with dirty dishes, such a profile remains open to further engagement. Like Jessa tagging her friend Anthony at a bar he would have liked, or leaving messages on his wall, these pages have a strange digital afterlife. This capacity to tag is particularly potent. As Paul Frosh argues, tagging on social media "reveals itself as an existentially significant technique for mediating the attachments of the body and the self in the face of possible unravelling and disintegration."[35] Tagging the dead marks an insistence on retaining a certain presence in the world produced by digital media, but it also points to the tenuous hold that the practice of tagging has on the deep relational work of maintaining attachments. Yet stranger still and far less visible than tagging and memorializing are the archival remainders of dead profiles, living on in Facebook's inaccessible and undisclosed data centers. Facebook's archive is not ephemeral but material, as Mél Hogan shows, constituted by "the electricity that powers the machines, and a virtual ethersphere that produces bigger records than the lived realities it records, as a politic of preservation that is, on the one hand, successfully inhabited and, on the other hand, dangerously reconfigured and protected as such."[36] Death on Facebook as both event and archive, as enduring public profile and invisible data cluster, is not apolitical but bound up with the politics of data centers and big data aggregation, and with the practices of attention, engagement, consumption, and preservation that shape digital sociality and selfhood.

Memorialized profiles manifest decreasing attention, a flurry of sorrowful posts that fades with time, sparking at moments of remembrance or past joy. Those left untended intrude unwittingly: an algorithm suggests you get in touch with a deceased friend, a reminder appears for their birthday, you are tagged in a photo with them. A brief foray onto Google reveals the complex multiplicity of experiences of digital death, from memorial pages for beloved pets to services that send letters from the afterlife to start-ups promising the first stage of a transhumanist transcendence of death through a postlife digital existence. On social media, death often intrudes unexpectedly, encountered in unfitting places: clicking on the profile of an acquaintance not seen for years, checking notifications on a bus on the way to work, wondering why your daughter hasn't called home from college. Individual stories present differing relations. Jessa Moore visits her friend's page each day to leave him messages; a widow wrestles with whether to leave her partner's page active. Death in the digital sphere is collaborative and delocalized, constituted by friends and family, by the algorithms of the encoded world. It repeats the intersubjectivity of digital identity, its formation not only through interpersonal connections but also via the technics and constraints of digital platforms themselves. "It's more for us than for him," said Jessa. Witnessing absence on Facebook is a relational practice, a means of forging communities of care around shared knowing and grieving, but one funneled through the extractive data regime of the social media platform.

Social media make visible and grant a kind of permanency to otherwise transitory relations: schoolmates, old work colleagues, fellow backpackers, or partygoers. Once, their deaths would have filtered into our lives sparingly, or not at all. Social media relations don't fade in quite the same way; even when someone might have disappeared from your newsfeed, an event of some magnitude or the foibles of the algorithm might push them to the fore, shunting aside the absence afforded by space and time. When testimonies to lost lives appear, they do so in the same flattened aesthetic as every other item. A friend pours grief for a dead parent into the status box, hits post, and their words appear alongside political rants, sports highlights, requests for advice on buying a new barbeque. Unless the link is broken, Facebook keeps connections active; more, it calls its users into action. Connect with Anushka, wish Peter a happy birthday, like the photo Siobhan just shared of her newborn child. To be thrown into shock or grief is no small thing, to encounter in a digital presence a radical absence of life can produce a bodily response of visceral intensity. Life is absent, yet also jarringly, movingly, or even thankfully present: its absence is radical in the sense that its traces are inescapable. Photographs, posts, comments, likes, events, check-ins, games—so much more cohesive, contained, and accessible than the material and ephemeral remnants of the predigital.

On Facebook, the dead are radically absent in part because engagements with them are so visible: mourning is not only public, but enduring.[37] Responding to death becomes a kind of public testimony: remembrances and condolences are not fleeting or offered in private, but within the performative space of the social network. Eliding geography and producing intimacy across distance, such grieving entails a kind of flattening of experience within the bland corporate aesthetic and ethos of the platform. Facebook becomes a constraining medium, giving a form to grief that limits or even denies something of experience, a more intensified form of the delimiting of affect that occurs in the writing of trauma.[38] All griefs are rendered equal, or near enough, and this can be traumatically affecting. Lines between rubbernecking and mourning are increasingly blurred, such that expressing grief in public can be undercut by the doubt of others. To lose a partner, a close friend, a son or sister, and then have countless others lay claim to them can reproduce loss as much as testify to life. Traumatic affect in digital death can be fleeting, a passing encounter with disappeared life. Or it can be unexpectedly intense, an encounter with loss that throws one's own life out of kilter, the actuality of death intersecting its virtual counterpart. An affectivity of absence produced within and by the ever-pressing potential of the digital, made material through nonhuman infrastructures of data collection, storage, processing, and distribution. Witnessing death as radical absence is all too human, yet this digital mediation ensures that it is inseparable from nonhuman technics, algorithms, data, and affects.

RADICAL ABSENCE (REDUX)

Screen-based media are only one slice of the pervasive digital mediation of contemporary life, but their ubiquity means everything from homes and shopping malls to buses and elevators has been infiltrated by the datalogical. To move through such spaces is to have our attention demanded and diverted, with digitized movement and sound calling us into a more temporal relation to the visual and aural than the static imagery of the past allowed. This demand for attention is also a bodily experience, from the adrenal surge that redirects the body in gaming to the haptic signals of smartwatches. Augmented and virtual reality hold the promise of interrupting our relation to the visual field, layering data over what we see or replacing our immediate surrounds entirely. Fantasies of neural link implants hint at a future of screen-body fusion. Even now, interpersonal interactions slip between online and off, or take place simultaneously in both domains.[39] Smartphones and their ilk have become what Bernard Stiegler calls "mnemotechnologies," doing the work of thinking, remembering, and processing our knowledge of the world.[40] What had been stable categories of causation no longer hold as relations between objects, humans, and different media become increasingly fluid and relative.[41]

Even if there are antecedents for the transformative effects of digital networks in the long human history of mediations, such as the telegraph's collapsing of distance or cinema's production of new modes of time, there can be little doubt that recent decades have seen an accelerated evolution in the imbrication of media technologies and human life. Nonhuman technics and the human sensorium are increasingly enfolded; affects flow between the corporeal and machinic, intensities surging across surfaces and substrates, modulating and shaping. In the words of Nigel Thrift, "There is no stable 'human' experience because the human sensorium is constantly being re-invented as the body continually adds parts to itself; therefore, how and what is experienced as experience is itself variable."[42] This cyborg tendency is not new, but it is accelerating and expanding. Drones and smartphones, for instance, are far from the only emergent forms of machinic perception. Sensors creep into running shoes and sidewalks, grocery aisles, and the skin of diabetics. Machine vision enables autonomous systems to power cars, surgical robots, and the logistics of ports. Learning algorithms analyze public health data and execute trades at scales, speeds, and frequencies far beyond human cognitive capacities. Chatbots generate text from the statistical analysis of patterns in data trawled from the internet. More than simply shifting how experience is composed, the ever-presence of these technovital mediations changes the ground of experience itself for the human and for nonhuman entities of all kinds. Media technologies, argues Marie-Luise Angerer, play an "active role in promoting a comprehensive relationality by setting and correlating the rhythms of large and small units and inward and outward sensations."[43] Sensations are not only produced bodily, but through the folded together mediations that make for a new fluidity of experience itself. As Brian Massumi and Erin Manning write, "The field of experience can be best described as relational-qualitative."[44] This is not to say that the human experience of the contemporary world is without grounding, that what was solid has melted into the networked ether, but rather that the ground truths of experience are more and more entangled in the systems and processes that produce the conditions of crisis in which so much life is lived.

Radical absences are made possible by this folding together of experience and digital mediation. They are themselves not rigid phenomena: videos circulate and then fade from view, flight paths are traced then slip away, posts in remembrance grow infrequent. Space and time bend and flex in odd ways. This combination of spatiality, temporality, and contingency matters. Mary Ann Doane writes of these phenomena in the context of the cinematic image, in which "chance and contingency have been assigned an important ideological role, supporting the fascination with the apparently alternative temporalities offered by the cinema."[45] Yet what occurs in the digital mediations of disappearance described here shows how the digital enables different experiences: chance, contingency, spatiality, and temporality are always and inescapably constitutive of encounters with radical absence. There is a tension in this between their intensity in the encounter and its durability over time and across space. Traumatic affects shaped by radical absence can be modulated, amplified, diminished, deferred, interrupted, and truncated in their passage across and between bodies. Radical absences are events rather than stand-alone phenomena, manifestations of encounter that are co-composed, emergently assembled. Experiences of radical absence are neither singular nor collective as such, but rather transindividual, "the collectivity at the heart of all individuations, before and beyond any spectating into individuals."[46]

Yet this emergence of the event—the potential encounter with the beheading video, the pervasive presence of a disappeared plane, the still-living of death on Facebook—is not solely dependent on the human. Technologies matter, processes matter, mediations matter—they matter in the doubled sense of carrying important information and making material. In this sense, radical absence performs an indexical function: it is the trace of the disappeared. Yet the indexicality of radical absence does more than point as close as can be to that which is not there: what makes these absences radical is the affectivity of encounter that materializes in lived experience that which is indexed in the digital. Radical absence collapses the seemingly limitless nature of media into its finitude, evoking the limits of what media can capture. Radical absence reminds us of the vitality of digital media, that its materiality does not reside solely in binary code but in how those codes work upon bodies and in the data centers, cables, transmitters, and repeaters that make their operation possible. Indeed, it is in this conjunction of (non)human(s) and media(tion) that particular encounters with digital disappearance become radical. More than agency as such, but a process of assemblage: "The directed intensity of a compositional movement that alters the field of experience."[47] Within encounters with radical absence, these compositional formations move most intensively in the tension between what is not and what almost might be, in the swarming of potential that withholds certain actuals. In short, radical absences are never static—closer to presences, yet not quite, possessed of a force that is exactly not presence.

Nor are they solely traumatic in their affectivity: much more than trauma circulates in the absences described here. Love, grief, fear, despair, alienation, and other affective formations are often at work. Histories, states, and moods of bodies matter too. To have a fear of flying and encounter a rising tide of MH370 posts and comments in your social media stream gives a particular angle or tenor to that encounter. Massumi calls this differential attunement: "bodies in encounter are both completely absorbed in the felt transition, but they are differently absorbed, coming at it asymmetrically, from different angles, living a different complexion of affecting-being affected, transitioning through the encounter to different outcomes."[48] This differential attunement means that the ways in which traumatic affect affects will vary: radical absences are not radical in quite the same way in every encounter that (re)constitutes them. Yet what they share is this traumatic affectivity—it is the qualitative relation that defines the encounter. Not traumatization as such, but a disjunctive, rupturing affectivity, in which affect's presignifying quality limits the capacity of the event to become meaningful. It is this felt-feeling of a refusal to cohere into sense-making that makes the potential encounter with beheading videos a force of disruption that is experienced bodily.

Radical absences do not call the body into them, but rather call the body alongside them, to encounter what has disappeared in the force of its absence: an all-too-human witnessing thrown into the domain of nonhuman technics. Entanglement without overlapping, a shared composition that produces a kind of synchrony that is not sameness. "Entanglements," Rey Chow reminds us, are "the linkages and enmeshments that keep things apart; the voidings and uncoverings that hold things together."[49] By calling attention to the disjunctive ways in which we are entangled with disappearances that manifest in the digital sphere, radical absence is an injunction to the necessity of nonhuman witnessing, of witnessing that exceeds the human, occurring not in the event itself but in the affectivity of its aftermath and in the material traces of its datafied afterlives. The strange time of digital media matters here, with its tension between liveness and belatedness, proximity and distance, and the vagaries of algorithmic determinations of significance that pluck events out of the past to bring them to attention. The time of witnessing in digital media—especially on social networks or in the preferences of Google's PageRank ordering—is subject to nonhuman contingencies, associations, circulations, and relations. Machinic affects compose clusters of relation that pull certain things to the fore, and then allow them to recede or dissolve. Witnessing radical absence has no present as such, not even in the moment of James Foley's death, or the plane's disappearance, or the memorialization of a Facebook page, or the aftermath of the violent expansion of a mine.

Radical absence thus constitutes a structure of relation to the disjunctive crises of the affective present, the present as it is affectively formed as something that can be made sensible despite its discontinuities. It is a form of attachment, a way in which subjectivities relate to contexts in modes ranging from the aesthetic to the political to the occasional. Radical absence is an attachment to that which has disappeared yet remains affectively present, digitally manifested, preserved in infrastructure. While traumatic affect—not to mention circulations of grief, fear, disgust, and outrage—animates its disjunctive force, such affect is not the thing itself. Traumatic affect is not necessarily contagious, but rather a form of relation conducive to affective conflagration: it is an affective structure formed within what Berlant calls "a crisis culture borrowing trauma's genres to describe what isn't exceptional at all in the continuous production and breakdown of life."⁵⁰ This structure is one of flows and vectors rather than scaffolds or walls. Radical absence stretches the boundaries of the subject, reconstituting selfhood within digital worldings shaped by the traumatic affects of intimately distant disappearances. It percolates through infrastructure, which Berlant calls "the living mediation of what organizes life: the lifeworld of structure."⁵¹ Witnessing absence is thus bound up with the witnessing of invisible infrastructures, or what "binds us to the world in movement and keeps the world practically bound to itself."⁵² The digital makes this intimate distance possible by enabling a collapse of space that simultaneously calls attention to its own occurrence: in the digital, we can touch the distant but always do so in an intensely mediated way.

If the digital continually extends and reworks subjectivity, as Thrift and others argue, then traumatic affect is increasingly folded into our digital becomings. Such traumatic affects are the vehicle for sensorial manifestations of radical absence, for the ways in which it is felt bodily. "The body doesn't just absorb pulses or discrete stimulations"; writes Massumi, "it infolds contexts, it infolds volitions and cognitions that are nothing if not situated."⁵³ Rather than an enfolding that envelopes the body, this infolding alters bodily states, including the angle at which the body senses events. Sensation "is the immanent limit at which perception is eclipsed by a sheerness of experience, as yet un-extended into analytically ordered, predictably reproducible, possible action."⁵⁴ Within the digital's ever-present pulsings and infoldings, radical absence holds its affectivity in this indeterminate zone between perception and sensation. This sensorial experience of radical absence gives it a visceral actuality, renders it more than a discrete media object. As affective structures, radical absences do something. They enact a relation of nonhuman witnessing to the terrain of national security, or to faith in technology, or to how one grieves, or to Country wounded by resource extractivism. Such nonhuman witnessing is more than material because it is always relational, always in the process of forging registrations, connections, and attachments when it seems that relationality itself is under assault, even by the most violent of ecological traumas.

FOURTH ABSENCE: SACRED SITES

On May 24, 2020, the mining giant Rio Tinto detonated two rock shelters in the Juukan Gorge in the Pilbara region of Western Australia, destroying sites sacred to the Puutu Kunti Kurrama and Pinikura (PKKP) peoples that provided evidence of more than forty-six thousand years of continuous occupation.⁵⁵ Charges had been laid for the extension of the Brockman 4 iron ore mine days before, but the Traditional Owners of the land were not notified despite formal consultations extending back to 2014. As media reports and outrage spread among First Nations people and settlers on social media, the irreparable damage became inescapable: the absent sacred sites became sharply, affectively present. Material witnesses to the enduring habitation of the land were lost: plaited hair four thousand years old, genetically linked to the present Traditional Owners, and bone and stone tools dating back more than twenty-eight thousand years, the oldest-known bone technologies in Australia. Worse still was the incalculable loss of sites sacred to the PKKP, places alive with ancestral spirits and an enduring vitality that has no equivalent in Western epistemologies. Testifying to this profound and visceral loss of living Country to the Standing Committee on Northern Australia's inquiry conducted in the wake of the blast, Traditional Owner Burchell Hayes told the committee:

> The Juukan Gorge is known to be a place where the spirits of our relatives who have passed away, even recently, have come to rest. It is a place that the very, very old people still occupy. Purlykuti has been specifically referred to by the old people as a place of pardu, which refers to the special language only spoken during ceremonies in the Pilbara. Our elders state that it is certain that the spirits are very disturbed, and their living relatives are also upset at this. This is why Juukan Gorge is important. It is in the ancient blood of our people and contains their DNA. It houses history and the spirits of ancestors and it anchors the people to this country.⁵⁶

Their absence would remain unbearably present, even as the cascading aftermath of the blasts brought a rare moment of scrutiny and accountability for extractive capitalism and its legal and political foundations.

Enabling the destruction were two proximate agents of what Aileen Moreton-Robinson calls "the possessive logic of patriarchal white sovereignty": the incompetence and negligence of Rio Tinto and the gross disparities of Western Australia's Aboriginal Heritage Act 1972, under which the destruction of the sites had been approved in 2013.⁵⁷ On the Rio Tinto side, the systematic sidelining of heritage reports and Traditional Owner concerns became evident, facilitated—or so it was claimed—by the geographic distance of the company's executives in London from its mining activities in Australia. This absence of communication protocols and heritage management practices combined with an institutionalized disdain for traditional ownership, exhibited by the company's sustained and systematic approach in seeking approval for the destruction of thousands of sacred sites over decades of mining in the Pilbara. Like its competitors BHP, Fortescue Metals Group, China Shenhua, Roy Hill, and others, Rio Tinto had made ruthless use of the Heritage Act to push through new mines and expansions with little regard for the Traditional Owners. Under the Heritage Act, the Aboriginal Cultural Heritage Committee is not required to consult with Traditional Owners, nor can its decisions be appealed. Even speaking publicly can threaten compensation for Aboriginal corporations through draconian gag clauses that enshrine stark inequities into the administrative process itself. Widely recognized as unfair and outdated, reform efforts for the Heritage Act had stalled. But the furor over what Yawuru man and federal senator Pat Dodson described as Rio Tinto's "incremental genocide" brought to mainstream attention the enduring coloniality of Australia's extractive capitalism and its supportive legal bedrock. Present in the radical absence of the sacred sites was settler colonialism as eliminationist structure.[58] The destruction of culture operated here as a way of breaking traditional bonds with Country, an expression of the shifting logics of racialization in response to political activism that stresses the significance of land to First Nations. The shared investment of settler government and corporation in the continuation of extractive industries in the face of First Nations resistance and global heating both depends upon and reproduces settler sovereignty. A mining giant founded in settler Australia but now headquartered in London (and subjects of the British Crown in either locale) had destroyed sites of sacred importance in the name of profit and with the imprimatur of law that explicitly and deliberately marginalizes and gags Aboriginal people. Here was the convergence of settler colonialism, extractive capitalism, and neoliberal corporate structures, suddenly all too present against the radical absence of the Juukan Gorge sites.

Even more rare than the visibility of infrastructures too often hidden in plain sight was the push to hold Rio Tinto to account from within the political establishment. Under the weight of public scrutiny and a formal inquiry by Parliament's Joint Standing Committee on Northern Australia, three executives and the chair of the board resigned, and the company committed to a range of remedial actions, internal reforms, and changes in its engagement with Traditional Owners—yet this might be read as the new normal of doing business in extractive industries rather than meaningful punishments. As with the rare prosecutions that follow police violence, the company's actions hardly constitute justice. Nor do they do anything to undo the underlying structure of resource income dependency for Traditional

Owners, profit maximization by multinational miners or even the specifically problematic Heritage Act, let alone the legal edifice stacked in favor of extractive fossil capitalism. The system endures, the sacred sites remain intensely, profoundly absent. After a brief hiatus, more continue to be blasted with shocking regularity. Indeed, the sites had borne witness already, examined for significance within an archaeological framework of knowledge legible to Rio Tinto and to the legal system of Western Australia. Rendered into evidence of enduring presence by scientific dating techniques, the sites were already testifying—material witnesses within an epistemic mode legible and contestable to the state. This material testimony was in turn accompanied by the witnessing of the Puutu Kunti Kurrama and Pinikura peoples in their years-long engagements about the significance of the sites. But all this witnessing found no purchase within the system until it was too late. The destruction of such sacred sites both enacts and legitimates the settler state, as resource extraction depends upon the continued denial and devastation of Country.

Throughout the first year of the coronavirus pandemic, the destruction of the sites at Juukan Gorge continued to reverberate. BHP paused the planned destruction of forty sites, but decided after a review of its permissions to permanently halt the destruction of just ten. Reports of Rio Tinto's negligence continued to mount. The Parliamentary Inquiry held sessions, took submissions, and eventually traveled to meet with PKKP Traditional Owners. In its final report released in October 2021, the Joint Standing Committee on Northern Australia delivered a scathing indictment of the legal architectures that facilitated the destruction at Juukan Gorge and many other places across the nation. It called for significant change, ranging from the codesign with First Nations of new national heritage legislation to addressing inequities in the negotiating positions of Traditional Owners with mining corporations and government. With its passionate evocation of First Nations culture—along with harsh words for Rio Tinto and the Western Australian government and heritage laws—the report made for startling reading: a rare recognition of the brutal violence of resource extraction and the facilitating legal regime of property rights and heritage laws that makes ecological trauma the normal condition in settler Australia.

Whether meaningful change will take place is difficult to say. By their own admission, members of the committee were deeply affected by their time on Puutu Kunti Kurrama and Pinikura Country and by their experiences with Elders and other community members. The social media presence of the inquiry itself was a background hum, occasionally punctuating the surface but never sparking back to the intensity of its first days, even when the final inquiry report was released to a brief flurry of media attention. For the peoples of the Pilbara, the wound remains achingly painful. Radical absence is often like this: it bursts and fades for many, remains intense for some. It is tempting to conclude that radical absence can be the necessary precondition for political accountability, but the nonhuman witnessing at work here was more complex than mere digital disappearance. Witnessing at Juukan Gorge occurred through geological vitality, a vitality that was itself all too absent from the digital mediation of the destruction. Witnessing absence at Juukan Gorge—and in the past, present, and future of the deliberate destruction of First Nations heritage—means attending not only to the radical force of the lost sacred sites but also to the presence of an entrenched interconnection of more-than-human institutions and infrastructures of law, capital, and settler-colonial control.

WITNESSING ABSENCE

"All attachments are optimistic," writes Berlant, and radical absence is itself a form of attachment, for all the grief and death to which it attends: a witnessing relation with what has disappeared, an attachment to what is no longer present that enables positive change.[59] A witnessing of absence in the absence of witnesses: such an attachment can be animated by traumatic affect yet still spark a reparative movement—even if small, tentative, and threatened by the very affectivity of the disappearances from which it might emerge.[60] While far from a panacea and by no means a politics in itself, nonhuman witnessing nevertheless widens the aperture from the human subject to assemblages of human and nonhuman entities. Witnessing radical absence is only possible due to the sheer materialities of networked infrastructures, the algorithms and network protocols that enable the flow of machinic affect. Witnessing radical absence means attending to those infrastructures, and to the ecologies they disrupt, the wars they enliven, the extractive industries they streamline. Witnessing absence in this way makes possible a different kind of response to systemic oppression than the voice of the testifying subject, or even the assembled evidentiary force of Schuppli's material witnesses. Witnessing absence asks that we hold onto the possibility of witnessing in nonnormative ways, working outside the frame of courts and public contestation. If we accept Berlant's proposition that all attachments contain some element of optimism, then an intensive attachment to absence might well contain within it new forms and dynamics of relation that contain new possibilities for becoming otherwise, for turning radical absence into reparative care.

At the heart of what distinguishes radical absence from other structures of relation to the affective present is its disjunctive mode of attachment. This disjuncture does not negate others or community, or not necessarily so. By calling disappearance into relation, radical absence affords the space for disjunction to produce change, to enact something new. For violent mediation to shift toward repair. "Without disjunction there would be no cut, no cleaving, no inflection, no minor gesture," writes Manning.[61] Without such cuts, the field of experience remains static. What Manning points to here is "the gestural force that opens experience to its potential variation," such that "its rhythms are not controlled by a preexisting structure, but open to flux."[62] Attending with an altered angle of approach to the wider field of fear within which execution videos circulate, or to the faith that we place in technology to protect our human fragility, or to the collectivity of loss enacted in digital memorials, or to the laws of the settler state, might be small acts but they are not insignificant. However minor, these gestures contribute to composing something else from what is going on around us. "Affect matters in a world that is always promising and threatening to amount to something," writes Kathleen Stewart. "Fractally complex, there is no telling what will come of it or where it will take persons attuned."[63] Traumatic affects that coalesce within encounters with radical absence can be an opening onto the reparative, but not because they afford the opportunity for treatment in any clinical sense. Arising from the digital, they bring to visceral life how mediation entangles experiences in unpredictable ways that vary in intensity and form as they flow and ebb in time.

Across these and other radical absences, such shifts might be small, even tentative, but it is the minor gestures of the everyday that constitute the first glimmerings of a political otherwise. It is a politics without the requirement for institutional engagement or party affiliation, for spatial or temporal contiguity. Rather, it is a politics that finds in radical absence a means to move beyond atomization and isolation, yet not insist on proximity as the foundation for collective feeling and action. Radical absence need not engender a collapse into a traumatic void, some ruptured space of digital loss. Rather, witnessing radical absence in all its more-than-human complexity might give the slow work of reparation and care an urgency they can otherwise lack. It might alter the trajectory with which one approaches the public feelings that circulate online and off. It might make corporeally real the imbrication of digital media and mediations into evermore crevices of human life and death.

Small movements, but not trivial ones. Finding in the potential for hurt, for negative inflection, for encounter with traumatic affect, that reside in such encounters with the violent mediations of digital disappearance some small space for renewed life. Working through the entrapments, dispossessions, and disempowerments of algorithmic enclosure requires grappling with the macroscale of digital capitalism, data colonialism, and platform politics, but that struggle can begin with a witnessing relation. Nonhuman witnessing tugs the human into altered relations with the infrastructural milieus that make up the material and affective present. Witnessing radical absence pulls to prominence continuums of experience: from presence to loss, life to death, and hope to fear—however faint and fleeting they might be. How, then, might the politics of nonhuman witnessing be theorized? It is that question to which the coda of this book is addressed.

CODA

toward a politics of nonhuman witnessing

COVID-19 HAS SHATTERED many of the fictions that sustained the global order, racial capitalism, and the supremacy of Man. These pandemic years have been a brutal reminder of the nonhuman agencies that impinge upon and transform us and our ways of living in profound and immeasurable ways. Writing on the growing intimacies with such nonhuman agencies in sites such as post-Fukushima Japan, Kath Weston argues that "ecointimacies are compositional," born of the "growing conviction that creatures co-constitute other creatures, infiltrating one another's very substance, materially and otherwise."[1] COVID-19 is that most intimate of infiltrators, absorbed through air and breath, accelerated and intensified by both the desire to share social and familial space, but even more so by an economic order that demands the production and distribution of goods passed through human hands in tightly packed spaces in which people have no choice but to breathe the same air. Regimes of testing, the continual monitoring for new strains, the (re)instantiation of borders of all kinds, the clear correlation between changing climate and new diseases—the pandemic has forced us to confront our entanglements, both with one another and with the nonhuman in all its technical and ecological variety. More just and equitable futures for human life depend not only on reckoning with COVID-19 but also with the enduring crises from which it is inseparable. Attending to the intimacies and estrangements through which life is composed is crucial to that task. If the virus teaches us of our constitutive entanglement within one another, it also insists on difference, complexity, and the incommensurate opacities through which life coexists.

Produced by new comingling of human and animal, the novel coronavirus emerged from the forces of expansion, extraction, and enclosure that actualize the compulsions of capital and its handmaiden the state.[2] But even as the pandemic disrupted the seemingly smooth flow of goods and people across the globe, it also accelerated the datafication and informationalization of life at all scales. From the profusion of Zoom meetings to the normalization of population health surveillance to the redistribution of carbon emissions away from air travel to data centers and compute resources, the pandemic has intensified the constitutive contradiction of contemporary life between the promise of a smooth and knowable World and the collective experience of disjunctive, agonistic worlds. Collapsing the geopolitical into everyday life, the stark inequities in access to COVID-19 vaccines and treatments across the globe—not to mention the very different capacity of wealthy nations to weather the economic storms of lockdowns, deaths, and soaring health care costs—are in turn reflected in the classist and racist application of restrictions within polities, backed by police and militaries. Here in Sydney, for example, armed police and active-duty soldiers were deployed en masse in the diverse working-class suburbs in the southwest of the city, while residents of the affluent east and north went largely untroubled. The biopolitics of health management fused with an incipient necropolitics of militarized policing, facilitated by the ontopolitical capacities of algorithmic analysis of the feral transmission of the virus itself.

Politics as we know it is not equipped to deal with the intimacies of the entangled and incommensurate, just as it is not equipped to reckon with crises at the planetary scale. "Only a politics rebuilt on aesthetic principles, that is, by remaking communications," writes Cubitt, "offers the possibility of changing the conduct of relations between human beings and nature, and between both of them and the technologies that so profoundly and multifariously mediate between them."[3] If the neoliberal moment of racial capitalism has produced a fragmented and ad hoc politics based around the marketization and informationalization of life, then an alternative politics must surely begin with communication within and across difference. As I have argued throughout this book, nonhuman witnessing is a distinctive communicative modality, one in which difference is not a problem to be solved but rather the grounds for flourishing. Many of the nonhuman entities and ecologies traced in this book lack speech, or lack an inherent verbal or visual language equivalent to the human, but they are nevertheless continually communicating. Uranium isotopes continue to communicate with the plants, animals, sand, and peoples at Maralinga, and with the Traditional Owners driven from Country. Communication such as this is aesthetic, in that it is at once sensing and sense-making, but it is also relational and epistemological.

Nonhuman witnessing makes a claim on what can be known, whether in the neural layers of machine learning systems, or in the breath of the artist blowing glass in the trail of nuclear fallout, or in the digital afterlife of the sacred sites blasted to extract iron ore. For philosopher Jacques Rancière, politics is disorder, an insistent challenge to the prevailing order, the demand that the part without a part—the dispossessed and denied—obtain agency over its own fate.[4] The problem at hand is not simply to expand who or what gets to stand for parliament, but to radically reimagine the conditions within which knowledge is made and the communicative modalities needed to reckon with the incommensurabilities and opacities that constitute life within worlds of infinite relation. Even as the politics of the pandemic have for the most part been grim in the extreme, I hold on to thin hope that these conditions of crisis contain within them the potential to witness worlds and what happens within and between them in ways that enable alternative politics in the flourishing of communication, of connection, and of relation across difference.

AFTER THE WORLD, MANY

Many peoples and worlds know deeply the destructive force of the World: damming rivers and flooding homelands in the name of progress; clearing bush for farmland; blasting mountain, hill, and stone to extract fossil fuels; dispossessing peoples and breaking apart families; and severing ties to land, country, and kin. Even if the World that, like Man, overrepresents itself as the totality of existence has come to an end as a plausible or coherent notion, its death throes continue to wrack the planet and life on it in catastrophic ways. No reckoning has yet been made, despite the urgency. Indebted to the Zapatista slogan "a world where many worlds fit," de la Cadena and Blaser describe "the practice of a world of many worlds, or what we call a pluriverse: heterogeneous worldings coming together as a political ecology of practices, negotiating their difficult being together in heterogeneity."[5] A pluriversal reconception of coexistence—from World to worlds—is the task at hand for that great swathe of humanity that has benefited from and maintained the fiction of Man. Pluriversality requires a new "political ontology," a "politics of reality" grounded in the presumption of "divergent worldings constantly coming about through negotiations, enmeshments, crossings, and interruptions."[6]

Pluriversality confronts a dominant politics set sharply against the very notion of many worlds. This politics "emerged (with science) to make a liveable universe," writes de la Cadena, "to control conflict among a single if culturally diversified humanity living in a single scientifically knowable nature."[7] This political field depends on divisions between friend and enemy, as well as between nature and culture. As de la Cadena argues, "These two antitheses—between humanity and nature, and between allegedly superior and inferior humans—declared the gradual extinction of other-than-human beings and the worlds in which they existed."[8] To engage in politics, one had to be recognized within the hierarchical domain of Humanity—of Man—and not assigned to Nature, a form of racialization many First Nations people have been, and continue to be, subjected to. Pluralizing politics, then, is not simply a question of inclusion within Man, but is to be found in the very dissolution of such a notion to begin with. As I argued in the introduction, witnessing has long operated as a coconspirator with Man, a guarantor to science, law, religion, and culture of the coherence and cogency of the World. As I have articulated the concept, nonhuman witnessing aims to break that binding of the Witness to Man and, with it, Man to World.

This refiguring of witness and witnessing does not facilitate the smooth aggregation of politics as usual with pluriversality but enables an adversarial pluralism, in which noncontiguous and mutually exclusive worlds can coexist—even if coexistence requires the end of the World of Man. Coexistence depends upon contact and relationality, not mutual exclusion. Incommensurate worlds can only coexist when contact with irreducible difference is the condition for a relational politics. Attending to the nonhuman in witnessing is one way to "slow down reasoning and provoke the kind of thinking that would enable us to undo, or more accurately, unlearn, the single ontology of politics," as de la Cadena puts it.[9] Nonhuman witnessing offers the means to trace how knowledge moves between or is animated across many worlds in a situation in which media, like all resources, are finite. Media and mediation hold the potential to generate the connective, communicative tissue between worlds. For Cubitt, communication constitutes the ground of a renewed politics, a politics that reckons with the exclusion of the nonhuman from the forms foisted on the world through the Enlightenment, colonialization, and marketization. To build alternative futures, the nonhuman must be understood as "an active agent of historical change."[10] For this to hold, humanity must reckon with the fact "that our environments are not only capable of communication, but are constantly communicating."[11] Communication—and mediation more generally—have long been too radically delimited by modernity's insistence on the radical distinction between human and environment, between nature and culture. Communication must embrace entities far beyond the human, not as sources of evidence or information but as agential and vital in and of themselves. In the aftermath of the end of the World, this communicative politics must reckon with the jostling and at times agonistic existence of countless worlds on this one planet. Setting agendas between worlds and resolving conflicts between species and things where outcomes might be lethal presents an immense challenge to such a proposition, and one that this book can only gesture toward. Pluriversal justice resides in the capacity for coexistence, and the active refusal of worlds predicated on martial, algorithmic, and ecological violence. Such a future requires a kind of faith in the incommensurate, a willingness to build a pluriversal politics of human and nonhuman that begins with the collective witnessing of what must remain opaque, unknowable, and incommunicable even as it seeks and nourishes connection and communication. A nonhuman witnessing of the opacity of existence constituted by human and nonhuman relationality.

WITNESSING OPACITY

Tracing nonhuman witnessing across entangled crises of war, data, and ecologies has meant repeated encounters with tensions and paradoxes. Not bound to the human subject or sensorium, nonhuman witnessing necessarily evokes agencies, entities, and aesthetics that cannot be readily resolved in the human communicative terrain of language, gesture, and image. Against the demand that the modern witness—the witness of science and the courts and the media—have their testimony be verifiable, nonhuman witnessing requires that the incommensurate and unknowable be taken as generative opportunities for crafting new relations and knowledges. Here we might recall the machine vision analysis of military drone images, but also the resistant potential of such systems when harnessed by the investigative aesthetics of Forensic Architecture and applied to state violence. Each of the analytic concepts developed in this book reckon in different ways with tension, incommensurability, and unknowability. Violent mediation seeks to describe how complexity, uncertainty, and the unknowable are erased and elided through instrumental processes of mediation. Machinic affect names those relational intensities that animate technoscientific apparatuses, ambivalent to the human and otherwise relegated to the mere operation of technical systems. Ecological trauma describes the rippling effects of the rupturing of relations within more-than-human ecologies, many of which elude human understanding and can only ever be partially made sensible to the ecological system itself. Radical absence brings these questions of the incommensurate into the quotidian experience of the digital and its nonhuman infrastructures, accounting for encounters with what has been rendered absent yet remains forcefully present. These analytics thus engage with the necessary opacity of existence, with the fundamental incapacity for entities to disclose themselves to one another even when bound in relation.

Here, then, I arrive at a final doubled meaning: witnessing opacity, or the nonhuman witnessing of opacity, and the opacity of nonhuman witnessing. Nonhuman witnessing seeks to bring opacity into the space of witnessing, not as a problem to be resolved but as a site of potential communicative relation. At the same time, nonhuman witnessing is constituted by its own opacity, its presence in zones of sensing and sense-making that cannot be decoded or even identified at all. The dissolution of the human as privileged witness depends on this potential for withdrawal from anthropocentric epistemology. Modernity—with its Enlightenment and colonial underpinnings—demands transparency, as Glissant argues: "This same transparency, in Western History, predicts that a common truth of Mankind exists and maintains that what approaches it most closely is action that projects, whereby the world is realized at the same time that it is caught in the act of its foundation."[12] Opacity works against this "reductive transparency."[13] It is not obscurity but rather "that which cannot be reduced, which is the most perennial guarantee of participation and confluence."[14] Opacity emerges with and is the condition of new and old worlds alike. Opacity does not produce irreconcilable difference between cultures, languages, or ways of living but rather makes possible the coexistence of multiplicities within a totality. "Opacities can coexist and converge, weaving fabrics," Glissant writes. "To understand these truly one must focus on the texture of the weave and not on the nature of its components."[15] This weave is Relation, or "what the world makes and expresses of itself."[16] Glissant's opening to Relation invokes "a poetics that is latent, open, multilingual in intention, directly in contact with everything possible," but in his account is very much tied to human subjectivities and the traumas they experience, particularly those of slavery's Middle Passage. Glissant's right to opacity is itself a response to dehumanizing violence and is, in a sense, already a politics of witnessing traumas that leave no trace, lost to the oceans. For Glissant, this unrecoverable trauma is both an end and beginning; a nonpassage for the drowned and an abyssal beginning for those who survive.

Opacity thus arises from this unknowable trauma and from the contact between worlds that it sets in motion. Racialization, in other words, is not a by-product of the World of Man, but rather its constitutive force that renders certain peoples nonhuman, producing both World and Man through that dehumanization. Responding to the historical enactment of violent trauma, Glissant's opacity offers a way of understanding the Other that does not require the relinquishing of Otherness. As such, it provides a generative way of thinking relations with more-than-human ecologies and technics that do not require their submission to human forms of knowing or being, but depend instead on their openness to communication, justice, and the flourishing of other worlds. In doing so, it will be necessary to reckon with the incommensurabilities of weaponized drones and military AI, for example, and ask whether in the coexistence of worlds such technics should continue. Witnessing opacity is itself a political project, with political struggles inherent to its articulation beyond these pages.[17]

Against the notion that transparency is the necessary antidote to difference between beings and worlds, witnessing opacity helps enable a pluriversal politics. Nonhuman witnessing—as an ethicopolitical, aesthetic, and epistemic mode of relation—provides the potential for a transversal communicative politics, one that works within and between a pluriverse of worlds. Nonhuman witnessing offers an aesthetics of rupture and repair, of connection and disconnection. The politics at hand here are not concerned with policy per se, or with the democratic organization of human societies. I am not proposing that nonhuman witnessing enable a parliament of things. Rather, my proposition is that nonhuman witnessing be mobilized in the name of a politics of the dispossessed, of the human and nonhuman, of those denied humanity and denied agency. Such a politics must contend with the incommensurate at every level, precisely because those denied political standing within the World of Man are also deemed to lack transparency or its potential when in fact what they possess is an unassailable opacity. Justice isn't made by enforced transparencies and disclosures, but through contact between opacities that are nonetheless generative of shared knowledges. Nonhuman witnessing's political potential resides in how a field of relations—human and non; technical, cultural, and ecological—composes itself in the face of the injunction that witnessing makes, an injunction to become communicative, to become both response-able and address-able even while holding the refusal that resides in the right to opacity.

THE POLITICS OF NONHUMAN WITNESSING

Nonhuman witnessing seeks to bring into being the conditions for an otherwise by producing communicative relations across and within difference that refuse to override the opaque and the incommensurate. Nonhuman witnessing is an ecological mode of communication that arises from the fields of relations that come together in the encounter between human and nonhuman, and most intensely so in contexts of violence, domination, and control. By refusing the supremacy of Man the Witness as the figure through which events obtain meaning or knowledge is produced, nonhuman witnessing gives standing to diverse actors and entities, whether people denied humanity or machinic intelligences or wounded ecologies in the aftermath of war. What the nonhuman bears witness to might well be ruin, death, and trauma—and the witness itself might be a perpetrator—but the fundamental implication of nonhuman witnessing is to remake the human and the witnessing that we do. Nonhuman witnessing can be mobilized to heal and empower, to bring to light change in its emergence, and to insist on attending to voices, bodies, patterns, and materialities denied standing in the present order. Nonhuman witnessing is not a panacea, but rather a practice of forging relations with the incommensurate. Its lure is becoming more human through the witnessing of our constitutive nonhumanity.

The politics of nonhuman witnessing, then, is not one of rights, human or otherwise. Expanding the domain of rights—granting rights to rivers and other earth beings, for example—is a worthy enough endeavor but not one that changes the conditions under which politics takes place. If a machine were to bear witness as a rights-bearing subject, what rights would obtain to it and what would their articulation mean for the rights that already accrue to the "human"? Rights, for all the protections they provide, are part and parcel of the existing order of racial capitalism and neoliberal governance, guarantors of human privilege and individual autonomy within the epistemic domain of the Enlightenment. Rather than extending rights that humans have to the nonhuman, the task at hand is to invite nonhumans subjectivities and agencies into the space of politics and, in doing so, seek to recompose what politics is for the human. Cubitt again: "It is we ourselves who must become other in order to produce an other world. The correlative is that we must cease to be human, and most of all cease to exist as exclusively human polity, which is the medium of communication par excellence. The road to that goal, however, must lead through the polis, the humanity of humans, and most of all through our communications in order to imagine a way out of stasis."[18] Such a politics nurtures a radical solidarity between human and nonhuman, nourished by a shared capacity to witness violence and wonder, trauma and healing, and to do so in and across incommensurate time, space, scales, subjectivities, and materialities. There is no blueprint for such a politics, no white paper or policy guidance. It is a politics that can only become thinkable in its particularities through the poesis of its emergence. That emergence will produce its own challenges, not least those of setting agendas, establishing the grounds for lethality, and resolving conflicts. But to impose its forms in advance would be to foreclose futures that cannot be imagined from within the epistemic dominance of the Anthropos. At this critical conjuncture of history, the transformative potential of the politics of nonhuman witnessing remains unrealized.

There are already and have always been many worlds, both prior to and existing alongside or in the shadow of the World of the Anthropos, the World of the Anthropocene. First Nations worlds, but also worlds on the periphery of empire, or in the underbelly of cities, or in speculative futures, or in fugitive subjects escaping constraints of all kinds. Worlds of nonhuman beings, of animals and bacteria and plants and rocks. Worlds of earth beings, as de la Cadena describes the animacies of mountains, lakes, and forests.[19] And now worlds of technical agencies, and even—against the odds and despite the hidden human labor that often powers them—machinic intelligences and perceptual machines. Not all of these worlds would be readily recognized as such, and it might well be that the existence of some constitutes a risk to the existence of others. Yet such worlds jostle, cohabiting terrains and atmospheres, competing for energy, voice, space, and even time.

To begin with a political ontology that allows for such pluriversality is itself a radical move, since it means the End of the World, and of life and politics as we know it. "The idea of a pluriverse is utopian indeed," writes de la Cadena, "not because other socionatural formations and their earth-practices do not take place, but because we have learned to ignore their occurrence, considering it a thing of the past or, what is the same, a matter of ignorance and superstition."[20] Like all utopian projects, a world of many worlds can't wind the clock back, undo the damage, or raise the dead. But a world of many worlds does require a communicative modality that reaches toward the incommensurability of crowding worlds, even as it respects the necessity of ineradicable difference. Rather than rights or democratic participation, the politics of nonhuman witnessing concerns the emergent composition of fields of relations out of which incommensurate collectivities and paradoxical knowledges might form. The politics of nonhuman witnessing is, in this sense, an ecological poesis, an attunement to and calibration of the human and the nonhuman that dwells in and with opacity. It is a politics of and for the future, even as it provides the means to reimagine the past.

The politics of nonhuman witnessing is a politics of the commons, but not the commons in a universal, global, or homogenous sense—rather it is a profusion of commons, bound by their common commitment to neither begin with nor seek to resolve homogeneity.[21] Such a commons can only ever be emergent and unfixed, since it must compose itself a new in the ongoing antagonisms, negotiations, sympathies, and alliances between worlds. Commons are necessarily communicative. Nonhuman witnessing offers the potential for a distinct communicative mode, one that insists not simply upon communication but on the demand for response and address. Such terms carry with them a certain anthropocentrism, but in adopting them I am not returning to narrow notions of speech or recognition. Address and response form instead a communicative relation and generative aesthetic. Fuller and Weizman describe the emergence of an investigative commons in the new collectivities of forensic architecture, open-source investigation, and distributed human rights research, which in turn draws on the existence of an aesthetic commons, in which processes of sensing and sensing-making fold into further such processes.[22] If nonhuman witnessing animates or emerges within particular commons, it also does so at the level of aesthetics and in league with such instrumental investigative modes. But it also exceeds those deliberate, human interventions, describing too the poesis that can arise in the strange agonisms and fleeting alliances of machines, ecologies, animals, and people.

To return to the Pacific Forum that opened chapter 3 of this book, nonhuman witnessing might galvanize a commons of islands and oceans, people and winds, garbage and atmospheric sensing. Nonhuman witnessing would not paper over the incapacities of speech or the ephemerality of certain agencies but would be alive to what emerges in the intensive connections that can arise when worlds are anchored, nurtured, and fought for. It is for this reason that I have attended in this book not only to material events and actually existing technologies, but also to speculative imaginaries and creative works. Such phenomena, objects, practices, and processes are often not at all contiguous or willing to reveal their workings. Nor should they be. What they reveal is the contingent and always incomplete nature of nonhuman witnessing, how its politics depend on the work of refiguring the human in the face of catastrophic crises.

This book is, too, a necessarily incomplete gesture. A pursuit of something happening all around us yet refusing to be fixed in place. War, in its all its turbulent and violent becoming, now escapes the human more than ever before, yet it cannot and will not leave us behind. Algorithmic and data technologies enclose life and seek to make it operative. Ecological catastrophe pushes the planet itself to the brink of becoming unlivable. In the shadow of what refuses to be grasped, that won't submit to contained and discrete ways of knowing, can't sit still long enough to become knowable to the human alone, nonhuman witnessing widens the ambit through which meaning comes to matter, responsibility is forged, and more-than-human epistemic communities become possible. Yet while its politics are never far from the surface, their form and force remain to be realized in the work that lies before us, humans and otherwise.

NOTES

INTRODUCTION. NONHUMAN WITNESSING

1 Like many, I first encountered the horrifying strike of February 21, 2010, through the excerpts from the transcript that open Grégoire Chamayou's *Drone Theory*, but it also plays a similar role in journalist Andrew Cockburn's *Kill Chain* and in international relations scholar Lauren Wilcox's brilliant analysis of racializing and gendering in the drone apparatus. In writing this account I am deeply indebted to the remarkable work of Derek Gregory, particularly a series of posts on his Geographical Imaginations site titled "Under Afghan Skies." In my rendition, I have sought to attend to the points of contact between technoscientific systems, human actions, and the environment. Chamayou, *Drone Theory*; Cockburn, *Kill Chain*; Wilcox, "Embodying Algorithmic War."
2 Whyte, "Indigenous Science (Fiction) for the Anthropocene."
3 Wynter, "Unsettling the Coloniality of Being/Power/Truth/Freedom."
4 Wynter differentiates between an original Man1 arising from the Renaissance and a later Man2 reshaped by the colonial encounter with the Americas and Darwinian biology, but as the distinctions between these two positions are not central to my argument, I am using "Man" to encapsulate this overrepresentation as the human in more general terms.
5 I understand affect in the Spinozan tradition: as the bodily capacity to affect and be affected. Here, as elsewhere in my work, affect gels with a

capacious conception of what counts as a body: texts, plants, drones, swans, databases, publics and waters can all be bodies as readily as individuated humans. Bodies—human and non, multiple and individuated—are enabled and constrained by the relations in which they are webbed, the resources and capacities for change, connection, signification and more. Those relations are the stuff of affect. Affect is thus not an exclusively human mode of experience akin to emotion, but the relational dynamics of bodies situated in contexts, entrained within environments, assembled in machinic processes, and so on. As Massumi writes, "The body is as immediately abstract as it is concrete; its activity and expressivity extend, as on their underside, into an incorporeal, yet perfectly real, dimension of pressing potential." *Parables*, 31. Affect can be modulated, amplified, intensified and otherwise transformed by media: this is precisely what makes ubiquitous media so powerful. But affect can break, sheer, stretch, distend and rupture bonds between bodies as much as strengthen or intensify them. See Massumi, "Autonomy of Affect"; Gibbs, "Panic!"; Gibbs, "Contagious Feelings"; Angerer, *Ecology of Affect*; Schaefer, *Evolution of Affect Theory*; Gregg and Seigworth, *Affect Theory Reader*; Clough, *Affective Turn*; Deleuze, "Ethology."

6 De la Cadena and Blaser, *A World of Many Worlds*.
7 Amazon, "All In"; Greenpeace, "Clicking Clean Virginia."
8 Sherwood, "Inside Lithium Giant SQM's Struggle to Win Over Indigenous Communities in Chile's Atacama."
9 Gilmore, *Golden Gulag*; Robinson, *Black Marxism*.
10 Kelley, "Racial Capitalism."
11 Packer and Reeves, *Killer Apps*, 5. On the history of computation, screens, and enemy production, see also Geoghegan, "An Ecology of Operations."
12 Puar, *Right to Maim*; Mbembe, *Necropolitics*.
13 Browne, *Dark Matters*.
14 Halpern, *Beautiful Data*, 8.
15 Furuhata, "Multimedia Environments and Security Operations," 72.
16 Edwards, *A Vast Machine*; Edwards, *The Closed World*.
17 Hogan and Vonderau, "The Nature of Data Centers."
18 On infrastructural violence, see Khalili, *Sinews of War and Trade*; Cowen, *The Deadly Life of Logistics*; and Easterling, *Extrastatecraft*. On slow and structural violence, see Nixon, *Slow Violence*; Farmer, "Structural Violence." On algorithmic violence, see Bellanova et al., "Critique of Algorithmic Violence."
19 Whyte, "Against Crisis Epistemology."
20 Vigh, "Crisis and Chronicity," 10.
21 Berlant, *Cruel Optimism*, 10.
22 Murphie, "On Being Affected," 24.
23 Murphie, "On Being Affected," 20.
24 Massumi, *Ontopower*, vii–viii.

25 As such, "politics, colonialism, settlement, capitalism, ecological destruction, racism, and misogynies are not wars by other means—they are war." Grove, *Savage Ecology*, 61.
26 Grove, *Savage Ecology*, 10.
27 Cubitt, *Finite Media*, 3; and Cubitt, *The Practice of Light*.
28 Kember and Zylinska, *Life after New Media*, xv. On mediation as performative and lively enactment, see also Parks, *Rethinking Media Coverage*, 2.
29 Drawing on German and Canadian media theory, John Durham Peters defines media as "ensembles of natural and human elements" and "our infrastructures of being, the habitats and materials through which we act and are." Andrew Murphie argues that "we move into relations with media that quite literally move us/the world and with which we can move the world." Even the planet can be understood as a medium, argues Chris Russill, most clearly in the monitoring apparatuses of climate change and atmospheric military sensor networks. Peters, *The Marvellous Clouds*, 3, 15; Murphie, "World as Medium," 17; Russill, "Is the Earth a Medium?"; Russill, "Earth Imaging."
30 Cubitt, *Finite Media*, 7.
31 Russill, "The Road Not Taken."
32 Patrick Wolfe has written persuasively about the relationship between settler colonialism and genocide, arguing that "settler colonialism is inherently eliminatory but not invariably genocidal" in "Settler Colonialism and the Elimination of the Native," 388. Today, Aboriginal children are currently being removed from their families at even higher rates than they were in the 1950s, an era of systemic destruction of culture and peoples that made what became known as the Stolen Generation and for which the Australian government issued a formal apology in 2008. Cashless debit cards to control welfare benefits are being rolled out to Indigenous communities, many still living under permutations of the military occupation launched in 2007 by an ailing government looking to stoke anti-Indigenous resentment. Black deaths in custody have returned to their heights from the 1980s, while Aboriginal people are massively overrepresented in prisons and Indigenous women are far more likely to be subject to sexual violence.
33 Whyte, "Indigenous Science (Fiction) for the Anthropocene," 226.
34 Estes, *Our History Is the Future*, 135.
35 De la Cadena and Blaser, *A World of Many Worlds*, 12.
36 Although, as of writing, it has not yet been recognized by either the International Commission on Stratigraphy nor the International Union of Geological Sciences as a division of geologic time.
37 Demos, *Against the Anthropocene*, 85. For a detailed discussion of Crutzen and Stoermer's conception of the Anthropocene, see Grove, *Savage Ecology*, 36–40.
38 Moore, *Anthropocene or Capitalocene?*; Grove, *Savage Ecology*; Haraway, "Anthropocene, Capitalocene, Plantationocene, Chthulucene"; de la Cadena, "Uncommoning Nature."

39 Writing on what she calls "minimal ethics," Joanna Zylinska argues that the response demanded by the Anthropocene is "strongly post-anthropocentric... in the sense that it does not consider the human to be the dominant or the most important species, nor does it see the world as arranged solely for human use and benefit." Zylinska, *Minimal Ethics for the Anthropocene*, 20.

40 Davis and Todd, "On the Importance of a Date," 763. By contrast, see, for example, McNeill and Engelke, *The Great Acceleration*.

41 Stewart, "Atmospheric Attunements," 445.

42 Kaplan, *Aerial Aftermaths*, 17–18.

43 Or, as as Kathryn Yusoff points out, if the end of the world of apocalyptic imagining is the end of this colonialist and capitalist one for some, then it is also "the prerequisite for the possibility of imagining 'living and breathing again' for others." Yusoff, *A Billion Black Anthropocenes or None*, 13.

44 Rather than look outside the narrow frame of knowledges that helped get us into this mess—loosely grouped under the rubrics of the humanist tradition and Western scientific rationality—we are called to attend ever more earnestly to those very knowledges in the search for solutions to the damage they have wrought. See Snaza, "The Earth Is Not 'Ours' to Save," 339.

45 Weizman, *Forensic Architecture*.

46 Fuller and Weizman, *Investigative Aesthetics*.

47 Schuppli, *Material Witness*, 19.

48 Schuppli, *Material Witness*, 34.

49 Pugliese, *State Violence and the Execution of Law*, 14.

50 Peters, "Witnessing."

51 Frosh and Pinchevski, "Why Media Witnessing?," 1.

52 Chouliaraki, *The Spectatorship of Suffering*.

53 See, for example, Reading, "Mobile Witnessing"; Andén-Papadopoulos, "Citizen Camera-Witnessing"; Andén-Papadopoulos, "Crowd-Sourced Video"; Papailias, "Witnessing in the Age of the Database"; Chouliaraki, "Digital Witnessing in Conflict Zones"; Gray, "Data Witnessing."

54 Wu and Montgomery, "Witnessing in Crisis Contexts"; Rae, Holman, and Nethery, "Self-Represented Witnessing"; Ristovska, *Seeing Human Rights*.

55 For more on torture in ancient Greece and Rome, see Ballengee, *Wound and Witness*; DuBois, *Torture and Truth*; Peters, *Torture*.

56 On the religious roots of witnessing, see Peters, "Witnessing," 708. On the emergence of new legal norms, see Langbein, *Law of Proof*.

57 Ballard, "And They Are like Wild Beasts," 19. See also Bennett, *Vibrant Matter*, 8–10.

58 Langbein, *Law of Proof*.

59 Spillers, "Mama's Baby, Papa's Maybe," 69.

60 Dispossession, stigmatisation and deprivation of First Nations served "both to 'verify' the overrepresentation of Man as if it were the human, and to

legitimate the subordination of the world and well-being of the latter to those of the former." Wynter, "Unsettling the Coloniality of Being/Power/Truth/Freedom," 268.
61 Law, as Zakkiyah Jackson explains, "denies those it deems 'inhuman' access to speech and law, thereby producing the inhumanity it excludes," showing how the standard of the "human" witness is actually "fundamental to law's injustice for both people of color and animals." Jackson, "Animal," 675, 676.
62 Fassin, "The Humanitarian Politics of Testimony," 534, 541.
63 Daston and Galison, *Objectivity*.
64 On the relationship of science, testimony, and the production of knowledge in a classic vein, see Coady, *Testimony*. On the role of trust and social conformity, see Adler, "Testimony, Trust, Knowing"; and Hardwig, "The Role of Trust in Knowledge."
65 Daston and Galison, *Objectivity*.
66 Haraway, *Modest–Witness*, 24. In her book, Haraway proposes her own feminist modest witness who is suspicious, situated, knowing, ignorant, partial, and more.
67 Haraway, *Modest–Witness*, 24.
68 Haraway, "Situated Knowledges."
69 "Witnessing became a domestic act.... Television sealed the twentieth century's fate as the century of witness." Ellis in Peters, "Witnessing," 708.
70 Frosh and Pinchevski, "Why Media Witnessing?," 9.
71 Peters, "Witnessing."
72 Boltanski, *Distant Suffering*; Chouliaraki, *The Spectatorship of Suffering*; Kozol, *Distant Wars Visible*.
73 On the significance of witnessing and testimony to the a host of scholarly disciplines and institutional practices, see Wieviorka, *The Era of the Witness*; Felman and Laub, *Testimony*; Frosh and Pinchevski, *Media Witnessing*; Givoni, "Witnessing/Testimony"; Guerin and Hallas, *The Image and the Witness*.
74 The German media theorist Friedrich Kittler was the leading proponent of this argument, which I am drawing on here by way of Sean Cubitt. See Cubitt, *The Practice of Light*, 7–12.
75 For the distilled argument, see the introduction to Cubitt, *The Practice of Light*.
76 As Halpern puts it, there emerged "a new set of investments in process, communication, and circulation, now encoded into built environments, machines, and attention spans." See *Beautiful Data*, 84.
77 Gray, "Data Witnessing."
78 McCosker, "Drone Media"; McCosker, "Drone Vision"; Andén-Papadopoulos, "Citizen Camera-Witnessing"; Chouliaraki and al-Ghazzy, "Flesh Witnessing"; Gil-Fournier and Parikka, "Ground Truth to Fake Geographies."
79 The limits of representation in witnessing has been a significant theme in my own research, see Richardson, *Gestures of Testimony*; Richardson and

Schankweiler, "Affective Witnessing"; Richardson, "Drone's-Eye View." See also, Pinchevski, *Transmitted Wounds*; Ettinger, *The Matrixial Borderspace*.

80 Oliver, *Witnessing*, 195, 20.

81 Givoni, "Witnessing/Testimony," 165.

82 There are now many valuable interventions in how to rethink the human. Dana Luciano and Mel Y. Chen draw on queer theory to argue that the "inhuman"—or inhumanisms—"points to the violence that the category of the human contains within itself" by "resonating against the 'inhumane'" in "Has the Queer Ever Been Human?," 197. In alliance with this queer inhumanism, Julietta Singh calls for dehumanism, a "practice of recuperation, of stripping away the violent foundations (always structural and ideological) of colonial and neocolonial mastery that continue to render some being more human than others." Singh, *Unthinking Mastery*, 4. Like the earlier "antihumanism" of Louis Althusser and the critical Marxist tradition, the "de-" and "in-" signal a critical desire to undo the structures of knowledge-making and world-making of the humanities in their traditional form, but are not so geared toward the expansive account of agencies needed to think about witnessing outside the frame of the human altogether, which is why some prefer the "more-than-human" and "other-than-human." See Springgay and Truman, *Walking Methodologies*, 8–11; Pugliese, *Biopolitics of the More-Than-Human*.

83 Grusin, "Introduction," ix–x.

84 "Humanity and nonhumanity have always performed an intricate dance with each other. There was never a time when human agency was anything other than an interfolding network of humanity and nonhumanity; today this mingling has become harder to ignore." Bennett, *Vibrant Matter*, 31.

85 Race in general, and blackness in particular, "cannot be escaped but only disavowed or dissimulated in prevailing articulations of movement 'beyond the human.'" Jackson, "Outer Worlds," 216. One consequence of this thinking, as Tavia Nyong'o points out, is that "posthumanist theory has tended to present the decentering of the human as both salutary and largely innocent of history." Nyong'o, "Little Monsters," 266.

86 Barad, "Posthumanist Performativity," 809. Stacy Alaimo describes this as "trans-corporeality," or how "the human is always intermeshed with the more-than-human world." Alaimo, *Bodily Natures*, 17.

87 Luciano and Chen, "Has the Queer Ever Been Human?," 192.

88 Sheikh, "The Future of the Witness," 148.

89 Zylinska, *Nonhuman Photography*, 15.

90 Cubitt, *Finite Media*, 151.

91 Vivian, *Commonplace Witnessing*.

92 See, for example, Caruth, *Unclaimed Experience*; Felman and Laub, *Testimony*; Kaplan, *Trauma Culture*; Abraham and Torok, *Shell*.

93 Felman writes that "testimony seems to be composed of bits and pieces of a memory that has been overwhelmed by occurrences that have not settled

into understanding or remembrance, acts that cannot be constructed as knowledge nor assimilated into full cognition, events in excess of our frames of reference." Felman and Laub, *Testimony*, 5.
94 LaCapra, *Writing History*; LaCapra, *Representing*.
95 Felman and Laub, *Testimony*, 24.
96 Agamben, *Remnants*, 141.
97 Arendt, *On Violence*, 50, 51.
98 Butler, *Precarious Life*.
99 Farmer, "Structural Violence," 308. The term "structural violence" originates with peace and conflict studies founder Johan Galtung but has been elaborated and extended by Farmer and others, particularly in anthropology.
100 Das et al., *Violence and Subjectivity*.
101 Wolfe, "Settler Colonialism and the Elimination of the Native."
102 Michael Taussig's account of paramilitary violence in Colombia is a particularly vibrant and nuanced account of the latter. Taussig, *Law in a Lawless Land*.
103 Reflecting on her own refusal to revivify spectacles of tortured slaves, Saidiya Hartman pursues instead the "diffusion of terror and violence perpetrated under the rubric of pleasure, paternalism and property." Hartman, *Scenes of Subjection*, 4.
104 Da Silva, "No-Bodies," 214.
105 Weizman, *Forensic Architecture*, 117.
106 Oliver, *Witnessing*, 7.
107 Oliver, *Witnessing*, 7.
108 Oliver, *Witnessing*, 7.
109 Oliver, *Witnessing*, 68.
110 Oliver, *Witnessing*, 223.
111 See Chow, *Age of the World Target*; Bousquet, *The Eye of War*.
112 Oliver, *Witnessing*, 224.

CHAPTER ONE. WITNESSING VIOLENCE

1 As Pailthorpe's work attests, aesthetic interventions into drone warfare can possess an ambivalent relation to their subject matter. Stubblefield argues that once drone art is restated in relation to the operative logics and processes of networked war, "a more nuanced reading emerges, one in which the apparent passivity of this genre is not only a conscious response to the specific conditions of drone power, but in fact the means for reimagining its relations of violence," Stubblefield, *Drone Art*, 2. Further valuable commentaries on drone art can be found in Rhee, *The Robotic Imaginary*; Danchev, "Bug Splat"; Bräunert and Malone, *To See Without Being Seen*.
2 Cubitt, *Finite Media*, 4.
3 Cubitt, *The Practice of Light*, 8.

4   Packer and Reeves, *Killer Apps*, 9.
5   For an extensive examination of the relationship between scientific epistemes and warfare, see Bousquet, *The Scientific Way of Warfare*.
6   Packer and Reeves, *Killer Apps*, 7.
7   Bousquet, *The Eye of War*, 8, 11.
8   In a similar vein, Amoore observes that "algorithmic war appears to make it possible for the imagination of an open global economy of mobile people, objects and monies, to be reconciled with the post-9/11 rendering of a securitized nation-state." Amoore, "Algorithmic War," 51.
9   All too human testimony takes place outside the strictures of rights-based discourses, of course. In Afghanistan, for example, the weaving of war rugs to represent the weaponry and martial dynamics of successive superpower invasions can be understood as a form of testimony.
10 Tahir, "The Ground Was Always in Play," 12.
11 Dawes, *That the World May Know*; Slaughter, *Human Rights, Inc.*
12 Givoni, *The Care of the Witness*.
13 Jess Whyte argues that neoliberals, threatened by socialist pushes for rights to social welfare and self-determination, set about developing an alternate framework of human rights that had the explicit intention of depoliticizing the social realm in order to protect private investment, strengthen liberal individualism, encourage market-based solutions, extend imperialism, and entrench a marketcentric international order. Whyte, *The Morals of the Market*.
14 Kaplan calls them "hybrid machines" that "make their worlds, materially and elementally" as "complex assemblages that gather and produce people, objects, discourses, information, terrains, atmospheres, and, in ways we must make more complicated, images." Kate Chandler argues that the unmanning at the center of drone warfare elides its coconstitution by human, media and machine elements that "not only come together but also fail to cohere and the attendant politics that emerge through these relations," Chandler, *Unmanning*, 7; Kaplan, "Drones and the Image Complex," 30.
15 McCosker and Wilken, *Automating Vision*, 89.
16 Parks and Kaplan, *Life in the Age of Drone Warfare*, 9.
17 See Kaplan, *Aerial Aftermaths*; Chandler, *Unmanning*; Wilcox, "Embodying Algorithmic War."
18 Kaplan, "Drone-o-Rama."
19 Grégoire Chamayou argues that this "temporary autonomous zone of slaughter," enacts "the idea of an invasive power based not so much on the rights of conquest as on the rights of pursuit: a right of universal intrusion or encroachment." Chamayou, *Drone Theory*, 55, 53. When first deployed in the 1991 Gulf War, the kill box was an area the size of New York City, but as both the concept and necessary geolocation and information communication technologies developed, kill boxes became three dimensional and increasingly granular in time and geographical specificity.

20 Bousquet, Grove, and Shah, "Becoming War," 1.
21 Bousquet, Grove, and Shah, "Becoming War," 5.
22 Gregory, "From a View to a Kill," 193. See also Grayson and Mawdsley, "Scopic Regimes in International Relations."
23 See Gregory, "From a View to a Kill"; Michel, *Eyes in the Sky*.
24 "Drone vision intervenes at the point of generating a new actionable kind of visibility or visual knowledge." McCosker and Wilken, *Automating Vision*, 99.
25 Andrejevic, *Automated Media*, 85.
26 Parks, *Rethinking Media Coverage*, 146.
27 Parks, *Rethinking Media Coverage*, 147.
28 For an outstanding history, see Michel, *Eyes in the Sky*.
29 On the history and contemporary practices of photogrammetry and vertical mediation, see Wilken and Thomas, "Vertical Geomediation."
30 Pong, *For the Duration*, 1.
31 Although Behram's photographs are often disbelieved and dismissed by supporters of the war. See Tahir, "The Ground Was Always in Play," 14.
32 Dorrian, "Drone Semiosis," 55.
33 For Stubblefield, Dorrian's observations are the hinge into reading the photographs as an inversion of drone vision. Stubblefield, *Drone Art*, 31.
34 Kapadia, *Insurgent Aesthetics*, 54–60.
35 Kaplan, *Aerial Aftermaths*, 33.
36 Kaplan, *Aerial Aftermaths*, 36.
37 In the Stanford/NYU "Living Under Drones" report, Hisham Abrar states: "When the weather is clear, three or four [drones] can be seen.... They are in the air 24 [hours a day], seven [days a week], but not when it's raining. Every time they are in the air, they can be heard. And because of the noise, we're psychologically disturbed—women, men, and children.... When there were no drones, everything was all right. [There was] business, there was no psychological stress and the people did what they could do for a living." Stanford Law School and NYU School of Law, "Living under Drones," 164.
38 Stanford Law School and NYU School of Law, "Living under Drones," 81.
39 Edney-Browne, "The Psychosocial Effects of Drone Violence," 1347.
40 Schuppli, *Material Witness*, 124.
41 Kapadia, *Insurgent Aesthetics*, 69–72.
42 Kapadia, *Insurgent Aesthetics*, 5.
43 Chishty's shadowy drones share some loose affinity with James Bridle's identically named and more well-known *Drone Shadows* (2012–18), in which 1:1 outlines of Reaper and Predator drones are painted onto public spaces in cities such as London and New York, insisting on the return of the presence of the drone to the places that authorize their deployment. Jennifer Rhee provides an excellent critique of the limitations of the politics of identification enacted by Bridle's works, demonstrating how such works rest on an obscur-

ing or forgetting of the racialized subjects of violence within those polities. Rhee, *The Robotic Imaginary*, 144–54.

44 Pakistan's Federally Administered Tribal Areas (FATA) operated under a separate legal and political regime to the rest of Pakistan, which is itself governed by structures inherited from the British colonial era. The securitization of FATA operates in two directions: by the United States and by the Pakistani state. As Madiha Tahir has powerfully argued, this violence (of torture, disappearance, and secrecy) constitutes part of the "distributed American empire," in which the state and military enact their own desires for power and control. Tahir, "The Distributed Empire of the War on Terror."
45 Pugliese, "Death by Metadata."
46 Andrejevic, *Automated Media*, 86.
47 Stanford Law School and NYU School of Law, "Living under Drones," 113.
48 Pugliese, "Drone Casino Mimesis."
49 Stanford Law School and NYU School of Law, "Living under Drones," 74.
50 Pugliese, *Biopolitics of the More-Than-Human*, 191. Pugliese quotes a Yemeni reporter: "Animals died, and the bodies of all those who died were disintegrated and scattered over a large area.... They were all exploded, and we could not identify them, their limbs ripped apart."
51 Da Silva, "No-Bodies"; Pugliese, "Death by Metadata," 11, 15. Of course, life in the Afghanistan-Pakistan borderlands remains much more complex and vibrant than the view through the drone suggests. See Bashir and Crews, *Under the Drones*.
52 Stanford Law School and NYU School of Law, "Living under Drones," 108.
53 Pugliese, *Biopolitics of the More-Than-Human*, 22.
54 See Pugliese, *Biopolitics of the More-Than-Human*, 197.
55 Parks, *Rethinking Media Coverage*, 9.
56 Mirzoeff, *How to See the World*; Greene, "Drone Vision."
57 Stahl, *Through the Crosshairs*, 68.
58 Not all drone witnessing is of aerial assault. In so-called overwatch missions, drone sensors might instead capture the violence of ground combat.
59 Starosielski, *Media Hot & Cold*, 168.
60 Fish, "Blue Governmentality."
61 Herscher, "Surveillant Witnessing."
62 UN News, "'Crimes of Historic Proportions' Being Committed in Aleppo, UN Rights Chief Warns."
63 Kurgan, "Conflict Urbanism, Aleppo," 74.
64 For a detailed reflection on this practice, see Kurgan, *Close up at a Distance*.
65 Weizman, *Forensic Architecture*, 28. The current 0.25m resolutions are for black-and-white imagery, with 1.6m limits on color.
66 Saldarriaga, Kurgan, and Brawley, "Visualizing Conflict," 104.
67 Gil-Fournier and Parikka, "Ground Truth to Fake Geographies."
68 Kurgan, "Conflict Urbanism, Aleppo," 76.

69 Chouliaraki and al-Ghazzy, "Flesh Witnessing."
70 Kaplan, *Aerial Aftermaths*, 8.
71 On drone-human sensoria, see Agostinho, Maurer, and Veel, "Sensorial Experience of the Drone"; Graae and Maurer, *Drone Imaginaries*.
72 Azoulay, "The Natural History of Rape," 167.
73 Azoulay, "The Natural History of Rape," 169.
74 Barnell et al., "Agile Condor."
75 Virilio, *War and Cinema*.
76 Virilio, *War and Cinema*.
77 Virilio, *War and Cinema*.
78 On power and the edge of perception, see Massumi, *Ontopower*.
79 Barnell et al. "Agile Condor," 2015; Barnell et al, "High-Performance Computing," 2018; Isereau et al "Utilizing High-Performance Embedded Computing," 2017.
80 See Halpern, *Beautiful Data*.
81 Andrejevic, *Automated Media*, 38.
82 Bousquet, *The Eye of War*, 12.
83 The Institute of Electrical and Electronics Engineers (IEEE) is an electrical engineering professional organization that runs some of the most important conferences, journals, and magazines for the development of computational and related technologies.
84 SRC Defense, "Agile Condor."
85 Andrejevic, *Automated Media*, 18.
86 Andrejevic, *Automated Media*, 27. Andrejevic describes four distinct modalities of automated media: preemption, operationalism, environmentality, and framelessness.
87 Bousquet, *The Eye of War*, 12.
88 Andrejevic, *Automated Media*, 47.
89 DeLanda, *War in the Age of Intelligent Machines*, 2.
90 DeLanda, *War in the Age of Intelligent Machines*, 3.
91 DeLanda, *War in the Age of Intelligent Machines*, 7.
92 DeLanda, *War in the Age of Intelligent Machines*, 7.
93 DeLanda, *War in the Age of Intelligent Machines*, 46.
94 Packer and Reeves, *Killer Apps*, 14.
95 Whittaker, "The Steep Cost of Capture."
96 Holmqvist, "Undoing War," 551.
97 See Sharkey in Bhuta et al., *Autonomous Weapons Systems*.
98 Packer and Reeves, "The Coming Humanectomy," 266.
99 Amoore, *Cloud Ethics*, 150.
100 Amoore, *Cloud Ethics*, 81.
101 On the relations between autonomous killing and liberal subjectivity, see Atanasoski and Vora, *Surrogate Humanity*.
102 Massumi, "Affective Fact," 53.

103 Andrejevic, *Automated Media*, 86.
104 Suchman, "Algorithmic Warfare and the Reinvention of Accuracy," 10.
105 Asaro, "Algorithms of Violence," 36.
106 Grove, *Savage Ecology*, 221. Elsewhere, Grove calls for a new "grammar" of geopolitics that reckons with the transformative ramifications of technological development, see Grove, "From Geopolitics to Geotechnics."

CHAPTER TWO. WITNESSING ALGORITHMS

1 Manjoo, "I Tried Microsoft's Flight Simulator. The Earth Never Seemed So Real."
2 Chayka, "The Weird Failures of Algorithm-Generated Images." In this vein, Clement Valla's *Postcards from Google Earth* project seeks to expose these strange and often beautiful moments of breakdown in the automated assembly of images. Valla, *Postcards from Google Earth*.
3 See, for example, Amoore and Raley, "Securing with Algorithms"; Bellanova et al., "Critique of Algorithmic Violence"; Noble, *Algorithms of Oppression*; Bucher, *If... Then*; Eubanks, *Automating Inequality*; Sadowski, *Too Smart*; Finn, *What Algorithms Want*; Benjamin, *Race After Technology*; Pasquale, *The Black Box Society*; Rouvroy and Berns, "Algorithmic Governmentality"; McKittrick, *Dear Science*.
4 Finn, *What Algorithms Want*, 5.
5 Machine learning algorithms are trained on data, but also optimized using a range of statistical functions. For example, Google's AlphaGo was optimized using various techniques of Bayesian optimization. Chen et al., "Bayesian Optimization in AlphaGo."
6 Mackenzie, *Machine Learners*.
7 Sadowski, "Potemkin AI."
8 Taffel, "Data and Oil."
9 Pasquale, *The Black Box Society*.
10 On algorithmic violence, see, for example, Bellanova et al., "Critique of Algorithmic Violence"; Safransky, "Geographies of Algorithmic Violence"; O'Malley and Smith, "'Smart' Crime Prevention?"; Asaro, "Algorithms of Violence."
11 Finn, *What Algorithms Want*, 5.
12 Halpern, *Beautiful Data*, 184.
13 Bucher, *If... Then*, 20.
14 Bucher, *If... Then*, 8.
15 Noble, *Algorithms of Oppression*; Phan and Wark, "What Personalisation Can Do for You!"
16 Offert and Phan, "A Sign That Spells."
17 Seaver, "Algorithms as Culture," 5.

18 "In spite of the rational straightforwardness granted to them by critics and advocates, 'algorithms' are tricky objects to know," such that "a determined focus on revealing the operations of algorithms risks taking for granted that they operate clearly in the first place." Seaver, "Algorithms as Culture," 2, 8.
19 Scannell, "What Can an Algorithm Do?"
20 Stark, "Facial Recognition Is the Plutonium of AI."
21 MacKenzie and Munster, "Platform Seeing," 2.
22 MacKenzie and Munster, "Platform Seeing," 8.
23 MacKenzie and Munster, "Platform Seeing," 6.
24 MacKenzie and Munster, "Platform Seeing," 4.
25 MacKenzie and Munster, "Platform Seeing," 3.
26 Amoore, *Cloud Ethics*, 16.
27 Amoore, *Cloud Ethics*, 9.
28 Amoore, *Cloud Ethics*, 135.
29 Amoore, *Cloud Ethics*, 66. Emphasis in the original.
30 Guattari's theorizing of the machine is complex and more nuanced than is necessary to elaborate here. See Guattari, *Chaosmosis*; Guattari, "On Machines."
31 My sincere thanks to one of the anonymous reviewers of the manuscript for the formulation of machinic affect as promiscuous in its adhesiveness.
32 Massumi, *Parables*, 35.
33 On potential, probability, possibility, and algorithmic systems, see Amoore, *Politics of Possibility*.
34 Amoore, *Cloud Ethics*, 109–29.
35 Massumi, *Parables*, 26.
36 Cole, "AI-Assisted Fake Porn."
37 Cole, "AI-Assisted Fake Porn."
38 Goodfellow et al., "Generative Adversarial Networks."
39 In 2017, University of Washington researchers trained a machine learning model to transform video footage of Barack Obama to photorealistically lip-sync to an audio input track. It was a key early indicator of the potential for AI-generated media to mimic real persons, including world leaders. See SyncedReview 2018 for an overview. Since then, concerns over generative AI have exploded. The questions sparked by the Obama lip-sync video take on a different hue in the context of generative models, but their implications are only just beginning to be understood as this book goes into production.
40 Not least, how to think about the knowledge produced in the scientific application of GANs. See Offert, "Latent Deep Space."
41 Maddocks, "'A Deepfake Porn Plot'"; Kikerpill, "Choose Your Stars and Studs"; Nagel, "Verifying Images"; Popova, "Reading out of Context." Samantha Cole has also made the point repeatedly in *Motherboard* that while the political implications of deepfakes have attracted the mainstream headlines,

the videos remain almost exclusively pornographic and targeted at women in practice.
42 Gerstner, "Face/Off"; Kirchengast, "Deepfakes and Image Manipulation"; Maras and Alexandrou, "Determining Authenticity."
43 Chesney and Citron, "Deepfakes and the New Disinformation War," 149. In a similar vein, deepfakes have been articulated as both new forms of "political warfare" and as a critical "multi-level policy challenge" for states. See also, Paterson and Hanley, "Political Warfare in the Digital Age."
44 McCosker, "Making Sense of Deepfakes."
45 Uliasz, "On the Truth Claims of Deepfakes," 25, 27.
46 See, for example, Whyte, "Deepfake News"; Fallis, "Epistemic Threat of Deepfakes"; Rini, "Epistemic Backstop."
47 WITNESS Media Lab, "Synthetic Media and Deepfakes," 15.
48 WITNESS Media Lab, "Synthetic Media and Deepfakes," 18.
49 Chouliaraki and al-Ghazzi, "Flesh Witnessing."
50 Uliasz, "On the Truth Claims of Deepfakes," 37.
51 Sear, "Xenowar."
52 Deleuze, *Cinema 1*; Tomkins, *Shame and Its Sisters*.
53 Anderson, *Technologies of Vision*, 21.
54 Anderson, *Technologies of Vision*, 23.
55 Experts remain divided on which side will win, most major platforms and numerous start-ups are developing detection—although questions remain about who will have access to them and whether they will be usable by people in the Global South. See https://lab.witness.org/backgrounder-deepfakes-in-2020/.
56 Miglio, "AI in Unreal Engine."
57 Pugliese, *Biopolitics of the More-Than-Human*, 15.
58 Weizman, *Forensic Architecture*, 65.
59 Weizman, *Forensic Architecture*, 58.
60 Weizman, *Forensic Architecture*, 58, 82.
61 There is, it should be noted, an increasingly significant domain within machine learning research that aims for "explainable" AI; however, this is far from the norm and contains problems of its own, such as the limited frames within which such systems might be "explained."
62 Amoore, *Cloud Ethics*, 119.
63 Massumi, *Ontopower*, 53.
64 Sontag, *Regarding Pain*; Kozol, *Distant Wars Visible*; Mirzoeff, *The Right to Look*.
65 Google's former CEO Eric Schmidt is a notable proponent of strengthening ties between big tech and the US military. He is the chair of the Defense Innovation Board and reportedly an influential voice in the Biden administration on the advantages of advance technology, often framing its importance with reference to China's capabilities.
66 Department of Defense, "AWCFT Memorandum."

67 Department of Defense, "AWCFT Memorandum."
68 *Bulletin of the Atomic Scientists*, "Project Maven."
69 Johnson, "Influx of Drone Footage."
70 Human Rights Watch, "A Wedding That Became a Funeral."
71 Amoore, *Cloud Ethics*, 128.
72 Amoore, *Cloud Ethics*, 127.
73 GovernmentCIOMedia, "AI to Help Pentagon."
74 See, for example, Mbembe, *Necropolitics*; Wilcox, "Embodying Algorithmic War"; Rhee, *Robotic Imaginary*; Wall and Monahan, "Surveillance and Violence from Afar"; Kapadia, *Insurgent Aesthetics*.
75 Benjamin, *Race after Technology*, 36.
76 Phan and Wark, "Racial Formations," 2.
77 Wilcox, "Embodying Algorithmic War," 21.
78 Bender et al., "On the Dangers of Stochastic Parrots." Coleader of the Ethical AI team Margaret Mitchell was fired a few weeks later, having been vocally and publicly supportive of Gebru and critical of her dismissal.
79 Dencik, et al., "Data Justice."
80 Sadowski, "When Data Is Capital."
81 Holmes, "Google's Off-Limits Data Farm."
82 Within industry and academia, AI ethics have become their own "economy of virtue" in which engagements with ethics and performances around the issue have become powerful currency. See Phan et al., *Economies of Virtue*.
83 OpenAI, "Proximal Policy Optimization."
84 Amoore, *Cloud Ethics*, 23.
85 Glissant, *Poetics*.

CHAPTER THREE. WITNESSING ECOLOGIES

1 Clarke, "Australia Shuts Down Climate Deal."
2 Lyons, "Fiji PM."
3 Westfall, "Australia Ranks Last on Climate Action."
4 DeLoughrey, *Allegories of the Anthropocene*, 25.
5 DeLoughrey, *Allegories of the Anthropocene*, 7.
6 McDonald, *Ecological Security*.
7 Jetñil-Kijiner, "Tell Them."
8 DeLoughrey, *Allegories of the Anthropocene*, 1.
9 DeLoughrey, *Allegories of the Anthropocene*, 5.
10 DeLoughrey, *Allegories of the Anthropocene*, 195.
11 Jetñil-Kijiner, "Tell Them."
12 Daston, "Epistemic Images," 17.
13 Cubitt, *Finite Media*, 4.
14 Fuller, *Media Ecologies*, 17.
15 Grove, *Savage Ecology*, 4.

16 Cubitt, *Finite Media*, 117.
17 Haraway, *Staying with the Trouble*.
18 Cubitt, *Finite Media*, 154.
19 Yusoff, *A Billion Black Anthropocenes*.
20 Turner, *From Counterculture to Cyberculture*.
21 Perhaps most powerfully manifest in the back to the land movement, which tended to be principally pursued by white middle-class youth who imagined a pure nature in which Indigenous people and knowledge was either absent or reduced to readily appropriated totems.
22 Edwards, "Entangled Histories," 34.
23 On the technical processes involved in earth imaging, including the role of satellites, tracking stations, pixels, and analysts, see Russill, "Earth Imaging," 245. In his study of the formation of the climate-monitoring system, Paul N. Edwards shows how the twinned dynamics of making data global (data from one place that could be analyzed in relation to data from elsewhere) and making global data (data about climatic change on a global scale) entailed significant labor, which he calls "data friction." Encompassing everything from adjusting recordings based on known instrument eccentricities to the sheer effort of transcribing handwritten records into digital spreadsheet, the challenge of data friction erodes the promise of bringing immense computational power to bear on climate and environmental analysis. Edwards, *A Vast Machine*. See also Yang et al., "Satellite Remote Sensing in Climate Change Studies"; Kidder and Haar, *Satellite Meteorology*.
24 Parks, *Rethinking Media Coverage*.
25 Russill, "Earth Imaging," 232.
26 Parks, *Cultures in Orbit*; Kurgan, *Close up at a Distance*; Russill, "Is the Earth a Medium?"
27 Russill, "Earth Imaging," 232. The shift toward using a range of datalogical technologies within human rights work, particularly via the emergence of open-source investigation, has necessitated new expertise in these media forms within human rights fields and produced new intermediary organizations, see Ristovska, *Seeing Human Rights*.
28 Furuhata, *Climatic Media*.
29 Weizman, *Forensic Architecture*, 20.
30 Rothe, "Seeing Like a Satellite," 340, 337.
31 Gabrys, *Program Earth*, 11.
32 Guattari, *The Three Ecologies*, 44.
33 Guattari, *The Three Ecologies*, 43.
34 Fuller, *Media Ecologies*, 20.
35 Clark, "Scale," 148.
36 Fuller, *Media Ecologies*, 147.
37 Fuller, *Media Ecologies*, 147.
38 Chakrabarty, "Climate of History," 206–7.

39 Clark, "Scale," 152.
40 Woods, "Scale Critique for the Anthropocene," 138.
41 Alaimo, *Exposed*, 168.
42 Raymond Williams proposed "structures of feeling" as a way of understanding how particular meanings and values are organized into the lived experience of the present. See Williams, *Marxism and Literature*.
43 Zylinska, *Nonhuman Photography*, 37.
44 Woods, "Scale Critique for the Anthropocene."
45 Clark, "Scale," 151.
46 Farrier, *Anthropocene Poetics*, 15.
47 Schankweiler, Straub, and Wendl, *Image Testimonies*; Guerin and Hallas, *The Image and the Witness*; Campt, *Listening to Images*.
48 Zylinska, *Nonhuman Photography*, 81.
49 Peters, "Witnessing," 722.
50 Tsing, "Nonscalability," 505.
51 James, *The Black Jacobins*; Taylor, *Empire of Neglect*; McKittrick, *Dear Science*; Rosenthal, *Accounting for Slavery*.
52 Tsing, "Nonscalability," 510.
53 Whyte, "Environmental Injustice," 125.
54 Nixon, *Slow Violence*.
55 Kaplan, *Climate Trauma*; Richardson, "Climate Trauma."
56 Morton, *Hyperobjects*, 1.
57 While Morton has elsewhere written about the necessity of addressing ecology without the overdetermining of Nature, the irony of their hyberobjects is that they risk replace replacing one problematic enclosure with another. As a theoretical endeavor, the object-oriented ontology movement, of which Morton is a prominent flag-waver, results in something of a political dead end, not least due to its insistence on the primacy of objects and the nonrelationality of existence.
58 On bushfires and their elemental properties, see Neale, Zahara, and Smith, "An Eternal Flame."
59 Massumi, *Ontopower*, 22.
60 Mittmann, "Maralinga."
61 Cited in Barnaby and Holdstock, *British Nuclear Weapons*, 99.
62 Ladd, "Lesser Known History"; Tynan, *Atomic Thunder*.
63 Tynan, "Sixty Years On"; Maralinga Rehabilitation Technical Advisory Committee, "Rehabilitation of Emu and Maralinga."
64 Barnaby and Holdstock, *British Nuclear Weapons*, 102. Authorized by Prime Minister Robert Menzies without cabinet consultation, the tests were overseen by the Atomic Weapons Test Safety Committee. The AWTSC was headed by scientists present at the 1952 trials (Project Hurricane), which was the first atomic bomb tested by the British in Australia (Arnold and Smith, *Britain, Australia, and the Bomb*, 27; Smith, *Clouds of Deceit*, 58). No regard was given to the effects on Indigenous inhabitants.

65 Tynan, "Sixty Years On."
66 Cook et al., "Pu-Bearing Particles at Maralinga."
67 ICAN: International Campaign to Abolish Nuclear Weapons, "Black Mist."
68 Quoted in Mittmann, "Maralinga," 10.
69 McLelland, *Report of the Royal Commission into British Nuclear Tests in Australia*, 574.
70 Cited in Alexis-Martin, "Nuclear Warfare and Weather (Im)Mobilities," 258.
71 Tynan, "What Is Relationality?," 1.
72 According to Moreton-Robinson, "White possessive logics are operationalized within discourses to circulate sets of meanings about ownership of the nation, as part of commonsense knowledge, decision making, and socially produced conventions." Moreton-Robinson, *The White Possessive*, xii.
73 The British government has admitted to using Australian servicemen in radioactivity experiments, ordering them to walk into blast zones after tests. Carter, *British Nuclear Tests in Australia*.
74 Mittmann, "Maralinga," 9.
75 On terra nullius and the cultural and legal logics of colonial possession in Australia, see Moreton-Robinson, *The White Possessive*.
76 Made popular by 1990s antinuclear activism, the term nuclear colonialism "designates contemporary dynamics of colonial exploitation, in which imperial countries militarily occupy and irreversibly pollute the lands and natural resources of communities, far away from their own economic and political centers, in order to further the development of their nuclear technologies." Maurer, "Snaring the Nuclear Sun," 372. See also Endres, "Rhetoric of Nuclear Colonialism"; Endres, "Most Nuclear-Bombed Place"; Edwards, "Nuclear Colonialism."
77 Maurer, "Snaring the Nuclear Sun," 373.
78 Hau'ofa, "Our Sea of Islands."
79 This co-option of Aboriginal language to name military sites was hardly new. The nearby town of Woomera was named for an Aboriginal spear-throwing implement after it was built to facilitate long-range weapons testing in 1947.
80 Hydrogen bombs, or thermonuclear weapons, use a combination of nuclear fission and nuclear fusion, a separate process in which the energy is released through smashing unstable atoms together.
81 Of the first nuclear detonation at White Sands Missile Test Range at Jornada del Muerto desert of New Mexico, Alexis-Martin writes: "This first nuclear weapon detonation marked the dawn of a freshly atomic Anthropocene, creating localized air temperatures so hot that silica sand seared into glassy trinitite, fossilizing the heat of the blast into puzzling." Alexis-Martin, "Nuclear Warfare and Weather (Im)Mobilities," 251.
82 Ray, "Myth of Empty Country," 5.
83 Scarce, Delany, and Australian Centre for Contemporary Art, *Missile Park*, 92.

84 The measure by which an isotopes radioactivity decreases (and the time it takes for it to fully transform into its product atom) is called a half-life. More specifically, it's the time that it takes for one half of the original radioactive isotope to decay. This means that as time passes, each successive half of the remaining radioactive isotope transforms and its level of radioactivity also decreases. If the half-life of an isotope (e.g., Thorium-90) is twenty-four days, it takes twenty-four days for half the isotope to disintegrate; followed by another twenty-four days for half of the remaining half, and so on. Depending on the isotope, the half-life could be years or minutes.
85 Vivian, *Commonplace Witnessing*.
86 Scarce, Delany, and Australian Centre for Contemporary Art, *Missile Park*, 126.
87 Ray, "Myth of Empty Country," 5.
88 Alexis-Martin, "Nuclear Warfare and Weather (Im)Mobilities," 251.
89 Harkin, "Anneal This Breath," 86.
90 Deleuze, *Logic of Sense*, 73.
91 Deleuze, *Pure Immanence*. Among other texts, this book contains the essay "Immanence: A Life...."
92 For more on plural worlds and William James, see Savransky, *Around the Day in Eighty Worlds*.
93 De la Cadena and Blaser, *A World of Many Worlds*.
94 De la Cadena, *Earth Beings*, 5.
95 Deleuze, *Pure Immanence*, 31.
96 Deleuze and Guattari, *A Thousand Plateaus*, 266.
97 Tynan, "What Is Relationality?," 5.
98 Deleuze, *Pure Immanence*, 31.
99 Deleuze, *Pure Immanence*, 31–32.
100 Caruth, *Unclaimed Experience*, 4.
101 Massumi, *Parables*, 35.

CHAPTER FOUR. WITNESSING ABSENCE

1 Kember and Zylinska, *Life after New Media*, 71–72.
2 Farwell, "Media Strategy of ISIS"; Ingram, "Islamic State's Information Warfare."
3 Hoskins and Illingworth, "Inaccessible War," 1.
4 Seigworth and Tiessen, "Mobile Affects."
5 Ahmed, *Cultural Politics of Emotion*, 71–80.
6 Bourke, "Public Beheading Fears."
7 Sparrow, "Plastic Sword."
8 Grusin, *Premediation*, 72.
9 Clery, "Six Handshakes, Then Silence."
10 Wise, "How Crazy Am I?"

11 Christopoulos and Ustinova, "Urgent Hypothesis on Plane MH370 Disappearance."
12 Day and Lury, "New Technologies of the Observer"; Bremner, "Technologies of Uncertainty in the Search for MH370"; Bremner, "Fluid Ontologies."
13 Gabrys, *Program Earth*.
14 Chris Ashton et al., "MH370."
15 See Day and Lury, "New Technologies of the Observer"; Taylor, "Fiction Machines."
16 Edwards, *Closed World*.
17 Scannell, *Television and the Meaning of Live*, 66.
18 Jue, *Wild Blue Media*.
19 Pinchevski, *Transmitted Wounds*, 14.
20 Pinchevski, *Transmitted Wounds*, 15.
21 Cubitt, *Practice of Light*, 2.
22 Berlant, "Feeling Historical," 6.
23 Gibbs, "Panic!"; Gibbs, "Contagious Feelings"; Richardson, "There's Something Going On."
24 Seltzer, "Wound Culture," 3.
25 Atkinson and Richardson, *Traumatic Affect*, 12.
26 Pinchevski, *Transmitted Wounds*, 22.
27 Murphie, "On Being Affected," 24.
28 Massumi, *Parables*, 35.
29 Richardson and Schankweiler, "Affective Witnessing as Theory and Practice."
30 Lapoujade, *William James*.
31 Kaleem, "Death on Facebook."
32 Öhman and Watson, "Are the Dead Taking over Facebook?"
33 Leaver, "Social Media Contradiction."
34 For many, Facebook is a site of testifying to lives lived and to the grief endured by survivors. See Keskinen, Kaunonen, and Aho, "Grief on Facebook."
35 Frosh, *Poetics of Digital Media*, 111.
36 Hogan, "Facebook Data Storage Centers," 11.
37 Brubaker, Hayes, and Dourish, "Beyond the Grave."
38 Gibbs, "Writing and Danger."
39 The very distinction between online and offline is, of course, problematic. "The notion of the offline as real and authentic is a recent invention, corresponding with the rise of the online." Jurgenson, *The Social Photo*, 68.
40 Stiegler, "Anamnesis and Hypomnesis."
41 Chow, *Entanglements*, 19.
42 Thrift, *Non-Representational Theory*, 2.
43 Angerer, *Ecology of Affect*, 24.
44 Manning and Massumi, *Thought in the Act*, 24.
45 Doane, *Cinematic Time*, 225.
46 Manning, *Minor Gesture*, 54.

47 Manning, *Minor Gesture*, 134.
48 Massumi, *Ontopower*, 95.
49 Chow, *Entanglements*, 12.
50 Berlant and Greenwald, "Affect in End Times," 82.
51 Berlant, "The Commons," 393.
52 Berlant, "The Commons," 394.
53 Massumi, *Parables*, 30.
54 Massumi, *Parables*, 98.
55 While the Puutu Kunti Kurrama and Pinikura peoples use the acronym PKKP, they are distinct socioterritorial groups. As their submission to the Joint Standing Committee on Northern Australia inquiry into Juukan Gorge states: "The Puutu Kunti Kurrama people and the Pinikura people are separate peoples with discrete rights and interests in country, though we have some shared laws and customs." Cited in Joint Standing Committee on Northern Australia, "A Way Forward," 2.
56 Joint Standing Committee on Northern Australia, "Never Again," 2.
57 Moreton-Robinson, *The White Possessive*, ix.
58 Wolfe, "Settler Colonialism and the Elimination of the Native."
59 Berlant, *Cruel Optimism*, 1.
60 This positive potential should not be overstated. As Jasbir Puar argues in response to optimistic sloganeering in response to depression and suicide among queer youth, the "tendentious mythologizing that 'it gets better'" after traumatic events obscures and even protects the systemic origins of violent oppression. Puar, "Cost of Getting Better," 149.
61 Manning, *Minor Gesture*, 151.
62 Manning, *Minor Gesture*, 1.
63 Stewart, "Worlding Refrains," 340.

CODA. TOWARD A POLITICS OF NONHUMAN WITNESSING

1 Weston, *Animate Planet*, 33.
2 See Davis, "How a Pandemic Happens."
3 Cubitt, *Finite Media*, 162.
4 Rancière, *Disagreement*.
5 De la Cadena and Blaser, *A World of Many Worlds*, 13. There is also a rich body of literature on pluriversality from both process philosophy and non-Western perspectives that I cannot do justice to here but that interested readers might wish to pursue. For example, Escobar, *Pluriversal Politics*; Escobar, *Designs for the Pluriverse*; Reiter, *Constructing the Pluriverse*; Savransky, *Around the Day in Eighty Worlds*; Yunkaporta, *Sand Talk*.
6 De la Cadena and Blaser, *A World of Many Worlds*, 15.
7 De la Cadena, "Indigenous Cosmologies," 359.
8 De la Cadena, "Indigenous Cosmologies," 345.

9 De la Cadena, "Indigenous Cosmologies," 361.
10 Cubitt, *Finite Media*, 178.
11 Cubitt, *Finite Media*, 177.
12 Glissant, *Poetics*, 62.
13 Glissant, *Poetics*, 62.
14 Glissant, *Poetics*, 191.
15 Glissant, *Poetics*, 190.
16 Glissant, *Poetics*, 160.
17 I am deeply indebted to Andrew Brooks for his wisdom and generous guidance through Glissant.
18 Cubitt, *Finite Media*, 6.
19 De la Cadena, *Earth Beings*.
20 De la Cadena, "Indigenous Cosmologies," 360.
21 "Our proposal is an invitation to think that instead of the sameness that recognition supposes, politics might not start from, nor resolve in ontologically homogeneous grounds. Rather, the grounds of adversarial dispute or of allied agreement would be what we call uncommons." De la Cadena and Blaser, *A World of Many Worlds*, 27.
22 Fuller and Weizman, *Investigative Aesthetics*, 165.

BIBLIOGRAPHY

Abraham, Nicolas, and Maria Torok. *The Shell and the Kernel.* Translated by Nicholas T. Rand. Vol. 1. Chicago: University of Chicago Press, 1994.
Adler, Jonathan E. "Testimony, Trust, Knowing." *Journal of Philosophy* 91, no. 5 (1994): 264–75.
Agamben, Giorgio. *Remnants of Auschwitz: The Witness and the Archive.* Translated by Daniel Heller-Roazen. New York: Zone, 2002.
Agostinho, Daniela, Kathrin Maurer, and Kristin Veel. "Introduction to the Sensorial Experience of the Drone." *Senses and Society* 15, no. 3 (September 2020): 251–58.
Ahmed, Sara. *The Cultural Politics of Emotion.* New York: Routledge, 2004.
Alaimo, Stacy. *Bodily Natures: Science, Environment, and the Material Self.* Bloomington: Indiana University Press, 2010.
Alexis-Martin, Becky. "Nuclear Warfare and Weather (Im)Mobilities: From Mushroom Clouds to Fallout." In *Weather: Spaces, Mobilities and Affects.* New York: Routledge, 2020.
Amazon. "All In: Staying the Course on Our Commitment to Sustainability," 2020. https://sustainability.aboutamazon.com/environment/sustainable-operations/carbon-footprint.
Amoore, Louise. "Algorithmic War: Everyday Geographies of the War on Terror." *Antipode* 41, no. 1 (January 2009): 49–69.
Amoore, Louise. *Cloud Ethics: Algorithms and the Attributes of Ourselves and Others.* Durham, NC: Duke University Press, 2020.

Amoore, Louise. *The Politics of Possibility: Risk and Security Beyond Probability.* Durham, NC: Duke University Press, 2013.

Amoore, Louise, and Rita Raley. "Securing with Algorithms: Knowledge, Decision, Sovereignty." *Security Dialogue* 48, no. 1 (February 2017): 3–10.

Andén-Papadopoulos, Kari. "Citizen Camera-Witnessing: Embodied Political Dissent in the Age of 'Mediated Mass Self-Communication.'" *New Media and Society*, 2013, 753–69.

Andén-Papadopoulos, Kari. "Media Witnessing and the 'Crowd-Sourced Video Revolution.'" *Visual Communication* 12, no. 3 (August 2013): 341–57.

Anderson, Steve F. *Technologies of Vision: The War between Data and Images.* Cambridge, MA: MIT Press, 2017.

Andrejevic, Mark. *Automated Media.* 1st ed. New York: Routledge, 2019.

Angerer, Marie-Luise. *Ecology of Affect: Intensive Milieus and Contingent Encounters.* Translated by Gerrit Jackson. Lüneborg: Meson, 2017.

Arendt, Hannah. *On Violence.* New York: Harcourt, Brace, Jovanovich, 1970.

Arnold, Lorna, and Mark Smith. *Britain, Australia and the Bomb: The Nuclear Tests and Their Aftermath.* 2nd ed. London: Palgrave Macmillan, 2006.

Asaro, Peter. "Algorithms of Violence: Critical Social Perspectives on Autonomous Weapons." *Social Research: An International Quaterly* 86, no. 2 (2019): 20.

Ashton, Chris, Alan Shuster Bruce, Gary Colledge, and Mark Dickinson. "The Search for MH370." *Journal of Navigation* 68 (2015): 1–22.

Atanasoski, Neda, and Kalindi Vora. *Surrogate Humanity: Race, Robots, and the Politics of Technological Futures.* Perverse Modernities. Durham, NC: Duke University Press, 2019.

Atkinson, Meera, and Michael Richardson, eds. *Traumatic Affect.* Newcastle upon Tyne: Cambridge Scholars, 2013.

Azoulay, Ariella. "The Natural History of Rape." *Journal of Visual Culture* 17, no. 2 (August 2018): 166–76.

Ballard, Su. "'And They Are like Wild Beasts': Violent Things in the Anthropocene." *Fibreculture* 226 (2019). https://thirty.fibreculturejournal.org/fcj-226-and-they-are-like-wild-beasts-violent-things-in-the-anthropocene/.

Ballengee, Jennifer R. *The Wound and the Witness: The Rhetoric of Torture.* New York: State University of New York Press, 2009.

Barad, Karen. "Posthumanist Performativity: Toward an Understanding of How Matter Comes to Matter." *Signs: Journal of Women in Culture and Society* 28, no. 3 (March 2003): 801–31.

Barnaby, Frank, and Douglas Holdstock. *The British Nuclear Weapons Programme, 1952–2002.* London: Routledge, 2004.

Barnell, Mark, Courtney Raymond, Christopher Capraro, et al. "Agile Condor: A Scalable High Performance Embedded Computing Architecture." Waltham, MA: 2015 IEEE High Performance Extreme Computing Conference (September 2015): pp. 1–5. https://doi.org/10.1109/HPEC.2015.7322447.

Barnell, Mark, Courtney Raymond, Chris Capraro, Darrek Isereau, Chris Cicotta, and Nathan Stokes. "High-Performance Computing (HPC) and Machine Learning Demonstrated in Flight Using Agile Condor®." Waltham, MA: 2018 IEEE High Performance Extreme Computing Conference (September 2018): 1–4. https://doi.org/10.1109/HPEC.2018.8547797.

Bashir, Shazad, and Robert D. Crews. *Under the Drones: Modern Lives in the Afghanistan-Pakistan Borderlands*. Cambridge, MA: Harvard University Press, 2012.

Bellanova, Rocco, Kristina Irion, Katja Lindskov Jacobsen, Francesco Ragazzi, Rune Saugmann, and Lucy Suchman. "Toward a Critique of Algorithmic Violence." *International Political Sociology* 15, no. 1 (2021): 121–50.

Bender, Emily M., Timnit Gebru, Angelina McMillan-Major, and Shmargaret Shmitchell. "On the Dangers of Stochastic Parrots: Can Language Models Be Too Big?" In *Proceedings of the 2021 ACM Conference on Fairness, Accountability, and Transparency*, 610–23. FAccT '21. New York: Association for Computing Machinery, 2021.

Benjamin, Ruha. *Race after Technology: Abolitionist Tools for the New Jim Code*. Medford, MA: Polity, 2019.

Bennett, Jane. *Vibrant Matter: A Political Ecology of Things*. Durham, NC: Duke University Press, 2010.

Berlant, Lauren. "The Commons: Infrastructures for Troubling Times." *Environment and Planning D: Society and Space* 34, no. 3 (2016): 393–419.

Berlant, Lauren. *Cruel Optimism*. Durham, NC: Duke University Press, 2011.

Berlant, Lauren. "Thinking about Feeling Historical." *Emotion, Space and Society* 1, no. 1 (2008): 4–9.

Berlant, Lauren, and Jordan Greenwald. "Affect in the End Times: A Conversation with Lauren Berlant." *Qui Parle* 20 (2012): 71–89.

Bhuta, Nehal, Susanne Beck, Robin Geiβ, Hin-Yan Liu, and Claus Kreβ, eds. *Autonomous Weapons Systems: Law, Ethics, Policy*. Cambridge: Cambridge University Press, 2016.

Boltanski, Luc. *Distant Suffering: Morality, Media and Politics*. Cambridge: Cambridge University Press, 1999.

Bourke, Latika. "Public Beheading Fears: Tony Abbott Confirms Police Believed Terrorists Planned 'Demonstration Killings.'" *Sydney Morning Herald*, September 18, 2014. https://www.smh.com.au/politics/federal/public-beheading-fears-tony-abbott-confirms-police-believed-terrorists-planned-demonstration-killings-20140918-10ilyq.html.

Bousquet, Antoine. *The Eye of War: Military Perception from the Telescope to the Drone*. Minneapolis: University of Minnesota Press, 2018.

Bousquet, Antoine. *The Scientific Way of Warfare: Order and Chaos on the Battlefields of Modernity*. New York: Columbia University Press, 2009.

Bousquet, Antoine, Jairus Grove, and Nisha Shah. "Becoming War: Towards a Martial Empiricism." *Security Dialogue* 51, nos. 2–3 (2020): 99–128.

Bräunert, Svea, and Meredith Malone. *To See without Being Seen: Contemporary Art and Drone Warfare*. Saint Louis, MO: Mildred Lane Kemper Art Museum, 2016.

Bremner, Lindsay. "Fluid Ontologies in the Search for MH370." *Journal of the Indian Ocean Region* 11 (2015): 8–29.

Bremner, Lindsay. "Technologies of Uncertainty in the Search for MH370." In *Art in the Anthropocene: Encounters among Aesthetics, Politics, Environments and Epistemologies*, edited by Heather Davis and Etienne Turpin. London: Open Humanities, 2015.

Browne, Simone. *Dark Matters: On the Surveillance of Blackness*. Durham, NC: Duke University Press, 2015.

Brubaker, Jed R., Gillian R. Hayes, and Paul Dourish. "Beyond the Grave: Facebook as a Site for the Expansion of Death and Mourning." *Information Society* 29 (2013): 152–63.

Bucher, Taina. *If... Then: Algorithmic Power and Politics*. Oxford Studies in Digital Politics. New York: Oxford University Press, 2018.

Bulletin of the Atomic Scientists. "Project Maven Brings AI to the Fight against ISIS." December 21, 2017. https://thebulletin.org/2017/12/project-maven-brings-ai-to-the-fight-against-isis/.

Butler, Judith. *Precarious Life: The Powers of Mourning and Violence*. New York: Verso, 2004.

Campt, Tina. *Listening to Images*. Durham, NC: Duke University Press, 2017.

Carter, Michael. *Australian Participants in British Nuclear Tests in Australia*. Canberra: Department of Veterans' Affairs, 2006. https://www.dva.gov.au/sites/default/files/dosimetry_complete_study_1.pdf.

Caruth, Cathy. *Unclaimed Experience: Trauma, Narrative, and History*. Baltimore: Johns Hopkins University Press, 1996.

Chakrabarty, Dipesh. "The Climate of History: Four Theses." *Critical Inquiry* 35, no. 2 (Winter 2009): 197–222.

Chamayou, Grégoire. *Drone Theory*. Translated by Janet Lloyd. London: Penguin, 2015.

Chandler, Katherine. *Unmanning: How Humans, Machines and Media Perform Drone Warfare*. War Culture. New Brunswick, NJ: Rutgers University Press, 2020.

Chayka, Kyle. "The Weird Failures of Algorithm-Generated Images." *Slate*, August 28, 2020. https://slate.com/technology/2020/08/uncanniness-of-algorithmic-style.html.

Chen, Yutian, Aja Huang, Ziyu Wang, Ioannis Antonoglou, Julian Schrittwieser, David Silver, and Nando de Freitas. "Bayesian Optimization in AlphaGo." ArXiv, arXiv:1812.06855 (December 2018). https://arxiv.org/abs/1812.06855v1.

Chesney, Robert, and Danielle Citron. "Deepfakes and the New Disinformation War: The Coming Age of Post-truth Geopolitics." *Foreign Affairs* 98, no. 1 (2019): 147–55.

Chouliaraki, Lilie. "Digital Witnessing in Conflict Zones: The Politics of Remediation." *Information, Communication and Society* 18, no. 11 (2015): 1362–77.

Chouliaraki, Lilie. *The Spectatorship of Suffering*. London: SAGE, 2006.

Chouliaraki, Lilie, and Omar al-Ghazzi. "Beyond News Verification: Flesh Witnessing and the Significance of Embodiment in Conflict News." *Journalism* 23, no. 3 (2022): 649–67.

Chow, Rey. *Entanglements, or Transmedial Thinking about Capture*. Durham, NC: Duke University Press, 2012.

Chow, Rey. *The Age of the World Target: Self-Referentiality in War, Theory, and Comparative Work*. Durham, NC: Duke University Press, 2006.

Christopoulos, Demetris T., and Galina K. Ustinova. "Urgent Hypothesis on Plane MH370 Disappearance." ResearchGate, 2014.

Clark, Timothy. "Scale." In *Theory in the Era of Climate Change*. Vol. 1, edited by Tom Cohen, 148–66. Ann Arbor, MI: Open Humanities, 2012.

Clarke, Melissa. "Australia Shuts down Climate Deal after Discussions Reduce Tongan PM to Tears." ABC News, August 15, 2019. https://www.abc.net.au/news/2019-08-15/no-endorsements-come-out-of-tuvalu-declaration/11419342.

Clery, Daniel. "Six Handshakes, Then Silence." *Science* 344 (May 2014): 964–65. https://www.science.org/doi/10.1126/science.344.6187.964.

Clough, Patricia Ticineto. *The Affective Turn: Theorizing the Social*. Durham, NC: Duke University Press, 2007.

Coady, C. A. J. *Testimony: A Philosophical Study*. Oxford: Oxford University Press, 1994.

Cockburn, Andrew. *Kill Chain: Drones and the Rise of High-Tech Assassins*. New York: Verso, 2015.

Cole, Samantha. "AI-Assisted Fake Porn Is Here and We're All Fucked." *Vice*, December 17, 2017. https://www.vice.com/en_us/article/gydydm/gal-gadot-fake-ai-porn.

Cook, Megan, Barbara Etschmann, Rahul Ram, Konstantin Ignatyev, Gediminas Gervinskas, Steven D. Conradson, Susan Cumberland, Vanessa N. L. Wong, and Joël Brugger. "The Nature of Pu-Bearing Particles from the Maralinga Nuclear Testing Site, Australia." *Scientific Reports* 11, no. 1 (2021): 10698.

Cowen, Deborah. *The Deadly Life of Logistics*. Minneapolis: University of Minnesota Press, 2014.

Cubitt, Sean. *Finite Media: Environmental Implications of Digital Technologies*. Durham, NC: Duke University Press, 2017.

Cubitt, Sean. *The Practice of Light: A Genealogy of Visual Technologies from Prints to Pixels*. Leonardo Book Series. Cambridge, MA: MIT Press, 2014.

Danchev, Alex. "Bug Splat: The Art of the Drone." *International Affairs* 92, no. 3 (2016): 703–13.

Das, Veena, Arthur Kleinman, Mamphela Ramphele, and Pamela Reynolds. *Violence and Subjectivity*. Berkeley: University of California Press, 2000.

da Silva, Denise Ferreira. "No-Bodies." *Griffith Law Review* 18, no. 2 (2009): 212–36.

Daston, Lorraine. "Epistemic Images." In *Vision and Its Instruments: Art, Science, and Technology in Early Modern Europe*, edited by A. Payne, 13–35. University Park: Pennsylvania State University Press, 2015.

Daston, Lorraine, and Peter Galison. *Objectivity*. New York: Zone, 2007.

Davis, Heather, and Zoe Todd. "On the Importance of a Date, or, Decolonizing the Anthropocene." *ACME: An International Journal for Critical Geographies* 16, no. 4 (2017): 761–80.

Davis, Mike. "How a Pandemic Happens: We Knew This Was Coming." *Literary Hub*, May 18, 2020. https://lithub.com/how-a-pandemic-happens-we-knew-this-was-coming/.

Dawes, James. *That the World May Know: Bearing Witness to Atrocity*. Cambridge, MA: Harvard University Press, 2007.

Day, Sophie, and Celia Lury. "New Technologies of the Observer: #BringBack, Visualization and Disappearance." *Theory, Culture and Society* 34, nos. 7–8 (2017): 51–74.

de la Cadena, Marisol. *Earth Beings: Ecologies of Practice across Andean Worlds*. Durham, NC: Duke University Press, 2015.

de la Cadena, Marisol. "Indigenous Cosmopolitics in the Andes: Conceptual Reflections beyond 'Politics.'" *Cultural Anthropology* 25, no. 2 (2010): 334–70.

de la Cadena, Marisol. "Uncommoning Nature: Stories from the Anthropo-Not-Seen." In *Anthropos and the Material*, edited by Penny Harvey, Christian Krohn-Hansen, and Knut G. Nustad, 35–58. Durham, NC: Duke University Press, 2019.

de la Cadena, Marisol, and Mario Blaser, eds. *A World of Many Worlds*. Durham, NC: Duke University Press, 2018.

DeLanda, Manuel. *War in the Age of Intelligent Machines*. New York: Zone, 1991.

Deleuze, Gilles. *Cinema 1: The Movement-Image*. Translated by Hugh Tomlinson and Barbara Habberjam. London: Continuum, 2005.

Deleuze, Gilles. "Ethology: Spinoza and Us." In *Incorporations*, edited by Jonathan Crary and Sanford Kwinter, translated by Robert Hurley, 625–33. New York: Zone, 1992.

Deleuze, Gilles. *The Logic of Sense*. New York: Columbia University Press, 1990.

Deleuze, Gilles. *Pure Immanence: Essays on a Life*. Translated by Anne Boyman. Cambridge, MA: Zone, 2001.

Deleuze, Gilles, and Félix Guattari. *A Thousand Plateaus: Capitalism and Schizophrenia*. Translated by Brian Massumi. Minneapolis: University of Minnesota Press, 1987.

DeLoughrey, Elizabeth M. *Allegories of the Anthropocene*. Durham, NC: Duke University Press, 2019.

Demos, T. J. *Against the Anthropocene: Visual Culture and Environment Today*. Berlin: Sternberg, 2017.

Dencik, Lina, Arne Hintz, and Jonathan Cable. "Towards Data Justice? The Ambiguity of Anti-surveillance Resistance in Political Activism." *Big*

Data and Society 3, no. 2 (July–December 2016). https://doi.org/10.1177/2053951716679678.

Department of Defense. "Memorandum for the Establishment of an Algorithmic Warfare Cross-functional Team (Project Maven)," April 26, 2017. https://www.govexec.com/media/gbc/docs/pdfs_edit/establishment_of_the_awcft_project_maven.pdf.

Doane, Mary Ann. *The Emergence of Cinematic Time: Modernity, Contingency, the Archive*. Cambridge, MA: Harvard University Press, 2002.

Dorrian, Mark. "Drone Semiosis." *Cabinet*, no. 54 (2014): 48–55.

DuBois, Page. *Torture and Truth*. New York: Routledge, 1991.

Easterling, Keller. *Extrastatecraft: The Power of Infrastructure Space*. New York: Verso, 2014.

Edney-Browne, Alex. "The Psychosocial Effects of Drone Violence: Social Isolation, Self-Objectification, and Depoliticization." *Political Psychology* 40, no. 6 (2019): 1341–56.

Edwards, Nelta. "Nuclear Colonialism and the Social Construction of Landscape in Alaska." *Environmental Justice* 4, no. 2 (2011): 109–14.

Edwards, Paul N. *The Closed World: Computers and the Politics of Discourse in Cold War America*. Cambridge, MA: MIT Press, 1996.

Edwards, Paul N. "Entangled Histories: Climate Science and Nuclear Weapons Research." *Bulletin of the Atomic Scientists* 68, no. 4 (2012): 28–40.

Edwards, Paul N. *A Vast Machine: Computer Models, Climate Data, and the Politics of Global Warming*. Cambridge, MA: MIT Press, 2010.

Endres, Danielle. "The Most Nuclear-Bombed Place: Ecological Implications of the US Nuclear Testing Program." In *Tracing Rhetoric and Material Life*, edited by Bridie McGreavy, Justine Wells, George F. McHendry, and Samantha Senda-Cook, 253–87. London: Palgrave Macmillan, 2018.

Endres, Danielle. "The Rhetoric of Nuclear Colonialism: Rhetorical Exclusion of American Indian Arguments in the Yucca Mountain Nuclear Waste Siting Decision." *Communication and Critical/Cultural Studies* 6, no. 1 (2009): 39–60.

Escobar, Arturo. *Designs for the Pluriverse: Radical Interdependence, Autonomy, and the Making of Worlds*. New Ecologies for the Twenty-First Century. Durham, NC: Duke University Press, 2018.

Escobar, Arturo. *Pluriversal Politics: The Real and the Possible*. Latin America in Translation. Durham, NC: Duke University Press, 2020.

Estes, Nick. *Our History Is the Future: Standing Rock versus the Dakota Access Pipeline, and the Long Tradition of Indigenous Resistance*. New York: Verso, 2019.

Ettinger, Bracha. *The Matrixial Borderspace*. Minneapolis: University of Minnesota Press, 2006.

Eubanks, Virginia. *Automating Inequality: How High-Tech Tools Profile, Police, and Punish the Poor*. New York: St. Martin's, 2018.

Fallis, Don. "The Epistemic Threat of Deepfakes." *Philosophy and Technology* 34, no. 4 (December 2021): 623–43. https://doi.org/10.1007/s13347-020-00419-2.

Farmer, Paul. "An Anthropology of Structural Violence." *Current Anthropology* 45, no. 3 (2004): 305–25.

Farrier, David. *Anthropocene Poetics: Deep Time, Sacrifice Zones, and Extinction*. Minneapolis: University of Minnesota Press, 2019.

Farwell, James P. "The Media Strategy of ISIS." *Survival* 56 (2014): 49–55.

Fassin, Didier. "The Humanitarian Politics of Testimony: Subjectification through Trauma in the Israeli Palestinian Conflict." *Cultural Anthropology* 23, no. 3 (2008): 531–58.

Felman, Shoshana, and Dori Laub. *Testimony: Crises of Witnessing in Literature, Psychoanalysis, and History*. New York: Routledge, 1992.

Finn, Ed. *What Algorithms Want: Imagination in the Age of Computing*. Cambridge, MA: MIT Press, 2017.

Fish, Adam. "Blue Governmentality: Elemental Activism with Conservation Technologies on Plundered Seas." *Political Geography* 93 (2022): 102528.

Frosh, Paul. *The Poetics of Digital Media*. Cambridge: Polity, 2019.

Frosh, Paul, and Amit Pinchevski. "Introduction: Why Media Witnessing? Why Now?" In *Media Witnessing: Testimony in the Age of Mass Communication*, edited by Paul Frosh and Amit Pinchevski, 1–19. Basingstoke, UK: Palgrave Macmillan, 2009.

Frosh, Paul, and Amit Pinchevski. *Media Witnessing: Testimony in the Age of Mass Communication*. Basingstoke, UK: Palgrave Macmillan, 2009.

Fuller, Matthew. *Media Ecologies: Materialist Energies in Art and Technoculture*. Leonardo. Cambridge, MA: MIT Press, 2005.

Fuller, Matthew, and Eyal Weizman. *Investigative Aesthetics: Conflicts and Commons in the Politics of Truth*. New York: Verso, 2021.

Furuhata, Yuriko. *Climatic Media: Transpacific Experiments in Atmospheric Control*. Elements. Durham, NC: Duke University Press, 2022.

Furuhata, Yuriko. "Multimedia Environments and Security Operations: Expo '70 as a Laboratory of Governance." *Grey Room* 54 (2014): 56–79.

Gabrys, Jennifer. *Program Earth: Environmental Sensing Technology and the Making of a Computational Planet*. Minneapolis: University of Minnesota Press, 2016.

Geoghegan, Bernard Dionysius. "An Ecology of Operations: Vigilance, Radar, and the Birth of the Computer Screen." *Representations* 147, no. 1 (2019): 59–95.

Gerstner, Erik. "Face/Off: DeepFake Face Swaps and Privacy Laws." *Defense Counsel Journal* 87, no. 1 (2020): 1–14.

Gibbs, Anna. "Contagious Feelings: Pauline Hanson and the Epidemiology of Affect." *Australian Humanities Review* 24 (2001). https://australianhumanitiesreview.org/2001/12/01/contagious-feelings-pauline-hanson-and-the-epidemiology-of-affect/.

Gibbs, Anna. "Panic! Affect Contagion, Mimesis and Suggestion in the Social Field." *Cultural Studies Review* 14 (2008): 130–45.

Gibbs, Anna. "Writing and Danger: The Intercorporeality of Affect." In *Creative Writing: Theory beyond Practice*, edited by Tess Brody and Nigel Krauth, 157–67. Tenerife, QLD: Post Pressed, 2006.

Gil-Fournier, Abelardo, and Jussi Parikka. "Ground Truth to Fake Geographies: Machine Vision and Learning in Visual Practices." *AI and Society* 36 (2020): 1253–62.

Gilmore, Ruth Wilson. *Golden Gulag: Prisons, Surplus, Crisis, and Opposition in Globalizing California*. Berkeley: University of California Press, 2007.

Givoni, Michal. *The Care of the Witness: A Contemporary History of Testimony in Crises*. Human Rights in History. Cambridge: Cambridge University Press, 2016.

Givoni, Michal. "Witnessing/Testimony." *Mafte'akh* 11, no. 2 (2011): 147–69.

Glissant, Édouard. *Poetics of Relation*. Translated by Betsy Wing. Ann Arbor: University of Michigan Press, 1997.

Goodfellow, Ian J., Jean Pouget-Abadie, Mehdi Mirza, Bing Xu, David Warde-Farley, Sherjil Ozair, Aaron Courville, and Yoshua Bengio. "Generative Adversarial Networks." ArXiv, arXiv:1406.2661 (June 2014). https://doi.org/10.48550/arXiv.1406.2661.

GovernmentCIOMedia. "AI to Help Pentagon Prep for Algorithmic Warfare." June 11, 2016. https://governmentciomedia.com/ai-help-pentagon-prep-algorithmic-warfare.

Graae, Andreas Immanuel, and Kathrin Maurer, eds. *Drone Imaginaries: The Power of Remote Vision*. Manchester: Manchester University Press, 2021.

Gray, Jonathan. "Data Witnessing: Attending to Injustice with Data in Amnesty International's Decoders Project." *Information, Communication, and Society* 22, no. 7 (2019): 971–91.

Grayson, Kyle, and Jocelyn Mawdsley. "Scopic Regimes and the Visual Turn in International Relations: Seeing World Politics through the Drone." *European Journal of International Relations* 25, no. 2 (2018).

Greene, Daniel. "Drone Vision." *Surveillance and Society* 13, no. 2 (2015): 233–49.

Greenpeace. "Clicking Clean Virginia: The Dirty Energy Powering Data Center Alley," February 13, 2019. https://www.greenpeace.org/usa/reports/click-clean-virginia/.

Gregg, Melissa, and Gregory J. Seigworth. *The Affect Theory Reader*. Durham, NC: Duke University Press, 2010.

Gregory, Derek. "From a View to a Kill: Drones and Late Modern War." *Theory, Culture and Society* 28, nos. 7–8 (2011): 188–215.

Gregory, Derek. "Under Afghan Skies (1)." Geographical Imaginations. March 27, 2020. https://geographicalimaginations.com/2020/03/27/under-afghan-skies-1/.

Gregory, Derek. "Under Afghan Skies (2)." Geographical Imaginations. April 1, 2020. https://geographicalimaginations.com/2020/03/31/under-afghan-skies-2/.

Gregory, Derek. "Under Afghan Skies (3)." Geographical Imaginations. April 3, 2020. https://geographicalimaginations.com/2020/04/03/under-afghan-skies-3/.

Grove, Jairus. "From Geopolitics to Geotechnics: Global Futures in the Shadow of Automation, Cunning Machines, and Human Speciation." *International Relations* 34, no. 3 (2020): 432–55.

Grove, Jairus Victor. *Savage Ecology: War and Geopolitics at the End of the World*. Durham, NC: Duke University Press, 2019.

Grusin, Richard. "Introduction." In *The Nonhuman Turn*, edited by Richard Grusin, vii–xxix. Minneapolis: University of Minnesota Press, 2015.

Grusin, Richard. *Premediation: Affect and Mediality after 9/11*. New York: Palgrave Macmillan, 2010.

Guattari, Félix. *Chaosmosis: An Ethico-Aesthetic Paradigm*. Translated by Paul Bains and Julian Pefanis. Bloomington: Indiana University Press, 1995.

Guattari, Félix. "On Machines." *Journal of Philosophy and the Visual Arts* 6 (1995): 8–12.

Guattari, Félix. *The Three Ecologies*. New York: Continuum, 2005.

Guerin, Frances, and Roger Hallas. *The Image and the Witness: Trauma, Memory and Visual Culture*. London: Wallflower, 2007.

Halpern, Orit. *Beautiful Data: A History of Vision and Reason since 1945*. Durham, NC: Duke University Press, 2015.

Haraway, Donna. "Anthropocene, Capitalocene, Plantationocene, Chthulucene: Making Kin." *Environmental Humanities* 6, no. 1 (2015): 159–65.

Haraway, Donna. *Modest−Witness@Second−Millennium.FemaleMan−Meets−OncoMouse™: Feminism and Technoscience*. New York: Routledge, 1997.

Haraway, Donna. "Situated Knowledges: The Science Question in Feminism and the Privilege of Partial Perspective." *Feminist Studies* 14, no. 3 (1988): 575–99.

Haraway, Donna. *Staying with the Trouble: Making Kin in the Chthulucene*. Experimental Futures. Durham, NC: Duke University Press, 2016.

Hardwig, John. "The Role of Trust in Knowledge." *Journal of Philosophy* 88, no. 12 (1991): 693–708.

Harkin, Natalie. "Anneal This Breath." In *Missile Park*, edited by Australian Centre for Contemporary Art, 86–87, 2021.

Hartman, Saidiya V. *Scenes of Subjection: Terror, Slavery, and Self-Making in Nineteenth-Century America*. New York: Oxford University Press, 2010.

Hau'ofa, Epeli. "Our Sea of Islands." *Contemporary Pacific* 6, no. 1 (1994): 147–61.

Herscher, Andrew. "Surveillant Witnessing: Satellite Imagery and the Visual Politics of Human Rights." *Public Culture* 26, no. 3 (74) (2014): 469–500.

Hogan, Mél. "Facebook Data Storage Centers as the Archive's Underbelly." *Television and New Media* 16, no. 1 (2015): 3–18.

Hogan, Mél, and Asta Vonderau. "The Nature of Data Centers." *Culture Machine* 19 (2019). https://culturemachine.net/vol-18-the-nature-of-data-centers/the-nature-of-data-centers/.

Holmes, Kevin. "An Artist and a Helicopter Capture Google's Off-Limits Data Farm." *Vice*, February 14, 2015. https://www.vice.com/en/article/aen3xk/artist-and-helicopter-capture-off-limits-data-farm.

Holmqvist, Caroline. "Undoing War: War Ontologies and the Materiality of Drone Warfare." *Millennium* 41, no. 3 (2013): 535–52.

Hoskins, Andrew, and Shona Illingworth. "Inaccessible War: Media, Memory, Trauma and the Blueprint." *Digital War* 1 (2020): 74–82.

Human Rights Watch. "A Wedding That Became a Funeral: US Drone Attack on Marriage Procession in Yemen." Human Rights Watch, February 19, 2014. https://www.hrw.org/report/2014/02/19/wedding-became-funeral/us-drone-attack-marriage-procession-yemen.

ICAN: International Campaign to Abolish Nuclear Weapons. "Black Mist: The Impact of Nuclear Weapons on Australia," January 2014. https://icanw.org.au/wp-content/uploads/BlackMist-FINAL-Web.pdf.

Ingram, Haroro J. "Three Traits of the Islamic State's Information Warfare." *RUSI Journal* 159 (2014): 4–11.

Isereau, Darrek, et al. "Utilizing High-Performance Embedded Computing, Agile Condor, for Intelligent Processing: An Artificial Intelligence Platform for Remotely Piloted Aircraft." London: 2017 Intelligent Systems Conference (IntelliSys) (September 2017): 1155–59. https://doi.org/10.1109/IntelliSys.2017.8324277.

Jackson, Zakiyyah Iman. "Animal: New Directions in the Theorization of Race and Posthumanism." *Feminist Studies* 39, no. 3 (2013): 669–85.

Jackson, Zakiyyah Iman. "Outer Worlds: The Persistence of Race in Movement 'Beyond the Human.'" *GLQ: A Journal of Lesbian and Gay Studies* 21, no. 2 (2015): 215–18.

James, C. L. R. *The Black Jacobins: Toussaint l'Ouverture and the San Domingo Revolution*. 2nd ed., rev. New York: Vintage, 1989.

Jetñil-Kijiner, Kathy. "Tell Them." 2011. https://jkijiner.wordpress.com/2011/04/13/tell-them/.

Johnson, Ted. "To Handle Its Influx of Drone Footage, Military Should Teach AI to Watch TV." *Wired*, November 26, 2017. https://www.wired.com/story/the-military-should-teach-ai-to-watch-drone-footage/.

Joint Standing Committee on Northern Australia. "Never Again: Interim Report into the Destruction of Indigenous Heritage Sites at Juukan Gorge." Canberra: Parliament of the Commonwealth of Australia, December 2020.

Joint Standing Committee on Northern Australia. "A Way Forward: Final Report into the Destruction of Indigenous Heritage Sites at Juukan Gorge." Canberra: Parliament of the Commonwealth of Australia, October 2021.

Jue, Melody. *Wild Blue Media: Thinking through Seawater*. Elements. Durham, NC: Duke University Press, 2020.

Jurgenson, Nathan. *The Social Photo: On Photography and Social Media*. New York: Verso, 2019.

Kaleem, Jaweed. "Death on Facebook Now Common as 'Dead Profiles' Create Vast Virtual Cemetery." *Huffington Post*, October 1, 2015. https://www.huffpost.com/entry/death-facebook-dead-profiles_n_2245397.

Kapadia, Ronak K. *Insurgent Aesthetics: Security and the Queer Life of the Forever War*. Durham, NC: Duke University Press, 2020.

Kaplan, Caren. *Aerial Aftermaths: Wartime from Above*. Durham, NC: Duke University Press, 2018.

Kaplan, Caren. "Drone-o-Rama: Troubling the Spatial and Temporal Logics of Distance Warfare." In *Life in the Age of Drone Warfare*, edited by Lisa Parks and Caren Kaplan, 161–77. Durham, NC: Duke University Press, 2017.

Kaplan, Caren. "Drones and the Image Complex: The Limits of Representation in the Era of Distance Warfare." In *Mediating the Spatiality of Conflicts: International Conference Proceedings*, edited by Armina Pilav, Marc Schoonderbeek, Heidi Sohn, and Aleksandar Staničić, 29–43. Delft, Netherlands: BK, 2020.

Kaplan, E. Ann. *Climate Trauma: Foreseeing the Future in Dystopian Film and Fiction*. New Brunswick, NJ: Rutgers University Press, 2016.

Kaplan, E. Ann. *Trauma Culture: The Politics of Terror and Loss in Media and Literature*. New Brunswick, NJ: Rutgers University Press, 2005.

Kelley, Robin D. G. "What Did Cedric Robinson Mean by Racial Capitalism?" *Boston Review*, January 12, 2017. https://bostonreview.net/race/robin-d-g-kelley-what-did-cedric-robinson-mean-racial-capitalism.

Kember, Sarah, and Joanna Zylinska. *Life after New Media: Mediation as a Vital Process*. Cambridge, MA: MIT Press, 2012.

Keskinen, Niina, Marja Kaunonen, and Anna Liisa Aho. "How Loved Ones Express Grief after the Death of a Child by Sharing Photographs on Facebook." *Journal of Loss and Trauma* 24, no. 7 (2019): 609–24.

Khalili, Laleh. *Sinews of War and Trade: Shipping and Capitalism in the Arabian Peninsula*. New York: Verso, 2020.

Kidder, Stanley Q., and Thomas H. Vonder Haar. *Satellite Meteorology: An Introduction*. Cambridge, MA: Academic Press, 1995.

Kikerpill, Kristjan. "Choose Your Stars and Studs: The Rise of Deepfake Designer Porn." *Porn Studies* 7 no. 4 (2020): 1–5.

Kirchengast, Tyrone. "Deepfakes and Image Manipulation: Criminalisation and Control." *Information and Communications Technology Law* 29, no. 3 (2020): 308–23.

Kozol, Wendy. *Distant Wars Visible: The Ambivalence of Witnessing*. Minneapolis: University of Minnesota Press, 2014.

Kurgan, Laura. *Close up at a Distance: Mapping, Technology, and Politics*. New York: Zone, 2013.

Kurgan, Laura. "Conflict Urbanism, Aleppo: Mapping Urban Damage." *Architectural Design* 87, no. 1 (2017): 72–77.

LaCapra, Dominick. *Representing the Holocaust: History, Theory, Trauma*. Ithaca, NY: Cornell University Press, 1994.

LaCapra, Dominick. *Writing History, Writing Trauma*. Baltimore: Johns Hopkins University Press, 2001.

Ladd, Mike. "The Lesser Known History of the Maralinga Nuclear Tests—and What It's like to Stand at Ground Zero." *Australian Broadcasting Corporation*, March 24, 2020. https://www.abc.net.au/news/2020-03-24/maralinga-nuclear-tests-ground-zero-lesser-known-history/11882608.

Langbein, John. *Torture and the Law of Proof*. Chicago: University of Chicago Press, 1977.

Lapoujade, David. *William James, Empiricism and Pragmatism*. Translated by Thomas LaMarre. Thought in the Act. Durham, NC: Duke University Press, 2020.

Leaver, Tama. "The Social Media Contradiction: Data Mining and Digital Death." *M/C Journal* 16 (2013). https://journal.media-culture.org.au/index.php/mcjournal/article/view/625.

Liu, Cixin. *Death's End*. Bk. 3 of *The Three-Body Problem*, Translated by Ken Liu. London: Head of Zeus, 2016.

Luciano, Dana, and Mel Y. Chen. "Has the Queer Ever Been Human?" *GLQ: A Journal of Lesbian and Gay Studies* 21, nos. 2–3 (2015): 183–207.

Lyons, Kate. "Fiji PM Accuses Scott Morrison of 'Insulting' and Alienating Pacific Leaders." *Guardian*, August 17, 2019. https://www.theguardian.com/world/2019/aug/16/fiji-pm-frank-bainimarama-insulting-scott-morrison-rift-pacific-countries.

Mackenzie, Adrian. *Machine Learners: Archaeology of a Data Practice*. Cambridge, MA: MIT Press, 2017.

Mackenzie, Adrian, and Anna Munster. "Platform Seeing: Image Ensembles and Their Invisualities." *Theory, Culture and Society* 36, no. 5 (2019): 3–22.

Maddocks, Sophie. "'A Deepfake Porn Plot Intended to Silence Me': Exploring Continuities between Pornographic and 'Political' Deep Fakes." *Porn* (2020): 1–9.

Manjoo, Farhad. "I Tried Microsoft's Flight Simulator. The Earth Never Seemed So Real." *New York Times*, August 19, 2020. https://www.nytimes.com/2020/08/19/opinion/microsoft-flight-simulator.html.

Manning, Erin. *The Minor Gesture*. Durham, NC: Duke University Press, 2016.

Manning, Erin, and Brian Massumi. *Thought in the Act: Passages in the Ecology of Experience*. Minneapolis: University of Minnesota Press, 2014.

Maralinga Rehabilitation Technical Advisory Committee. "Rehabilitation of Former Nuclear Test Sites at Emu and Maralinga (Australia)." Canberra: Department of Education, Science, and Training, 2003. https://www.industry.gov.au/sites/default/files/July%202018/document/pdf/rehabilitation-of-former-nuclear-test-sites-at-emu-and-maralinga.pdf?acsf_files_redirect.

Maras, Marie-Helen, and Alex Alexandrou. "Determining Authenticity of Video Evidence in the Age of Artificial Intelligence and in the Wake of Deepfake Videos." *International Journal of Evidence and Proof* 23, no. 3 (2019): 255–62.

Massumi, Brian. "The Autonomy of Affect." *Cultural Critique* 31 (1995): 83–109.

Massumi, Brian. "The Future Birth of the Affective Fact: The Political Ontology of Threat." In *The Affect Theory Reader*, edited by Melissa Gregg and Gregory J. Seigworth. Durham, NC: Duke University Press, 2010.

Massumi, Brian. *Ontopower: War, Powers, and the State of Perception*. Durham, NC: Duke University Press, 2015.

Massumi, Brian. *Parables for the Virtual: Movement, Affect, Sensation*. Post-contemporary Interventions. Durham, NC: Duke University Press, 2002.

Maurer, Anaïs. "Snaring the Nuclear Sun: Decolonial Ecologies in Titaua Peu's Mutismes: E 'Ore Te Vāvā." *Contemporary Pacific* 32, no. 2 (2020): 371–97.

Mbembe, Achille. *Necropolitics*. Durham, NC: Duke University Press, 2019.

McCosker, Anthony. "Drone Media: Unruly Systems, Radical Empiricism and Camera Consciousness." *Culture Machine* 16 (2015). https://culturemachine.net/vol-16-drone-cultures/drone-media/.

McCosker, Anthony. "Drone Vision, Zones of Protest, and the New Camera Consciousness." *Media Fields Journal* 9 (2015). http://www.mediafieldsjournal.org/drone-vision-zones-of-protest/2015/8/21/drone-vision-zones-of-protest-and-the-new-camera-consciousne.html.

McCosker, Anthony. "Making Sense of Deepfakes: Socializing AI and Building Data Literacy on GitHub and YouTube." *New Media and Society* (May 2022). https://doi.org/10.1177/14614448221093943.

McCosker, Anthony, and Rowan Wilken. *Automating Vision: The Social Impact of the New Camera Consciousness*. New York: Routledge, 2020.

McDonald, Matt. *Ecological Security*. Cambridge: Cambridge University Press, 2021.

McKittrick, Katherine. *Dear Science and Other Stories*. Errantries. Durham, NC: Duke University Press, 2021.

McLelland, J. R. *The Report of the Royal Commission into British Nuclear Tests in Australia*. Vol. 1. Parliamentary Paper. Canberra: The Parliament of the Commonwealth of Australia, 1985. https://parlinfo.aph.gov.au/parlInfo/download/publications/tabledpapers/HPP032016010928/upload_pdf/HPP032016010928.pdf.

McNeill, J. R., and Peter Engelke. *The Great Acceleration: An Environmental History of the Anthropocene since 1945*. Cambridge, MA: Harvard University Press, 2014.

Michel, Arthur Holland. *Eyes in the Sky: The Secret Rise of Gorgon Stare and How It Will Watch Us All*. Boston: Houghton Mifflin Harcourt, 2019.

Miglio. "AI in Unreal Engine: Learning through Virtual Simulations." *Unreal Engine Blog*, April 13, 2018. https://www.unrealengine.com/en-US/tech-blog/ai-in-unreal-engine-learning-through-virtual-simulations.

Mirzoeff, Nicholas. *How to See the World: An Introduction to Images, from Self-Portraits to Selfies, Maps to Movies, and More*. New York: Penguin, 2015.

Mirzoeff, Nicholas. *The Right to Look: A Counterhistory of Visuality*. Durham, NC: Duke University Press, 2011.

Mittmann, J. D. "Maralinga: Aboriginal Poison Country." *Agora* 25 (2017): 7.

Moore, Jason W., ed. *Anthropocene or Capitalocene? Nature, History, and the Crisis of Capitalism*. Oakland, CA: PM, 2016.

Moreton-Robinson, Aileen. *The White Possessive*. Minneapolis: University of Minnesota Press, 2015.

Morton, Timothy. *Hyperobjects: Philosophy and Ecology after the End of the World*. Minneapolis: University of Minnesota Press, 2013.

Murphie, Andrew. "On Being Affected: Feeling in the Folding of Multiple Catastrophes." *Cultural Studies* 32, no. 1 (2018): 18–42.

Murphie, Andrew. "World as Medium: A Whiteheadian Media Philosophy." In *Immediation*, edited by Erin Manning, Anna Munster, and Bodil Marie Stavning Thomsen, 16–46. Detroit: Open Humanities, 2019.

Nagel, Emily van der. "Verifying Images: Deepfakes, Control, and Consent." *Porn Studies* 7, no. 4 (2020): 424–29.

Neale, Timothy, Alex Zahara, and Will Smith. "An Eternal Flame: The Elemental Governance of Wildfire's Pasts, Presents and Futures." *Cultural Studies Review* 25, no. 2 (2019): 115–34.

Nixon, Rob. *Slow Violence and the Environmentalism of the Poor*. Cambridge, MA: Harvard University Press, 2011.

Noble, Safiya Umoja. *Algorithms of Oppression: How Search Engines Reinforce Racism*. New York: New York University Press, 2018.

Nyong'o, Tavia. "Little Monsters: Race, Sovereignty, and Queer Inhumanism in *Beasts of the Southern Wild*." *GLQ: A Journal of Lesbian and Gay Studies* 21, no. 2–3 (2015): 249–72.

Offert, Fabian. "Latent Deep Space: Generative Adversarial Networks (GANs) in the Sciences." *Media+Environment* 3, no. 2 (2021).

Offert, Fabian, and Thao Phan. "A Sign That Spells: DALL-E 2, Invisual Images and the Racial Politics of Feature Space." ArXiv, arXiv:2211.06323 (October 2022). http://arxiv.org/abs/2211.06323.

Öhman, Carl J., and David Watson. "Are the Dead Taking over Facebook? A Big Data Approach to the Future of Death Online." *Big Data and Society* 6, no. 1 (2019). https://doi.org/10.1177/2053951719842540.

Oliver, Kelly. *Witnessing: Beyond Recognition*. Minneapolis: University of Minnesota Press, 2001.

O'Malley, Pat, and Gavin J. D. Smith. "'Smart' Crime Prevention? Digitization and Racialized Crime Control in a Smart City." *Theoretical Criminology* 26, no. 1 (2020): 40–56.

OpenAI. "Proximal Policy Optimization." July 20, 2017. https://openai.com/blog/openai-baselines-ppo/.

Packer, Jeremy, and Joshua Reeves. "Taking People Out: Drones, Media/Weapons, and the Coming Humanectomy." In *Life in the Age of Drone Warfare*, edited by Lisa Parks and Caren Kaplan, 261–81. Durham, NC: Duke University Press, 2017.

Packer, Jeremy, and Joshua Reeves. *Killer Apps: War, Media, Machine*. Durham, NC: Duke University Press, 2020.

Papailias, Penelope. "Witnessing in the Age of the Database: Viral Memorials, Affective Publics, and the Assemblage of Mourning." *Memory Studies* 9, no. 4 (2016): 437–54.

Parks, Lisa. *Cultures in Orbit: Satellites and the Televisual.* Console-Ing Passions. Durham, NC: Duke University Press, 2005.

Parks, Lisa. *Rethinking Media Coverage: Vertical Mediation and the War on Terror.* New York: Routledge, 2018.

Parks, Lisa, and Caren Kaplan, eds. *Life in the Age of Drone Warfare.* Durham, NC: Duke University Press, 2017.

Pasquale, Frank. *The Black Box Society: The Secret Algorithms That Control Money and Information.* 1st ed. Cambridge, MA: Harvard University Press, 2015.

Paterson, Thomas, and Lauren Hanley. "Political Warfare in the Digital Age: Cyber Subversion, Information Operations and 'Deep Fakes.'" *Australian Journal of International Affairs* 74, no. 4 (2020): 439–54.

Peters, Edward. *Torture.* New York: Basil Blackwell, 1985.

Peters, John Durham. *The Marvelous Clouds.* Chicago: University of Chicago Press, 2015.

Peters, John Durham. "Witnessing." *Media, Culture and Society* 23, no. 6 (2001): 707–23.

Phan, Thao, and Scott Wark. "Racial Formations as Data Formations." *Big Data and Society* 8, no. 2 (2021).

Phan, Thao, and Scott Wark. "What Personalisation Can Do for You! Or: How to Do Racial Discrimination without 'Race.'" Culture Machine, 2021. https://culturemachine.net/vol-20-machine-intelligences/what-personalisation-can-do-for-you-or-how-to-do-racial-discrimination-without-race-thao-phan-scott-wark/.

Phan, Thao, Jake Goldenfein, Monique Mann, and Declan Kuch, editors. *Economies of Virtue—the Circulation of "Ethics" in AI.* Amsterdam: Institute of Network Cultures, 2022.

Pinchevski, Amit. *Transmitted Wounds: Media and the Mediation of Trauma.* New York: Oxford University Press, 2019.

Pong, Beryl. *British Literature and Culture in Second World Wartime: For the Duration.* Oxford Mid-century Studies. New York: Oxford University Press, 2020.

Popova, Milena. "Reading out of Context: Pornographic Deepfakes, Celebrity, and Intimacy." *Porn Studies* 7 no. 4 (2019): 1–15.

Puar, Jasbir. "The Cost of Getting Better: Suicide, Sensation, Switchpoints." *GLQ: A Journal of Lesbian and Gay Studies* 18 (2012): 149–58.

Puar, Jasbir. *Right to Maim: Debility, Capacity, Disability.* Durham, NC: Duke University Press, 2017.

Pugliese, Joseph. *Biopolitics of the More-Than-Human: Forensic Ecologies of Violence.* Durham, NC: Duke University Press, 2020.

Pugliese, Joseph. "Death by Metadata: The Bioinformationalisation of Life and the Transliteration of Algorithms to Flesh." In *Security, Race, Biopower: Essays on Technology and Corporeality*, edited by Holly Randell-Moon and Ryan Tippet, 3–20. London: Palgrave Macmillan, 2016.

Pugliese, Joseph. "Drone Casino Mimesis: Telewarfare and Civil Militarization." *Journal of Sociology* 52, no. 3 (2016): 500–21.

Pugliese, Joseph. *State Violence and the Execution of Law: Biopolitical Caesurae of Torture, Black Sites, Drones*. New York: Routledge, 2013.

Rae, Maria, Rosa Holman, and Amy Nethery. "Self-Represented Witnessing: The Use of Social Media by Asylum Seekers in Australia's Offshore Immigration Detention Centres." *Media, Culture and Society* 40, no. 4 (2018): 479–95.

Rancière, Jacques. *Disagreement: Politics and Philosophy*. Translated by Julie Rose. Minneapolis: University of Minnesota Press, 1999.

Ray, Una. "The Myth of Empty Country and the Story of 'Deadly' Glass." *Di'van*, no. 9 (2021): 42–55.

Reading, Anna. "Mobile Witnessing: Ethics and the Camera Phone in the 'War on Terror.'" *Globalizations* 6, no. 1 (2009): 61–76.

Reiter, Bernd, ed. *Constructing the Pluriverse: The Geopolitics of Knowledge*. Durham, NC: Duke University Press, 2018.

Rhee, Jennifer. *The Robotic Imaginary: The Human and the Price of Dehumanized Labor*. Minneapolis: University of Minnesota Press, 2018.

Richardson, Michael. "Climate Trauma, or the Affects of the Catastrophe to Come." *Environmental Humanities* 10, no. 1 (2018): 1–19.

Richardson, Michael. "Drone's-Eye View: Affective Witnessing and Technicities of Perception." In *Image Testimonies: Witnessing in Times of Social Media*, edited by Kerstin Schankweiler, Verena Straub, and Tobias Wendl, 64–74. New York: Routledge, 2018.

Richardson, Michael. *Gestures of Testimony: Torture, Trauma, and Affect in Literature*. New York: Bloomsbury Academic, 2016.

Richardson, Michael. "There's Something Going On." *Capacious* 1, no. 2 (2018): 149–54.

Richardson, Michael, and Kerstin Schankweiler. "Affective Witnessing." In *Affective Societies: Key Concepts*, edited by Jan Slaby and Christian von Scheve, 166–177. New York: Routledge, 2019.

Richardson, Michael, and Kerstin Schankweiler. "Introduction: Affective Witnessing as Theory and Practice." *Parallax* 26, no. 3 (2020): 235–53.

Rini, Regina. "Deepfakes and the Epistemic Backstop." *Philosophers' Imprint* 20, no. 24 (2020): 1–16.

Ristovska, Sandra. *Seeing Human Rights: Video Activism as a Proxy Profession*. Information Policy. Cambridge, MA: MIT Press, 2021.

Robinson, Cedric J. *Black Marxism: The Making of the Black Radical Tradition*. Chapel Hill: University of North Carolina Press, 2000.

Rosenthal, Caitlin. *Accounting for Slavery: Masters and Management*. Cambridge, MA: Harvard University Press, 2019.

Rothe, Delf. "Seeing Like a Satellite: Remote Sensing and the Ontological Politics of Environmental Security." *Security Dialogue* 48, no. 4 (2017): 334–53.

Rouvroy, Antoinette, and Thomas Berns. "Algorithmic Governmentality and Prospects of Emancipation." *Reseaux* 177, no. 1 (2013): 163–96.

Russill, Chris. "Earth Imaging: Photograph, Pixel, Program." In *Ecomedia: Key Issues*, edited by Stephen Rust, Salma Monani, and Sean Cubitt, 228–50. New York: Routledge, 2015.

Russill, Chris. "Is the Earth a Medium? Situating the Planetary in Media Theory." *Ctrl-z.Net.Au* 7 (2017). http://www.ctrl-z.net.au/articles/issue-7/russill-is-the-earth-a-medium/.

Russill, Chris. "The Road Not Taken: William James's Radical Empiricism and Communication Theory." *Communication Review* 8, no. 3 (2005): 277–305.

Sadowski, Jathan. "Potemkin AI." *Real Life*, August 6, 2018. https://reallifemag.com/potemkin-ai/.

Sadowski, Jathan. *Too Smart: How Digital Capitalism Is Extracting Data, Controlling Our Lives, and Taking over the World*. Cambridge, MA: MIT Press, 2020.

Sadowski, Jathan. "When Data Is Capital: Datafication, Accumulation, and Extraction." *Big Data and Society* 6, no. 1 (2019).

Safransky, Sara. "Geographies of Algorithmic Violence: Redlining the Smart City." *International Journal of Urban and Regional Research* 44, no. 2 (2020): 200–18.

Saldarriaga, Juan Francisco, Laura Kurgan, and Dare Brawley. "Visualizing Conflict: Possibilities for Urban Research." *Urban Planning* 2, no. 1 (2017): 100–107.

Savransky, Martin. *Around the Day in Eighty Worlds: Politics of the Pluriverse*. Thought in the Act. Durham, NC: Duke University Press, 2021.

Scannell, Josh. "What Can an Algorithm Do?" *DIS Magazine*. Accessed July 14, 2016. http://dismagazine.com/discussion/72975/josh-scannell-what-can-an-algorithm-do/.

Scannell, Paddy. *Television and the Meaning of Live: An Enquiry into the Human Situation*. Cambridge, UK: Polity, 2014.

Scarce, Yhonnie, Max Delany, and Australian Centre for Contemporary Art. *Missile Park*, 2021.

Schaefer, Donovan O. *The Evolution of Affect Theory: The Humanities, the Sciences, and the Study of Power*. Cambridge Elements. Cambridge: Cambridge University Press, 2019.

Schankweiler, Kerstin, Verena Straub, and Tobias Wendl, eds. *Image Testimonies: Witnessing in Times of Social Media*. New York: Routledge, 2018.

Schuppli, Susan. *Material Witness: Media, Forensics, Evidence*. Cambridge, MA: MIT Press, 2020.

Sear, Tom. "Xenowar Dreams of Itself." *Digital War*, 1 (2020). https://doi.org/10.1057/s42984-020-00019-6.

Seaver, Nick. "Algorithms as Culture: Some Tactics for the Ethnography of Algorithmic Systems." *Big Data and Society* 4, no. 2 (2017).

Seigworth, Gregory J., and Matthew Tiessen. "Mobile Affects, Open Secrets, and Global Illiquidity: Pockets, Pools, and Plasma." *Theory, Culture and Society* 29 (2012): 47–77.

Seltzer, Mark. "Wound Culture: Trauma in the Pathological Public Sphere." *October* 80 (1997): 3–26.

Sheikh, Shela. "The Future of the Witness: Nature, Race and More-than-Human Environmental Publics." *Kronos* 44, no. 1 (2018): 145–62.

Sherwood, Dave. "Inside Lithium Giant SQM's Struggle to Win Over Indigenous Communities in Chile's Atacama." Reuters, January 15, 2021. https://www.reuters.com/article/us-chile-lithium-sqm-focus-idUSKBN29K1DB.

Singh, Julietta. *Unthinking Mastery: Dehumanism and Decolonial Entanglements.* Durham, NC: Duke University Press, 2018.

Slaughter, Joseph R. *Human Rights, Inc.: The World Novel, Narrative Form, and International Law.* New York: Fordham University Press, 2007.

Smith, Joan. *Clouds of Deceit: The Deadly Legacy of Britain's Bomb Tests.* London: Faber, 1985.

Snaza, Nathan. "The Earth Is Not 'Ours' to Save." In *Interrogating the Anthropocene: Ecology, Aesthetics, Pedagogy, and the Future in Question*, edited by Jan Jagodzinski, 339–57. Palgrave Studies in Educational Futures. Cham, Switzerland: Springer International, 2018.

Sontag, Susan. *Regarding the Pain of Others.* London: Penguin, 2003.

Sparrow, Jeff. "Plastic Sword the Least of ASIO's Bungles in 'Terror Raid.'" Crikey, October 9, 2014. https://www.crikey.com.au/2014/10/09/plastic-sword-the-least-of-asios-bungles-in-terror-raid/.

Spillers, Hortense J. "Mama's Baby, Papa's Maybe: An American Grammar Book." *Diacritics* 17, no. 2 (1987): 65–81.

Springgay, Stephanie, and Sarah E. Truman. *Walking Methodologies in a More-than-Human World: WalkingLab.* New York: Routledge, 2018.

SRC Defense. "Agile Condor™ High-Performance Embedded Computing Architecture." YouTube video, 1:57, October 14, 2016. https://www.youtube.com/watch?v=sc1aOFmb3AI.

Stahl, Roger. *Through the Crosshairs: War, Visual Culture, and the Weaponized Gaze.* New Brunswick, NJ: Rutgers University Press, 2018.

Stanford Law School and NYU School of Law. "Living under Drones: Death, Injury, and Trauma to Civilians from US Drone Practices in Pakistan." International Human Rights and Conflict Resolution's Clinic at Stanford Law School and Global Justice Clinic at NYU School of Law, 2012.

Stark, Luke. "Facial Recognition Is the Plutonium of AI." *XRDS: Crossroads, the ACM Magazine for Students* 25, no. 3 (2019): 50–55.

Starosielski, Nicole. *Media Hot and Cold.* Elements. Durham, NC: Duke University Press, 2021.

Stewart, Kathleen. "Afterword: Worlding Refrains." In *The Affect Theory Reader*, edited by Melissa Gregg and Gregory J. Seigworth, 339–53. Durham, NC: Duke University Press, 2010.

Stewart, Kathleen. "Atmospheric Attunements." *Environment and Planning D: Society and Space* 29, no. 3 (2011): 445–53.

Stiegler, Bernard. "Anamnesis and Hypomnesis." Ars Industrialis, March 7, 2016. https://arsindustrialis.org/anamnesis-and-hypomnesis.

Stubblefield, Thomas. *Drone Art: The Everywhere War as Medium*. Oakland, CA: University of California Press, 2020.

Suchman, Lucy. "Algorithmic Warfare and the Reinvention of Accuracy." *Critical Studies on Security* 8, no. 2 (2020): 175–87.

SyncedReview. "Barack Obama Is the Benchmark for Fake Lip-Sync Videos." Medium, January 17, 2018. https://medium.com/syncedreview/barack-obama-is-the-benchmark-for-fake-lip-sync-videos-d85057cb90ac.

Taffel, Sy. "Data and Oil: Metaphor, Materiality, and Metabolic Rifts." *New Media and Society*, 25, no 5 (2021): 980–98.

Tahir, Madiha. "The Distributed Empire of the War on Terror." *Boston Review*, September 9, 2021. https://bostonreview.net/global-justice/madiha-tahir-war-on-terror-empire-pakistan.

Tahir, Madiha. "The Ground Was Always in Play." *Public Culture* 29, no. 1 (2017): 5–16.

Taussig, Michael T. *Law in a Lawless Land: Diary of a "Limpieza" in Colombia*. Chicago: University of Chicago Press, 2005.

Taylor, Christopher. *Empire of Neglect: The West Indies in the Wake of British Liberalism*. Radical Américas. Durham, NC: Duke University Press, 2018.

Taylor, Simon. "Fiction Machines: How Drones Read Oceanic Volumes through 'Technically-Induced Hallucination.'" In *Drone Aesthetics: War, Cultures, Ecologies*, edited by Beryl Pong and Michael Richardson. London: Open Humanities, 2024.

Thrift, Nigel. *Non-representational Theory : Space, Politics, Affect*. 1st ed. Hoboken, NJ: Taylor and Francis, 2008.

Tomkins, Silvan. *Shame and Its Sisters: A Silvan Tomkins Reader*. Durham, NC: Duke University Press, 1995.

Tsing, A. L. "On Nonscalability: The Living World Is Not Amenable to Precision-Nested Scales." *Common Knowledge* 18, no. 3 (2012): 505–24.

Turner, Fred. *From Counterculture to Cyberculture: Stewart Brand, the Whole Earth Network, and the Rise of Digital Utopianism*. Chicago: University of Chicago Press, 2006.

Tynan, Elizabeth. *Atomic Thunder: The Maralinga Story*. Sydney: NewSouth, 2016.

Tynan, Elizabeth. "Sixty Years on, Maralinga Reminds Us Not to Put Security over Safety." *Conversation*, September 25, 2016. http://theconversation.com/sixty-years-on-maralinga-reminds-us-not-to-put-security-over-safety-62441.

Tynan, Lauren. "What Is Relationality? Indigenous Knowledges, Practices, and Responsibilities with Kin." *Cultural Geographies*, 28, no. 4 (2021): 597–610.

Uliasz, Rebecca. "On the Truth Claims of Deepfakes: Indexing Images and Semantic Forensics." *Journal of Media Art Study and Theory* 3, no. 1 (2022): 63–84.

UN News. "'Crimes of Historic Proportions' Being Committed in Aleppo, UN Rights Chief Warns." *UN News*, October 21, 2016. https://news.un.org/en/story/2016/10/543432-crimes-historic-proportions-being-committed-aleppo-un-rights-chief-warns.

Valla, Clement. Postcards from Google Earth, 2012. http://www.postcards-from-google-earth.com/.

Vigh, Henrik. "Crisis and Chronicity: Anthropological Perspectives on Continuous Conflict and Decline." *Ethnos* 73, no. 1 (2008): 5–24.

Virilio, Paul. *War and Cinema: The Logistics of Perception*. New York: Verso, 1989.

Vivian, Bradford. *Commonplace Witnessing: Rhetorical Invention, Historical Remembrance, and Public Culture*. New York: Oxford University Press, 2017.

Wall, T., and T. Monahan. "Surveillance and Violence from Afar: The Politics of Drones and Liminal Security-Scapes." *Theoretical Criminology* 15, no. 3 (2011): 239–54.

Weizman, Eyal. *Forensic Architecture: Violence at the Threshold of Detectability*. New York: Zone, 2017.

Westfall, Sammy. "Australia Ranks Last on Climate Action in U.N. Report." *Washington Post*, July 2, 2021. https://www.washingtonpost.com/world/2021/07/02/australia-climate-action-un-sustainable-development/.

Weston, Kath. *Animate Planet: Making Visceral Sense of Living in a High-Tech, Ecologically Damaged World*. ANIMA. Durham, NC: Duke University Press, 2017.

Whittaker, Meredith. "The Steep Cost of Capture." *Interactions* 28, no. 6 (2021): 50–55.

Whyte, Christopher. "Deepfake News: AI-Enabled Disinformation as a Multi-level Public Policy Challenge." *Journal of Cyber Policy* 5, no. 2 (2020): 199–217.

Whyte, Jessica. *The Morals of the Market: Human Rights and the Rise of Neoliberalism*. New York: Verso, 2019.

Whyte, Kyle. "Against Crisis Epistemology." In *Routledge Handbook of Critical Indigenous Studies*, edited by Brendan Hokowhitu, Aileen Moreton-Robinson, Linda Tuhiwai-Smith, Chris Andersen, Steve Larkin, and Brendan Hokowhitu, 52–64. New York: Routledge, 2021.

Whyte, Kyle. "Indigenous Science (Fiction) for the Anthropocene: Ancestral Dystopias and Fantasies of Climate Change Crises." *Environment and Planning E: Nature and Space* 1, nos. 1–2 (2018): 224–42.

Whyte, Kyle. "Settler Colonialism, Ecology, and Environmental Injustice." *Environment and Society* 9, no. 1 (2018): 125–44.

Wieviorka, Annette. *The Era of the Witness*. Ithaca, NY: Cornell University Press, 2006.

Wilcox, Lauren. "Embodying Algorithmic War: Gender, Race, and the Posthuman in Drone Warfare." *Security Dialogue* 48, no. 1 (2017): 11–28.

Wilken, Rowan, and Julian Thomas. "Vertical Geomediation: The Automation and Platformization of Photogrammetry." *New Media and Society* 24, no. 11 (2022): 2531–47.

Williams, Raymond. *Marxism and Literature*, Oxford: Oxford University Press, 1977.

Wise, Jeff. "How Crazy Am I to Think I Actually Know Where That Malaysia Airlines Plane Is?" *New York Magazine*, February 23, 2015. https://nymag.com/intelligencer/2015/02/jeff-wise-mh370-theory.html.

WITNESS Media Lab. "Mal-Uses of AI-Generated Synthetic Media and Deepfakes: Pragmatic Solutions Discovery Convening." WITNESS, June 11, 2018.

Wolfe, Patrick. "Settler Colonialism and the Elimination of the Native." *Journal of Genocide Research* 8, no. 4 (2006): 387–409.

Woods, Derek. "Scale Critique for the Anthropocene." *Minnesota Review* 2014, no. 83 (2014): 133–42.

Wu, Xiaoping, and Martin Montgomery. "Witnessing in Crisis Contexts in the Social Media Age: The Case of the 2015 Tianjin Blasts on Weibo." *Media, Culture and Society* 42, no. 5 (2020): 675–91.

Wynter, Sylvia. "Unsettling the Coloniality of Being/Power/Truth/Freedom: Towards the Human, After Man, Its Overrepresentation—an Argument." *CR: The New Centennial Review* 3, no. 3 (2003): 257–337.

Yang, Jun, Peng Gong, Rong Fu, Minghua Zhang, Jingming Chen, Shunlin Liang, Bing Xu, Jiancheng Shi, and Robert Dickinson. "The Role of Satellite Remote Sensing in Climate Change Studies." *Nature Climate Change* 3, no. 10 (2013): 875–83.

Yunkaporta, Tyson. *Sand Talk: How Indigenous Thinking Can Save the World*. Melbourne: Text, 2019.

Yusoff, Kathryn. *A Billion Black Anthropocenes or None*. Minneapolis: University of Minnesota Press, 2018.

Zylinska, Joanna. *Minimal Ethics for the Anthropocene*. Ann Arbor, MI: Open Humanities, 2014.

Zylinska, Joanna. *Nonhuman Photography*. Cambridge, MA: MIT Press, 2017.

INDEX

Italicized page numbers refer to figures.

Aboriginal peoples, 18, 146–47, 205n55; Aboriginal Heritage Act of 1972 (Australia), 168–70; military cooptation of Aboriginal languages, 202n78; nuclear weapons testing and, 133–39, 141–42, 144–45; Stolen Generation, 187n32. *See also* First Nations peoples; Indigenous peoples; *individual nations and peoples*

Abrar, Hisham, 193n37

activism, 104, 119, 154, 192n13, 200n27; of Aleppo Media Center, 60, 63–64; antinuclear, 137, 144, 202n75; call for cloud ethics, 110; of Forensic Architecture, 20–21, 87, 93–99, 109, 178; humanitarian testimony and, 4, 22, 24, 32, 42–43, 95, 183, 192n9; of Indigenous peoples, 6, 18, 20–21, 115, 137, 144, 169; prodemocracy protests in Daraa, 59; protests at US–Mexico border, 94; of WITNESS, 90–91. *See also* aesthetic interventions and artwork

aesthetic interventions and artwork, 13, 98; about nuclear testing, 21, 115, 138–45; drones in, 34–35, 37–39, 53, 107–10, 191n1, 192n9, 193n33, 193n43; ecological trauma and, 117, 125–29, 138–46, 149, 154; insurgent aesthetics, 53; significance to the book, 9, 21, 23; and trauma theory, 29–30. *See also individual artworks and artists*

affect theory, 6–7, 185n5. *See also* machinic affect; traumatic affect

Afghanistan, 32, 38, 46, 52–53, 55, 57, 150, 192n9; Pakistan border, 50, 101–2, 194n51; Uruzgan Province, 1–3, 7, 67

Agile Condor (SRC Inc.), 43, 49, 59, 66–74, 76

Air Force Research Laboratory (AFRL), 66; Moving and Stationary Target Acquisition and Recognition (MSTAR), 69–70

Alaimo, Stacy, 122, 190n86

al-Asad, Bashir, 59–60

Aleppo Media Center, 60, 63–64

Aleppo, Syria: aftermath of war in, 43, 59–65, 98, 119; Battle of Aleppo, 60; Conflict Urbanism project and, 60–63, 65

Alexander, David R., 68
Alexis-Martin, Becky, 202n80
Al-Ghazzi, Omar, 63
algorithmic enclosure, 4–6, 8, 11, 118, 192n8; autonomous warfare and, 2, 12–14, 42, 56, 79, 83; ethics and, 84–88, 91–92
Algorithmic Warfare Cross-Functional Team (AWCFT), 99–100, 102, 109. *See also* Project Maven
Althusser, Louis, 190n82
Amazon, 11–12, 14, 75
Amoore, Louise, 77, 85–86, 96, 101, 110, 192n8
ancestral dystopias, 6
Anderson, Stephen F., 92
Andrejevic, Mark, 46, 69, 72, 78, 195n86
Angerer, Marie-Luise, 164
anthropocentrism, 33, 116, 179, 182–83; atomic bomb and, 202n80; climate change and, 6, 13, 121–23, 126, 128, 130–32, 149; minimal ethics and, 188n39; naming of the Anthropocene, 19, 121–23; trauma theory and, 30
Arab Spring, 59
ArcGIS, 100
Arendt, Hannah, 31
Armenia–Azerbaijan war (2020), 75
artificial intelligence (AI), 26, 38, 40, 75, 110, 180, 199n82; Agile Condor targeting system, 43, 49, 59, 66–74, 76; Azure platform, 80; ChatGPT, 82, 105–6; convolutional neural networks (CNNs), 88, 96, 100; Dall-E 2, 83, 92; deepfakes and, 88, 90–91, 197n39; FAccT conference, 105; Figure Eight, 100; generative adversarial networks (GANs), 88–90, 92, 197n40; Google Brain, 88; Google Ethical AI team, 104, 199n78; human labor and, 76, 82, 85, 100–101; Mechanical Turk, 82; Midjourney, 83; Potemkin AI, 82; Project Maven, 99–100, 103; Stable Diffusion, 92; Synthesis.ai, 93. *See also* machine learning
Asaro, Peter, 79
Atacama salt flats, Chile, 123. *See also* Atacan community of Chile

Atacan community of Chile, 12
Atkinson, Meera, 158
Australia, 18, 37, 104, 107, 115; Aboriginal Heritage Act of 1972, 168–70; Atomic Weapons Test Safety Committee (AWTSC), 201n63; Brockman 4 iron ore mine, 168; climate crisis and, 17, 112–13, 132, 148; "Digital Earth Australia," 125; Eora Nation, 7; Juukan Gorge, 167–71, 205n55; Maralinga, 133–39, 141–42, 144, 176; Stolen Generation, 187n32; terrorist raids in, 152; Woomera, 138, 142, 202n78
author positionality, 7, 17–18
Autonomous Real-Time Ground Ubiquitous Surveillance Imaging System (ARGUS-IS), 47–48, 100
Azoulay, Ariella, 64–65

Baichal, Jennifer, 123
Bainimarama, Frank, 112
Ballard, Su, 23
Barad, Karen, 27
Behram, Noor, 50–51, 193n31
Benjamin, Ruha, 102–3
Berlant, Lauren, 15, 158, 166–67, 171
Biden, Joe, 198n65
Bidjigal people of Eora Nation, 7
biopolitics, 12, 16, 22, 29, 35; COVID-19 pandemic and, 175–76. *See also* ontopower
Biopolitics of the More-Than-Human (Pugliese), 22
black boxing, 68, 77, 82, 86, 104–5, 110, 156
Blaser, Mario, 7, 18, 146, 176
"Blue Marble," 117
bnngina (slang for drones), 52
"Boiling Milk" (Halperin), 127–29, 145
Borges, Jorge Luis: "On Exactitude in Science," 80
Boulminwi, Joy, 104
Bousquet, Antoine, 41, 45, 69, 73
Brand, Stewart: *Whole Earth Catalogue*, 118
Bridle, James: *Drone Shadows*, 193n43
Brimblecombe-Fox, Kathryn: *Theatre of War: Photons Do Not Care*, 34–35
British Royal Commission into Nuclear Testing (1984), 133, 144

Browne, Simone, 13
Browning, Daniel, 139
Bucher, Taina, 83
Burtynsky, Edward: "Clear Cut #3," 123; "Morenci Mine #2," *124*; "Salt Pan #18," 123
Butler, Judith, 31

capitalism, 18, 25, 43, 114, 133, 148, 187n25, 188n43; algorithms and, 79, 104, 152, 160; extractive industries and, 12, 31, 130–31, 168–71; racial, 12–14, 19, 174–75, 181. *See also* settler colonialism; slavery
Caruth, Cathy, 147
Center for Spatial Research, Columbia University: Conflict Urbanism: Aleppo project, 60–61
Chakrabarty, Dipesh, 121
Chamayou, Grégoire, 185n1, 192n19
Chandler, Kate, 192n14
ChatGPT (OpenAI), 82, 105–6
Chayka, Kyle, 81
Chen, Mel Y., 28, 190n82
Chile, 12, 123
Chishty, Mahwish: *Drone Art Paintings*, 53; *Drone Shadows*, 53–54, 193n43; *Reaper*, 53–54
Chouliaraki, Lilie, 22, 63
Chow, Rey, 166
Christianity, 6, 24–25
Clark, Timothy, 121, 124
"Clear Cut #3" (Burtynsky), 123
climate crisis, 11, 133; artwork about, 123–30; climate trauma, 132; climatic media and, 119; Marshall Islands and, 112–15, 148; scale of, 13, 121–22, 125; settler colonialism and, 14–15, 18–19, 110, 113, 131. *See also* ecological trauma
closed world computation, 13, 156
Cockburn, Andrew, 185n1
Cold War era, 113, 117–18; closed world computation and, 13, 156
Cole, Samantha, 88, 197n41
Columbian Exchange (1610), 19
communicative aesthetics, 29
communicative commons, 115

communicative politics: and nonhuman witnessing, 3, 8, 20, 116, 175–83
Computer Learns Automation (Tan), 106–10
computer vision, 39, 58, 77, 93, 99–100, 108–9. *See also* drone vision; machine vision; surveillance
Conflict Urbanism project, 60–63, 65
convolutional neural networks (CNNs), 88, 96, 100
Cooke, Grayson: "Open Air," 125–26
corporate violence, 5, 20, 38, 87, 93, 119. *See also* state violence; structural violence
COVID-19 pandemic (2020), 17, 26, 80, 158, 170, 174–76
Creech Air Force Base (US), 1
crisis epistemologies, 14–15
crisis ordinariness, 15, 158–59
CrowdFlower platform, 100
Crutzen, Paul, 19
Cubitt, Sean, 16–17, 39–40, 116–17, 157, 175, 177, 181–82; *The Practice of Light*, 26, 28, 189n74
cyborg tendency, 26, 63, 164

da Silva, Denise Ferreira, 31, 56
Daston, Lorraine, 24, 115
data friction, 12, 71, 76, 200n23
data justice, 104–5, 110. *See also* activism
Davis, Heather, 19
Death Zephyr (Scarce), 139, 141
deepfakes, 9, 25, 87–92, 102, 197n41; of Barack Obama, 197n39; political warfare and, 198n43. *See also* synthetic media
Defense Advanced Research Projects Agency (DARPA), 13, 47; Moving and Stationary Target Acquisition and Recognition (MSTAR), 69–70; OFFSET program, 75; role in internet creation, 118; Systems of Neuromorphic Adaptive Plastic Scalable Electronics (SyNAPSE), 69
de la Cadena, Marisol, 7, 18, 146, 176–77, 182
DeLanda, Manuel, 73–75
Deleuze, Gilles, 6, 45, 74, 91, 145–49
DeLoughrey, Elizabeth, 113–14
Dencik, Lina, 104
de Pencier, Nicholas, 123

disappearances. *See* radical absence
disinformation, 21, 90. *See also* deepfakes
Doane, Mary Ann, 164
Dodson, Pat, 169
Dorrian, Mark, 50, 193n33
Dowdell, Anthony, 160–61
Drone Art Paintings (Chishty), 53
drones and drone warfare, 8–9, 14–15, 20, 99, 164, 178, 180; AeroVironment RQ-11 Raven, 44; Bayraktar TB2, 38; *bnngina* (slang), 52; Castle Bravo, 137; Datta Khel airstrike, 50, 101–2; gendering and, 50, 56, 102–3, 185n1; Global Hawks, 38, 46; global increase in, 12; kill boxes and, 44–45; life under, 32, 38, 46, 51–52, 55–58, 193n37, 194n51; Operation Kamikazi, 137; Predator, 1–3, 38, 44, 46, 53, 75, 193n43; racialization and, 50–51, 56, 102–3, 185n1, 193n43; Reaper, 37–39, 44, 46, 53–54, 58, 66, 70, 75–76, 100, 193n43; search for Malaysian Airlines Flight 370, 156–57; spatial dynamics and, 35, 37–38, 47, 50, 52, 57, 59–65, 68, 192n19; temporality and, 44, 47–49, 59, 61–62, 64, 68, 78, 192n19; unmanning and, 44, 192n14; Uruzgan airstrike, 1–3, 7, 67. *See also* aesthetic interventions and artwork; drone vision; surveillance; violent mediations
drone vision, 193n24, 193n33, 194n51; warfare and, 46, 50, 57–59, 61, 65, 109, 194n58. *See also* computer vision; machine vision; surveillance

Earth imaging, 118–21; "Blue Marble," 117; "Digital Earth Australia," 125; "Earthrise," 117; Google Earth and, 80, 100, 196n2; Landsat and, 61–62, 115, 125–26
earwitnessing, 52
ecological trauma, 10, 30, 116–17, 132–33, 149; Aboriginal peoples and, 135, 142, 144–45; aesthetic interventions and, 117, 125–29, 138–45; First Nations peoples and, 115, 131; Pacific Islands and, 113–15, 148; radical absence and, 154, 158, 167, 170, 179; wounding and, 145–48. *See also* trauma; traumatic affect

edge computing, 29, 49, 68
Edney-Browne, Alex, 52
Edwards, Paul N., 13, 156, 200n23
Ellis, John, 25, 189n69
empiricism, 7, 22, 76, 87; radical, 6, 17, 45, 117, 132
Enlightenment, the, 7, 23–24, 31, 177, 179, 181
Epic Games: Unreal Engine, 93, 95–96
Estes, Nick, 18
ethics, 28, 42, 59, 77, 102, 120; algorithms and, 84–88, 91–92; of care, 129, 147; cloud ethics, 110; Google Ethical AI team, 104, 199n78; humanism and, 23, 32–33; memory and, 29; minimal, 188n39; video editing and, 151
Eubanks, Virginia, 104
Eye in the Sky, 58

FAccT conference, 105
Facebook (Meta), 75, 151, 155–56; bias and, 82–83, 159; digital death and, 153, 160–62, 165–66, 204n34
facial recognition, 11, 70, 72, 84; bias and, 104; deepfakes and, 88, 90–91
Farid, Idris, 56
Farmer, Paul, 31, 191n99
Farrier, David, 128
Federally Administered Tribal Areas (FATA), Pakistan, 55, 194n44
feminist critique, 16, 24–25, 64–65, 117, 189n66, 197n41
Finn, Ed, 83
First Nations peoples, 6–8, 20, 24, 158, 177, 182; crisis epistemologies and, 14–15; mining sacred sites of, 167–71, 176; nuclear weapons testing and, 9, 115; settler colonialism and, 17–18, 131, 136, 138, 188n60. *See also* Aboriginal peoples; Indigenous peoples; *individual nations and peoples*
Foley, James, 150–52, 166
Forensic Architecture (Goldsmiths, University of London), 20, 87, 102, 178; *Triple Chaser*, 21, 93–99, 109
forensic ecology, 22, 56
Freedom of Information Act (US), 3
Frosh, Paul, 22, 25, 161

Fuller, Matthew, 116, 120–21; *Investigative Aesthetics*, 21–23, 183
Furuhata, Yuriko, 13, 119

Gabrys, Jennifer, 120, 156
Gadigal people of Eora Nation, 7
Galison, Peter, 24
Galtung, Johan, 191n99
gaming. *See* video games
Gebru, Timnit, 104, 199n78
gender, 24, 53; deepfakes and, 90, 197n41; drone systems and, 50, 56, 102–3, 185n1; sexual violence and, 64–65, 187n32; targeting of "military-aged males," 2, 58, 102
General Atomics, 68; Reaper drones, 37–39, 44, 46, 53, 58, 66, 70, 75–76, 100, 193n43
generative adversarial networks (GANs), 88–90, 92, 197n40
geographic information systems (GIS), 100
Gerrard, John: "The Farm," 105
GILGAMESH, 2, 55
GitHub repository, 88, 90, 94
Givoni, Michal, 27
Glissant, Édouard, 110, 179–80
Google (Alphabet), 2, 11, 13–14, 105, 198n65; bias and, 83, 104; Brain, 88; digital death and, 161; Earth, 80, 100, 105, 196n2; Ethical AI team, 104, 199n78; machine learning and, 75, 88, 196n5; PageRank, 166; Project Maven, 99–100, 103
Gregory, Derek, 46, 185n1
ground truth, 26, 56, 70, 91, 164; aftermath in Aleppo and, 61–62
Grove, Jairus, 16, 42, 45, 79, 116, 187n25, 196n106
Grusin, Richard, 27, 153
Guattari, Félix, 86, 120, 147, 197n30
Gulf War (1991), 46, 192n19

Halperin, Ilana: "Boiling Milk," 127–29, 145
Halpern, Orit, 13, 26, 83, 189n76
Haraway, Donna, 24–25, 117, 189n66
Harkin, Natalie, 144; "mine and refine this float . . . ," 145
Hartman, Saidiya, 31, 191n103
Hayes, Burchell, 168

Hellfire missiles, 2, 30, 50, 57, 66
Hogan, Mél, 161
Holmqvist, Caroline, 75
Hoskins, Andrew, 151

Illingworth, Shona, 151
imperialism, 80, 156, 192n13; First Nations and, 18, 113, 136, 144, 182; insurgent aesthetics and, 53; violence and, 12, 18, 24, 29, 44, 113, 115, 194n44
Indigenous peoples, 18, 23–24, 146–47, 201n63; back-to-the-land movement and, 200n21; genocide and, 11–12, 187n32; nuclear weapons testing and, 136, 144. *See also* Aboriginal peoples; First Nations peoples; *individual nations and peoples*
Institute of Electrical and Electronics Engineers (IEEE), 69, 195n83
insurgent aesthetics, 53. *See also* aesthetic interventions and artwork
Investigative Aesthetics (Fuller and Weizman), 21–23, 183
invisual perception, 85, 101, 103, 108. *See also* computer vision
Iraq, 42; Islamic State in Iraq and Syria (ISIS) and, 59–60, 100, 103, 150, 152; US invasion of, 57
Iron Dome technology (Israel), 74
Islamic State in Iraq and Syria (ISIS), 59–60, 100, 103, 150, 152

Jackson, Zakiyyah Iman, 27, 189n61
James, C. L. R., 130
James, William, 17, 45, 146, 160
Jetñil-Kijiner, Kathy, 148; "Tell Them," 113–14
Joint Standing Committee on Northern Australia, 168–70, 205n55
Juukan Gorge sacred sites, 167–71, 205n55

Kainaki II Declaration, 112
Kanders, Warren B., 94
Kapadia, Ronak, 53
Kaplan, Caren, 20, 44, 50, 63, 192n14
Kausar, Mohammed, 52
Kelley, Robin D. G., 12

Kember, Sarah, 16, 151
kill boxes, 44–45, 192n19
Kittler, Friedrich, 189n74
Kurgan, Laura, 60

Landsat (NASA), 61–62, 115, 126; "Digital Earth Australia," 125
Lapoujade, David, 159–60
law, Western, 21, 52, 76, 90, 104, 194n44; Aboriginal peoples and, 135–37, 168–70; extractive capitalism and, 31, 168–70; First Nations peoples and, 20, 24, 136, 169–71; *terra nullius* doctrine, 136, 202n74; witnessing in, 23, 42–43, 56–57, 98, 144, 178, 189n61
Liu, Cixin: *The Three-Body Problem*, 129–30
liveness, 25, 59, 166
"Living Under Drones" report (Stanford University and New York University), 56, 193n37
Luciano, Dana, 28, 190n82

machine learning, 68–69, 80–81, 83–84, 119, 196n5, 198n61; aesthetic interventions and, 93–99, 105–9; deepfakes and, 88–89, 92, 102, 197n39; human labor and, 1–2, 12, 77, 79, 82, 96, 100, 106–8. *See also* artificial intelligence (AI); machinic affect
machine vision, 26, 49, 73, 75, 164, 178. *See also* computer vision; drone vision; surveillance
machinic affect, 10, 84, 101–3, 197n31; *Computer Learns Automation* and, 109, 110; deepfakes and, 91; definition, 86–87; ecological trauma and, 114–15, 149, 179, 181; invisual perception and, 108; radical absence and, 154, 158, 163–64, 166, 171; *Triple Chaser* and, 94, 96, 98. *See also* affect; machine learning
Mackenzie, Adrian, 82, 84–85, 108
Malaysian Airlines Flight 370 (MH370), 154–57, 165
Man, the Witness, 6, 19, 23–25, 28–29, 32, 35–36, 185n4, 188n60; climate crisis and, 115–17, 126–27, 149; concept of the World and, 176–77, 180–81; COVID-19 pandemic

and, 174; opacity and, 179–80; racialization and, 31, 177, 180
Manjoo, Farhad, 80
Manning, Erin, 164, 172
Māori peoples, 20
Maralinga, Australia, 133–39, 141–42, 144, 176
Marshall Islands, 113–14, 137, 148
martial gaze, 41–42, 44, 56, 69, 103
Massumi, Brian, 78, 159; on ontopower, 15, 72, 87; theorizing affect, 7, 96, 132, 148, 164–65, 167, 185n5
Material Witness (Schuppli), 21
McCosker, Anthony, 44
media studies, 16, 25; witnessing subfield, 22–23
mediation, 26, 98, 120, 175, 177; and absence, 151–67, 171–73; and deepfakes, 91; definition, 16; and drones, 2–3, 22, 35, 39–79; and ecology, 116–19, 125–28, 132; and machinic affect, 86, 101, 114; and nonhuman witnessing, 7, 28; and nuclear testing, 21, 114, 144–45; violent, 10, 22, 39–79, 101, 114, 119, 132, 146, 149, 178–79
media witnessing, 25–26, 91, 158, 189n69; definition, 22. *See also* social media; violent mediations
Menzies, Robert, 133, 201n63
Meta. *See* Facebook (Meta)
Microsoft, 75; AirSim, 93; Bing, 105; Flight Simulator, 80–81, 105, 109; Planetary Computer, 119
military-aged males, targeting of, 2, 58, 102
"mine and refine this float . . ." (Harkin), 145
misinformation, 21, 88. *See also* deepfakes
Missile Park (Scarce), 139, 142–43
Mitchell, Margaret, 199n78
Mittman, J. D., 135–36
mnemotechnologies, 163. *See also* drones and drone warfare
Moore, Jessa, 160–62
"Morenci Mine #2" (Burtynsky), *124*
Moreton-Robinson, Aileen, 135, 168, 202n71
Morgan, Nyarri, 135
Morrison, Scott, 112–13
Morton, Timothy, 132, 201n56

MQ-9 *Reaper I–III* (Pailthorpe), 37–39
Multi-Spectral Targeting System (MSTS), 1–2
Munster, Anna, 84–85, 108
Murphie, Andrew, 15, 159, 187n29

NASA: Earth Resources Technology Satellite, 126; Landsat, 61–62, 115, 125–26
Nature, 116, 147, 177, 201n56
natureculture, 10, 117
necropolitics, 12, 16, 29, 35, 68, 78, 175. *See also* biopolitics; ontopower
neuromorphic computing, 69–71
9/11 attacks (September 11, 2001), 12, 25–26, 158; aftermath of, 46, 150, 152, 192n8
Nixon, Rob, 131
Noble, Safiya, 83, 104
nonhuman witnessing, definition, 3–11, 16–17, 23–29
nonhuman witnessing, politics of, 175–84
nuclear colonialism, 19, 136–38, 142, 144–45, 202n75
nuclear weapons testing, 67, 118, 202n79; artworks about, 21, 113–14, 138–45; in Australia, 9, 115, 133–39, 201n63, 202n72, 202n78; on Marshall Islands, 113–14, 137, 148; "Operation Antler," 134; "Operation Buffalo," 134, 137–38; White Sands Missile Testing Range (US), 202n80. *See also* nuclear colonialism
Nvidia, 95
Nyong'o, Tavia, 190n85

Obama, Barack, 90, 150, 197n39
Oceti Sakowin peoples of Dakota, 18
Öhman, Carl J., 160
Oliver, Kelly, 26–27, 32–33, 36, 101
ontopower, 29, 35, 68, 78–79, 87, 175; definition, 15–16, 72
opacities, 86, 100, 175–76, 178–81, 183. *See also* black boxing
OpenAI, 107; ChatGPT, 82, 105–6; Two-Minute Papers YouTube channel, 105–6
"Open Air" (Cooke and Walker), 125–26
open-source tools, 20, 60, 90, 93–94, 183, 200n27

Pacific Islands Forum (2019), 112, 183
Packer, Jeremy, 12, 40–41, 74, 76
Paglen, Trevor, 105
Pailthorpe, Baden, 191n1; MQ-9 *Reaper I–III*, 37–39
Pakistan, 42, 53, 194n51; Federally Administered Tribal Areas (FATA) of, 55, 194n44; Waziristan, 50, 101–2
Parks, Lisa, 44, 47, 57
Pasquale, Frank, 82
Pax for Peace, 119
Pearl, Daniel, 152
Peters, John Durham, 22, 25, 130, 187n29
Phan, Thao, 103
Pinchevski, Amit, 22, 25, 157, 159
pluralism, 146
pluriversal politics, 3, 11, 19, 110, 153, 176–78, 180, 182, 205n5
Pohiva, Akilisi, 112
Poitras, Laura: *Triple Chaser*, 21, 93–99, 109
police brutality, 30, 152, 158, 169, 175, 187n32
"Polymorphism" (Tan), 105
Pong, Beryl, 49
porn studies, 90
posthumanist theory, 27, 190n85
Project Maven (Google and US Department of Defense), 99–100, 103
proximal policy optimization (PPO), 107–8
Puar, Jasbir, 12, 205n60
Pugliese, Joseph, 23, 43, 56, 94–95, 194n49; *Biopolitics of the More-Than-Human*, 22
Puutu Kunti Kurrama and Pinikura (PKKP) peoples, 167–71, 205n55

queer critique, 27–28, 104, 190n82, 205n60

race and racialization, 16, 31, 118, 180, 190n85; Aboriginal peoples and, 145, 187n32; algorithmic bias and, 82–83, 103–4, 110–11, 159; drone warfare and, 50–51, 56, 102–13, 185n11, 193n43; First Nations peoples and, 169, 177; insurgent aesthetics and, 53; racial capitalism, 12–14, 19, 174–75, 181; surveillance logics and, 13, 44. *See also* settler colonialism; slavery

radical absence, 10, 50, 153–54, 163–67, 172–73, 179; digital death and, 153, 160–63, 165–66, 204n34, 204n39; execution of James Foley and, 150–52; Malaysian Airlines Flight 370 and, 155–57; sacred sites and, 168–71; traumatic affect and, 157–60
radioactivity, 137, 141–42, 176, 202n72, 202nn79, 203n83
Ramstein Air Base, Germany, 1
Rancière, Jacques, 176
rape, 42, 64–65
Ray, Una, 139, 142
Reeves, Joshua, 12, 40–41, 74, 76
Rhee, Jennifer, 193n43
Rio Tinto, 167–70
Rise of the Drones (PBS), 48
Rothe, Delf, 119–20
Russill, Chris, 17, 118, 187n29

Sadowski, Jathan, 82
Safariland, 94–96
"Salt Pan #18" (Burtynsky), 123
savage ecology, 116, 120
Scannell, Paddy, 156–57
Scarce, Yhonnie, 115, 138, 144–45; *Death Zephyr*, 139, 141; *Missile Park*, 139, 142–43; *Thunder Raining Poison*, 139–40
Schmidt, Eric, 14, 198n65
Schuppli, Susan, 22–23, 43, 52, 63, 171; *Material Witness*, 21
Sear, Tom, 91
Seaver, Nick, 83
Seltzer, Mark, 158
September 11, 2001 (9/11), attacks, 12, 25–26, 158; aftermath of, 46, 150, 152, 192n8
settler colonialism, 11, 19–20, 29, 111, 117, 121, 148, 185n4, 187n25, 188n43; author positionality and, 7, 17–18; environmental injustice and, 5, 12, 115, 131; genocide and, 19, 169, 187n32; possessive logics of, 39, 135–36, 169–70, 202n74; racist othering and, 24–25, 44, 82–83, 103, 190n82; resistance to, 13, 53, 110, 137–39, 142, 145, 168–69, 172, 177, 202n75; structural nature of, 5, 14, 23, 31, 35, 113, 144, 169–71, 194n44
sexual violence, 42, 64–65, 187n32

Shah, Nisha, 45
Shanahan, John, 100
Sharkey, Noel, 76
Sheikh, Shela, 28
Singh, Julietta, 190n82
slavery, 12–13, 23–24, 29, 31, 179–80, 191n103; plantations and, 18–19, 130–31. See also capitalism
social media, 13, 17, 20, 98, 109, 111, 130, 154; bias and, 82–83, 159; digital death and, 153, 160–62, 165–66, 204n34; disappearance of Malaysian Airlines Flight 370 and, 155–57; execution of James Foley and, 150–52; grief and, 203n34; mining sacred sites and, 168, 170–71, 176; traumatic affect and, 159–60, 162–63, 166. See also *individual platforms*
Sotloff, Steven, 151
spatial dynamics, 16, 20, 25, 88, 93, 96, 114, 142; climate crisis and, 9, 118, 120–23, 126–32; drone warfare and, 35, 37–38, 47, 50, 52, 57, 59–65, 68, 192n19; radical absence and, 154, 157–59, 162–64, 172, 174
Spiking Neural Networks, 69
Spillers, Hortense, 24, 31
SRC Inc., 66, 69–70. See also Agile Condor
Stahl, Roger, 57
Starosielski, Nicole, 58
state violence, 5, 12–16, 20, 31–32, 79, 84, 119, 178. See also drones and drone warfare; settler colonialism; structural violence
Stewart, Kathleen, 19–20, 172
Stiegler, Bernard, 163
Stoermer, Eugene, 19
Stolen Generation, 187n32
structural violence, 5, 14, 31, 61, 190n82, 191n99. See also settler colonialism; slavery; state violence
structures of feeling, 122, 172, 201n41
Stubblefield, Thomas, 50, 191n1, 193n33
Suchman, Lucy, 78
surveillance, 44, 56, 155–56; Agile Condor, 43, 49, 59, 66–74, 76; ARGUS-IS, 47–48, 100; climate-monitoring systems, 9, 13–14, 20, 113, 119–20, 126, 187n29, 200n23; COVID-19 pandemic and, 174–75;

drones and, 12, 32, 46, 51–52, 59, 194n58; Earth imaging, 61–62, 80, 100, 115, 117–21, 125–26, 196n2; GILGAMESH, 2, 55; nuclear monitoring systems, 67, 118; SKYNET, 55; wide area motion imagery (WAMI) initiatives, 41, 47–49, 71, 100. *See also* computer vision; drone vision; machine vision

synthetic media, 66, 88, 90–91, 93–99. *See also* deepfakes

Syria, 42; aftermath of war in Aleppo, 43, 59–65, 98, 119; Islamic State in Iraq and Syria (ISIS) and, 59–60, 100, 103, 150, 152

Taffel, Sy, 82
Tahir, Madiha, 42, 194n44
Tan, Kynan: *Computer Learns Automation*, 106–10; "Polymorphism," 105
Taussig, Michael, 191n102
television, 25, 158, 189n69
"Tell Them" (Jetñil-Kijiner), 113–14
temporality, 16, 18, 87, 98, 147, 187n36; climate crisis and, 114, 117–23, 125–30, 132, 145, 149; drone warfare and, 44, 47–49, 59, 61–62, 64, 68, 78, 192n19; machine learning and, 100, 105, 107–8; of nuclear radiation, 116, 133, 141–42, 203n83; radical absence and, 154–55, 161–64, 172; significance to the book, 8–9
terra nullius, 18, 136
Theatre of War: Photons Do Not Care (Brimblecombe-Fox), 34–35
"The Farm" (Gerrard), 105
Thirft, Nigel, 163, 167
Three-Body Problem, The (Liu), 129–30
Thunder Raining Poison (Scarce), 139–40
Todd, Zoe S., 19
Tomkins, Silvan, 91
trans-corporeality, 190n86
trauma, 9, 15, 59; mythologizing and, 205n60; used to radicalize, 151; witnessing in response to, 4, 21, 29, 32–33, 180–82; wounding and, 50, 145–48. *See also* ecological trauma; traumatic affect; trauma studies

trauma studies, 29–30, 32, 147–48
traumatic affect, 151–54, 156–60, 164, 166–67, 171–73; digital death and, 162–63, 165. *See also* affect theory; trauma
Triple Chaser (Poitras and Forensic Architecture), 21, 93–99, 109
Tsing, Anna, 130
Tynan, Lauren, 135, 147

Ukraine, 2022 Russian invasion of, 38, 75
Uliasz, Rebecca, 90
uncommmons, 206n21
United Nations Institute for Training and Research (UNITAR): UNOSAT (United Nations Satellite Center), 60
US Defense Innovation Board, 14, 198n65
US Department of Defense (DoD), 198n65; Defense Intelligence Enterprise, 99–100; Project Maven, 99–100, 103; report on Uruzgan airstrike, 2–3
US Special Forces, 2, 68

Valla, Clement: *Postcards from Google Earth*, 196n2
video games, 38, 70, 162–63; Microsoft Flight Simulator, 80–81, 105, 109; OpenAI, 106; Second Life, 93; Unigene, 105; Unreal Engine, 93, 95–96
Vigh, Henrik, 15
violent mediations, 10, 101–2, 178–79; aftermath of drone warfare and, 2–3, 22, 49–50, 52, 57–65; climate crisis and, 114–16, 119, 132, 146, 149; drone systems and, 39–49, 67, 72–73, 76–79, 84; radical absence and, 151–54, 157–60, 172–73; rape and, 64–65
Virilio, Paul, 67
von Neumann, John, 118

Walker, Emma: "Open Air," 125–26
Wark, Scott, 103
war rugs, 53, 192n9
Watson, David, 160
Waup, Lisa, 142
Waziristan, Afghanistan–Pakistan border, 50, 101–2

Weizman, Eyal, 22, 32, 93, 95, 102, 119, 183; *Forensic Architecture*, 21; *Investigative Aesthetics*, 21–23, 183. *See also* Forensic Architecture
Weston, Kath, 174
Whanganui River, New Zealand, 20
white settler sovereignty, 135, 137, 168–69, 202n71. *See also* nuclear colonialism; settler colonialism
Whole Earth Catalog (Brand), 118
Whyte, Jess, 192n13
Whyte, Kyle Powis, 6, 14, 18, 131
wide area motion imagery (WAMI) initiatives, 41, 47–49, 71, 100
Wilcox, Lauren, 103, 185n1
Wilken, Rowan, 44
Williams, Raymond, 201n41
WITNESS, 90–91
Wolf, Asher, 104
Wolfe, Patrick, 31, 187n32

Woods, Derek, 122
Woomera, Australia, 138, 142, 202n78
Work, Robert, 99
worldings, 19–20, 176–77
wound culture, 158. *See also* trauma; violent mediations
Wynter, Sylvia, 6, 31, 116, 118, 185n4

xenowar, 91. *See also* deepfakes

Yami, Lester, 133, 135, 139, 144
YouTube, 58, 90, 156; aftermath in Aleppo and, 61, 63; Agile Condor videos, 71; execution of James Foley and, 150, 152; Two-Minute Papers channel (OpenAI), 105–6
Yusoff, Kathryn, 188n43

Zylinska, Joanna, 16, 28, 122, 128, 151; minimal ethics, 188n39

www.ingramcontent.com/pod-product-compliance
Lightning Source LLC
Chambersburg PA
CBHW070840160426
43192CB00012B/2259